NFL
UNPLUGGED

THE BRUTAL, BRILLIANT WORLD OF
PROFESSIONAL FOOTBALL

Anthony L. Gargano

WILEY

John Wiley & Sons, Inc.

Published by John Wiley & Sons, Inc., Hoboken, New Jersey
Published simultaneously in Canada

For general information about our other products and services, please contact our Customer Care Department within the United States at (800) 762-2974, outside the United States at (317) 572-3993 or fax (317) 572-4002.

Wiley also publishes its books in a variety of electronic formats. Some content that appears in print may not be available in electronic books. For more information about Wiley products, visit our web site at www.wiley.com.

Library of Congress Cataloging-in-Publication Data:

Gargano, Anthony L., date.
  NFL unplugged : the brutal, brilliant world of professional football / Anthony L. Gargano.
    p.   cm.
  Includes bibliographical references and index.
  ISBN 978-0-470-52283-7 (hardback); ISBN 978-0-470-64198-9 (ebk);
  ISBN 978-0-470-64199-6 (ebk); ISBN 978-0-470-64200-9 (ebk)
  1. National Football League.   2. Football–United States.   I. Title.   II. Title: National Football League unplugged.
  GV955.5.N35G37   2010
  796.332'64—dc22

                                                                      2010028342

Printed in the United States of America

10 9 8 7 6 5 4 3 2 1

For my dearest Tamara, my cherished wife
and partner in the trenches of life

Contents

Acknowledgments

The genesis of this book can be traced back to a single gray Sunday in late November 1977.

Wrapped in a homemade afghan on the floor too close to the RCA color television set, I vividly recall the awful plight of my quarterback. I remember thinking how comfortable I felt at that very moment nestled in the warmth of a good home and how this poor jersey number 7 had it so rough.

He tried desperately to make a play, only to be chased down like dinner in a pen. I imagined that each New England defensive player under his helmet resembled the cartoon "Pat" Patriot logo, which seemed too prevalent on the NFL sheets that covered my bed.

I was nine, and that's what I knew of New England back then: Plebeian Pat, who wore a scowl at the intersection of arching eyebrows, sturdy and muscular, readying to hike the ball.

I looked up the stats recently from that game. Number 7 was sacked eight times total, and that didn't count the hurries. They were horrible hurries, with 7 just firing the ball to a naked spot on the field before being flung like flotsam—undoubtedly the kind of horrible hurry that would have drawn a personal foul today.

But 7 stood tall amid the ambush. He limped and waddled back to the huddle every single time. He never left his team or the game. I deemed him gallant.

Ron Jaworski. The Polish Rifle.

The Eagles finished 4–10 that season, but three years later Jaworski led them to the Super Bowl. And while the Eagles were my boyhood team, I was especially pleased for Jaworski. I thought it a just world because he survived with fortitude that frightening day in Foxborough and was rewarded for it.

Such was the message of football I received.

So when I say I admire football players today, I do not mean it in a bleachers sort of way, rather than on a human level. I admire them the way I admire anyone who displays such courage and unrelenting desire. Throughout the years in my profession, I've gotten to know many pro football players. As a general rule, I have found them grounded and smart, with a farmer's work ethic. Goldbrickers don't last long in the NFL.

I wish to thank the scores of players who allowed me insight into their world, especially Ike Reese, Jon Runyan, and Hugh Douglas, three great grunts.

Thanks to my assistant, James Lynch Jr., who helped coordinate interviews for the project and showed the determination of a football player.

Thanks to Anthony R. Gargano, Mary Tomasetti, Joseph Tomasetti, Christina Gargano, Vince Portaro, Michael Deangelo, David Rodden, Joseph Benvignati, Bob Marino, Angelo Borgese, Gary Smith, Anthony Cardillo, Ray Didinger, Steve Martorano, Michael Missanelli, Angelo Cataldi, Glen Macnow, Robert Huber, Stan Hochman, Marc Rayfield, Andy Bloom, Jill Speckman, and Tom Srendenschek.

Thanks to a wonderful editor, Stephen S. Power, production editor, Kimberly Monroe-Hill, and believers Jackie Harris and Evan Goldfried.

Special thanks to the National Football League, the Philadelphia Eagles football club, Jeffrey Lurie, Joe Banner, and especially Andy Reid, Tom Heckert, Derek Boyko, Rick Burkholder, and my adopted uncle, Anthony "Mister Wolf" Buchanico.

Prologue

There's no lying in football because it's in your
face. There's no bullshit in football because you
have your brother's back. Because in football
you're held accountable.

—Former defensive end Hugh Douglas

T
he man who rides with me in the back of the stretch limousine
plays professional football. Though he warrants a handsome pay,
the game renders his identity irrelevant for purposes of celebrity
or the game's upward mobility. Nothing personal now. He plays offensive line, the position of sentry. Human wall. Trench dweller. And to
be exact, he mans the right tackle spot for a right-handed quarterback.

The Bland Side.

So while he lives with his wife and three children in a newly constructed dream home that peeks out of the woods in a most livable
suburb and sports an interior of thirteen thousand square feet if you
include the two in-law suites above the six-car garage—he actually just
refinanced his monthly mortgage payment to $22,632—the man is
merely an expensive contractor in the background. He will not revolu-
tionize the game or become a marketing appendage for the league.

1

Think about it. There's only one Peyton Manning. While Tom Brady commands a cadre of celebrity stalkers who purport with audacity his media status, especially with the model wife, he isn't even Peyton Manning when it comes to face. Only a few quarterbacks and assorted skill position types—a running back here, a wide receiver there, a Troy Polamalu because of the hair—ever reach the point of household recognition.

And despite manning the top spot in the country's most popular sport, Peyton pales as a pitchman to, say, LeBron James. Professional basketball has long since sold its soul to American idols and false messiahs. Major League Baseball now toes the line between game and individual, especially after the scandal of potions and lotions proved once more the fallibility of sluggers and their personal trainers.

Meanwhile, professional football extinguishes just about everyone who plays it. That's how the game is designed. Sum of all parts, you know? It has to be that way because just about everyone who plays the game won't last longer than a hiccup.

For example, Peyton Manning played with exactly sixty men his rookie season with the Colts in 1998. Entering the 2009 season, none of the sixty were still with the Colts.

Same thing with the fifty-six teammates of Manning's in 1999. You have to go back to 2000 to find one who still played with him—a long snapper by the name of Justin Snow. Heard of him? Justin Wade Snow? Out of Baylor? Attended Abilene Cooper High School in Fort Worth? Wife, Heather? Daughter, Kambrie, son, Hunter?

See, the game thrives mostly on the aspect of team, the colors and the laundry. Players with any sort of personality might as well be street-corner performers doing their little end zone or tackle dance when compared to the machine of the game. Does anybody in the world try harder than Chad Johnson? He successfully taught most of middle America how to say eight and five in Spanish (eighty-five would be *ochenta y cinco*), but what did he really accomplish other than good competition for Rosetta Stone?

The game sustains because of men like Justin Wade Snow, the faceless men, like our travel companion in the stretch limousine. I will share with you his forthcoming story of pain because it illustrates the lives of the players who shape the sport that we love. These are men who trade their sweat and potentially their bodies for excellent pay and more excellent fringe benefits, but little name recognition.

The unplugged version of professional football is what I sought in this book, the pain-filled Sundays and painful Mondays and glamourless Thursdays. Yes, sort of the Real Men of the National Football League. I spoke with many, many players to seek an accurate snapshot of modern-day life in the league, which takes into account what occurs in places on the field and in the locker room and at practice that cameras can't really capture. I tried to keep the compilation of stories fairly recent, with most of the players attached somehow to the last fifteen years, either currently playing or recently retired. Some spoke on the condition that their identity be withheld, though as you will see, that doesn't really matter in the story of the Disposable Men.

Life in pads knows no true hierarchy.

I must warn you that the language is best described as salty. I thought about sanitizing it, but how can you aptly depict the underbelly of football and bracket golly-goshes between quotation marks?

No matter how offensive the language, context comes in competition and confrontation. It's the nature of sport, whether it's Lambeau Field or a playground pickup game involving ten strangers or ten friends. Hard-core profanity. Racial swipes. Ethnic cuts. Sexual flouts. Mother jokes. Wicked taunts.

The words sound harsh because of vantage point, which also works the other way. We watch the game with a numbness, shrugging off, say, an off-tackle running play buried in the second quarter somewhere between the twenties that goes for three yards. For the players, however, the risk wasn't any less. The collisions presented the same potential for disaster. The lines collapsed against one another. Knees and limbs were exposed. Tendons and ligaments stretched. The play ended like every other in a pile of flesh.

The game seems fun from the couch. Like backyard football on Thanksgiving.

So one player talked to me about pinching in the pile, and how much it hurt. Pinching? Of all the misdeeds that occur deep in the pile, out of plain sight—the twisting of joints, bending back of fingers—he talked of pinching.

Pinching?

He lunged at me and snared what little flesh is on the back of my knee. He squeezed and then twisted as hard as he could for about fifteen seconds. It felt like a bee sting at first—then skin stripping from the bone.

I can tell you why we stayed in love with the game, long after we succumbed to the realization that it wasn't happening for a living, and by game, I mean any of them that we watch. It's what they effuse. Emotion. Alluring, combustible emotion that resides inherently in each of them, no matter the participants or their skill level or your allegiances. Emotion enhances drama and trumps aesthetics, even if hoops was better when big men roamed the post instead of the arc. While unquestionably significant, quality of play is quantifiable. That's just evolution or devolution, depending on your box seat. It's not essence. Emotion is essence.

Story lines recycle and rotate from person to person, the way seniors graduate and players file for free agency and coaches perish to unemployment, but what remains in football is a bundled energy that plays out over three hours just sixteen times in a regular season. And that's what makes the NFL so freaking compelling. That by comparison you don't have to wait for the playoffs to hang on every pitch or every possession, which is not to defile the other two great American games, only to speak of the league's greatest attribute. Abiding drama.

The players represent the league's second greatest attribute. A trail of them line the road to the NFL's immense popularity. The man in the limousine might as well be underneath it. You would guess he plays professional football because of his super size. He wears 5-sometimes-6X practice gray T-shirts, but he's so tall that he appears solidly in proportion—like one of those giant sequoias in the North Grove of Calaveras State Park.

He abhors the metaphor, by the way, and whenever anyone makes a stupid wisecrack about his size, he responds with a mock laugh—"huh, huh, huh"—that almost makes him sound like a giant from the fables because his voice is so deep. Lord knows, they don't mean to offend him. It's just that they're always so enamored by his bigness.

That size works against him now because he has to contort his frame into an odd position that looks like a crooked, camel-humped numeral seven. His torso roosts on the rear seat to one side, right elbow bearing his weight, while his lower legs and feet stretch across the carpeted floor to the section nearest the driver, with his ample buttocks fully suspended in air. He squirms, desperately seeking a position that makes the hour ride bearable.

He finds one and the pain begins to subside, but minutes later half of his body goes numb, and so he moves and the pain comes rushing back.

The body never feels good the day after a game. Everything hurts. Everything that ails awakens at the same time and throbs. But it's way worse on this day. It's agony. Because the other day, following practice, with some time to kill before a team meeting, he slipped on the second step down while getting into the cold tub and fractured his tailbone.

It was one of those comical slips, he says, the kind where you are on your back in the air, hanging for what feels like minutes, your whole body suspended. He came down at the very edge of the tub flush on his buttocks. He had his cell phone in his right hand and somehow kept it from getting wet. He kept thinking about saving his phone.

Then he heard it. A tick. Like when you flick your finger over a piece of plastic.

You know when you do something like that, he says, you're like, "Oh, shit, what did I just do?"

There was a three-second delay and then the pain came rushing forth. He climbed out of the cold tub and stood up real slow, the way you do when your back hurts. He began to walk back into the training room and the pain started to get worse and worse. He wonders now if he even breathed for two minutes. When he got back into the training room, he sat down in shock and began to sweat. A full, profuse sweat, the kind that comes after one of those full-contact training camp practices under the morning sun. He wasn't breathing. But he was shaking and he felt sick to his stomach. So clammy, he kept thinking something was very wrong, and he waited to pass out.

He sat there in the training room for twenty minutes and hoped the feeling would pass. Finally he forced himself to stand. "Up and at 'em," he said to himself and lifted his body to his feet. He thought he could will that horrible sensation away—you know, walk it off, just like a football player would do—and so he slogged over to the team meeting and the whole time felt like he was going to vomit. He was light-headed, dizzy, and spacey, and he found that odd because he hadn't hit his head.

The next two nights, the man could barely sleep, other than when the Vicodin kicked into his system. In fact, for more than a month he couldn't lie on his back, which meant he had to sleep on his side. But he's so damn big that sooner or later his shoulders began to throb. So he had to roll over, but that presented an enormous chore. First he had to dig his heels down on the bed and arch his back, and then flip in the air so he wouldn't roll over on his buttocks.

The man could barely walk when he entered the training room early that Sunday morning before the game. He felt nauseous from the throbbing and a lack of good sleep, and joked to his wife about the nausea, something about understanding childbirth. She said he still had no idea.

Now, you must know there is no real treatment for a fractured tailbone. It only heals with time and rest, which offered the man little solace since more than half the season remained. The doctors told him he couldn't do any further damage to the injury, and whether or not he could play depended solely on his pain threshold. He decided to gauge how he felt the morning of the game.

The fact that he always played ultimately made the decision, and damn, he says, the shots were almost more painful than the injury. Seven times he was stabbed by needles that morning to dull the pain.

"The area is already swollen and sensitive and now you're adding more fluid and pressure to it," the man explains. "To shoot the injury, they start down at the very tip and work their way back up, alternating sides, coming right up the tailbone. Talk about feeling violated.

"They gave me straight novocaine the first time and I was in a full sweat by the time they were done. It was horrible. After that, they added lidocaine to the mix and that was a lot better. Lidocaine works faster. It's almost instant. That's all an anesthesiologist is—a bartender. All they do is make cocktails. Then I got a shot of Toradol in the butt. I don't normally take it unless I have an injury. I figure I drink enough vodka to damage my liver. But I needed to have one before every game thereafter."

Twenty minutes later, the man couldn't feel anything. He had a numb spot in his buttocks—which was a relief until some of the novocaine seeped into the muscle. His glutes didn't fire the way they should have because the nerves were not connecting, being effectively deadened, the way they are during a root canal. Except the man needed his buttocks to run. So he played the game with a hitch in his step, all the while trying to protect the area, an awfully hard endeavor when you play lineman in the trenches.

What he totally dreaded, he says, was that bad boy wearing off. He knew the drugs would last for four hours, and slowly the pain crept back following the game. He took a heavy dose of Vicodin before he left the stadium.

That night, he again had trouble sleeping. At one point he thinks he dozed off at about two in the morning, only to wake up two hours later in agony. He says it was really, really bad. Nothing like he's ever felt, through many previous injuries and surgeries. So really, really bad that he began crying uncontrollably. He laughs about it recounting the story in the limo.

"Tears, dude," he says.

One of his kids is six, and she came into the bedroom, gently rubbed his shoulder, turned to her mother, and asked, "Why is Daddy crying? What's wrong with Daddy?"

So after that first game the training staff switched him from Vicodin to Percocet, every four hours, and he assures he was on time with it. The medication takes twenty to forty minutes before it begins to work, so he says he took it like his "life depended on it."

At that point, his day-to-day life was pretty miserable. "Taking all of those drugs," the man says, "you're not getting good rest because your body is fighting off those painkillers. You're not eating a lot. The painkillers kill your appetite. The painkillers also make your stool hard. So you're afraid to take a shit. You're afraid to push because you don't know if it's going to hurt. I don't think I shit for a week. It's not a fun situation."

It's not fun now, either, as the man tries gamely to reposition himself. He takes a deep breath, winces, and emits a long exhale.

Breathe through the pain.

He gathers himself. Now he wants to show off. Men like to display their scars and bruises as badges, especially when borne from a fight or the field. Such a permanent imperfection represents a trophy of combat, a sort of proof of valor to be compared like a poker hand in bars or locker rooms.

"Dude, not to be gay or anything," he says, "but take a look at this."

He pulls down his pants and undershorts to reveal a deep bruise that looks like an ink stain that begins from his lower back and covers most of his buttocks. It appears as though that area of his body has died.

Warrior bruise.

The trainer with his team describes it as "pitch-black from that side over. There was a collection of fluid right on the inside of the butt cheek—two, three inches long, and hard. I put my gloves on and rubbed electric stim to loosen it so I could drain it. I did it because I wouldn't make my assistants do it. I'm here with this big ol' hairy Sasquatch and I'm rubbing his butt cheek every night so he can get some sleep."

The man laughs at what his friend the trainer described and says, "I've been down that road before. When you pull your groin, you got a dude under your sac rubbing a muscle. Nothing you can do about it."

For the man, the worst was yet to come. The next game was on the road, a three-hour flight away. He started to walk down the aisle and the seats seemed to shrink further as he reached his row. Because of his size the man detests flying more than ripostes about his size, and now he had to sit? He tried it for ten minutes, moving side to side with all of his weight. One-cheeking it, he called it. So of course his back began to whine. He spent the rest of the flight either standing hunched or spread across a row of seats.

At the team meetings inside the hotel ballroom that night, he didn't sit down. Just too painful. So he stood in the back leaning on a table. Following another poor night of sleep, he suddenly found himself at the stadium.

You know when you're so mentally and physically drained, he says, you just wind up someplace without remembering how you got there?

One moment he was in a hotel bed with about eight pillows strategically aligned and the television still on—now showing some annoying infomercial—because he wanted some noise to divert his mind from the pain and fell asleep to it and dreamed about actually being in the cop show, and the next he was resting uncomfortably over a table inside a dingy visitor's training room that resembled a clinic. He wrestled with the notion of another cocktail of narcotics. He didn't feel up to all of those needles again and he didn't want to play football drugged.

"Totally whacked," he recalls from that first week. "You're basically high, so you have a tough time concentrating out there on the field."

He leaned over that table, lost in thought, debating whether to play. The pain really started to get to him. He looked a total mess, the general manager of the team told him.

"You gonna play today or not?" the general manager (GM) asked him. "We have to make some roster moves if you don't."

Finally, he shook his head. "Yeah, I'm gonna play."

"You sure?"

"Yeah."

The GM gave him that look—one of admiration mixed with fright, the kind where you question one's sanity.

"That game was the closest I came to not playing," he would say after the season. "It's weird. You wind up settling into a routine after a while with an injury. You get used to the pain and how to manage it. You get used to the injury and how to protect it. I went all the way to the middle of December before somebody hit me in the tailbone. I took a helmet right in my butt. When it happened, I had a buzzing feeling in it. The area was numb from the shots and what you feel is this weird buzzing in the area.

"I'm like, 'Oh, God, here we go.'"

Oddly, the serious pain never came that day and the man recalls that what actually hurt worse after that game was his finger. He had caught his ring finger in somebody's jersey in the first half and the "bone kept popping in and out." Torn ligament. So he taped all four fingers together like a claw so it was stable. Well after the season, the finger is permanently crooked and doesn't touch the middle finger. It still hurts when he puts his hand in his pocket.

"A lot of pain is mental," the man says. "It's the ability to cope with it and block it out. As long as the doctor says I won't injure myself further, I have to be able to play that mental game."

He talks of another time, long ago, when his line mate, who was also a friend, got into a scrum with a kid safety in practice. Those on the team didn't care much for the kid safety's brashness, and two plays later the man's line mate said to him in the huddle, "Let's get that motherfucker."

Sure enough, the man peeled off and eyed the kid safety's chest exposed. "I go to blow him up," he remembers. "I'm three steps away. Before I get to him, I take a helmet square in the rib cage. That was Thursday. Sunday, I'm real, real sore, and we're getting our asses handed to us by Baltimore. I'm blocking Peter Boulware, and by the middle of the fourth quarter my ribs hurt so much, I have to take a deep breath just to bend my knees to get into a two-point stance. We have two guys go down. We have no one left. I can't even jog off the field. I was in so much pain. I'm trying just to get in Boulware's way. I can't wrestle him. I'm trying to get into my stance and I'm like, 'Uuuuuugggg! Fuck!'

"I was crying on the bench. It hurt that much. I couldn't breathe or anything. When we got back home, they took me to hospital. They thought I bruised my liver."

Of all the man's injuries—two broken thumbs, two broken middle fingers, one broken index finger, torn ligaments in both ring fingers, ribs that became displaced, a broken ankle, a torn ACL (anterior cruciate ligament), and the broken tailbone—the worst of it, he says, came when he was sick.

The man was playing a game against the Seahawks in the Kingdome, and he awoke on game day feeling ill. He had a fever, his throat hurt, and his sinuses stabbed at him. The team doctor said he had a sinus infection and gave him an IV before the game. During the game, he vomited on the sideline several times. Strangely, he played well—popping the ball on one play from a defensive lineman who had recovered a fumble from his team and then re-recovering the football—but it came with a price.

He burned with fever after the game; at one point his body temperature reached 104 degrees. A chest X-ray later in the week revealed pneumonia, but the man says with pride, "I didn't miss the game. No meetings, no practice all week. I showed up for the walk-through on Saturday and played on Sunday."

Funny the trade-offs of the game that come to his mind. He laments not being able to take a sick day. "You get to stay in bed all day and eat soup," the man says. "We have to work."

That's what this book is about: the work.

1

Pregame

W hatever the similarities, football as war is a dishonest analogy. It's just that football doesn't feel like a game, say the way baseball does. It's why former linebacker Bill Romanowski talks of a dark place that he sought out before a football game, one sans compassion or humanity, where he "wanted to hurt people," and how that mentality brought forth a kinship with a former Navy SEAL.

A smile is not a smile before one plays football. It is a sneer wrapped in a smile, induced by adrenaline or some wicked thought. Pregame in other sports offers hot buffets, crossword puzzles, yoga stretches, television watching, and an organic progression into the game, like batting practice or layup lines.

Even before the most important baseball or basketball games, at the height of playoff nerves, there is not the forbidding feeling that lurks before kickoff. "It's the only game where an ambulance arrives three hours before the game," former offensive lineman Kevin Gogan offers with an underlying tone of pride.

We begin with a portrait of pregame because it is here that you learn about them—away from preconception and the grand production and their own pose, born from the attention and for the applause.

Fanfare stripped away, that's what they are, you know?

Just men. Ordinary men.

Men who represent every nook of the American culture. Men from the South Side of Chicago to Southern California to south-central Texas, places like Floresville, a whole 4.8 square miles of Wilson County, and towns even smaller and deeper country. Black men, white men. Young men, younger men. Some slight of build with chiseled features, others hulking with sharp-edged, rolling muscles that create the image of a mountain range, the veins that snake over and around them the rivers, still others round-faced, innocent, however massive, with blocks of flat flesh the size of a shipping crate.

Here in this window they move about totally unsheathed. Just men in preparation.

Saturday, 5:16 p.m.
Airport Marriott

Pregame in America actually begins here in the lobby of an upscale chain hotel, usually tucked away on the outskirts of town. The ones by the airport offer good seclusion, away from the distractions of downtown and the hassles of Saturday night hotel happenings where the fine diners and wedding parties converge amid an air of revelry. Weekends at the airport, meanwhile, feel relaxed, the deep breath between Friday afternoon and Monday morning offering only a few stragglers, usually layovers during perhaps longer journeys abroad.

Though hardly the lavish living of, say, the Mandarin Oriental overlooking Central Park or the Peninsula Beverly Hills, the hotel is quite pleasing for those overnighting on business. And for the handful of ordinary men who now wander over to a table where a woman with a clipboard stands, away from the check-in counter for the rest of the guests in the center of the lobby, it's strictly business. Football is a game of itineraries, and the next twenty-four hours will be strictly regimented.

Whether at home or on the road, the players stay in a hotel the night before a game. If it is a road game with a destination two time zones away or less (a cross-country trip elicits a Friday afternoon departure), barring flight delays for weather, the team would have just arrived in its opponent city. Players and personnel would have deplaned, boarded two oversized charter buses, and arrived here at the lobby in one large group.

The men before you play at home tomorrow. They happen to play for the Philadelphia Eagles, though such a seemingly important detail doesn't matter all that much in the story of pregame. Across the league, the snapshot appears nearly identical. Right about now, two hours by car south of here, members of the Ravens will enter the lobby of the Hyatt Regency Baltimore on Light Street in the Inner Harbor. And farther south, at the Westin on South College Street in the financial district of downtown Charlotte, walking distance from the city's historic South End and Bank of America Stadium, two companion Carolina Panthers will receive their hotel key from another woman with a clipboard.

Depending on ownership, each team may seek slightly different amenities from their pregame hotel. For example, the Steelers demand that Heinz provide the ketchup for team meals, which makes perfect sense seeing how Heinz paid $57 million for the naming rights of the stadium in Pittsburgh. Since the Rooney family is devoutly Catholic, the team also requests a priest and the use of a meeting room for mass.

Depending on the head coach, the timeline may vary slightly, but the schedule is remarkably similar for every team. Preparation for Sunday is a game of details, a series of check-offs in what amounts to a to-do tome.

Meanwhile, the line of players receiving their room keys grows. Because it's a home game, they drove to the hotel on their own with a check-in time between 5 and 7 p.m., the onus on earlier. The evening schedule is filled with meetings.

The stream of players becomes more steady now. One by one they walk past, so very different-looking but with a sameness surrounding them beyond the obvious—the earbud necklace dangling around all of their necks that's attached to their cell phone or iPod. Part of it is their pricey contemporary dress, more nightclub than business casual, and that they are draped in accessories—thick watches with oversized wide faces, gold chains, silver chains, rings, bracelets, hoop earrings in one or both ears, diamond studs the size of buttons. They all seem to wheel a designer bag behind them.

And they wield presence—a "we're here" presence, accentuated by purposeful, somebody strides, prompting rubbernecking from the other guests. The latter don't recognize most of the players because other than a handful of mostly quarterbacks, the game offers little identity, down to the uniform steeped in padding and a helmet. The game is wholly a sum of all parts, the players cogs in a machine, except for now when they are real people just checking into a hotel room, eliciting knowing stares because of their youth and robust size.

Saturday, 7:31 p.m.
Defense Meeting

A security guard looking rather bored balances his chair on its two back legs outside the Grand Ballroom on the hotel's subfloor, a maze of ballrooms and meeting rooms of various sizes used for business or social functions. Tonight, however, the football team occupies the whole floor, and there's a sign resting on an easel at the foot of the stairwell that wards off trespassers.

Two hours of Saturday night meetings are under way. Special teams was first, beginning shortly after 7 p.m., and now the team is divided into units, split into separate rooms by offense and defense. The final briefings of the game plan for tomorrow's contest against the New York Giants, these meetings are the most lengthy.

Saturday, 8:42 p.m.
Team Meeting

The final mandatory session of the evening is about to start in the Grand Ballroom with the overall team meeting. Standing in front of the room, his players seated before him in high-backed banquet chairs, Andy Reid clears his throat to silence the last remnants of personal conversation.

Wearing a black 5X Eagles golf shirt, Reid looks like a football coach the way the accountant resembles an accountant or the detective resembles a detective. Beyond his imposing stature—that of a former offensive tackle who's put on weight since his college playing days—it's the bushy half-circle, half-inch-thick mustache that matches his cropped spiky red hair. While most men today look creepy or cheesy wearing one, the mustache still works for the football coach. Reid's mustache is the cafeteria lady's hairnet.

He also has the right eyes, sunk deep within the folds of his face, small but piercing, which gives him a wonderful stare. Good football coaches are expressive without yelling, saving their voice from landing on deaf ears. They can bore through a player. Depending on the transgression, Reid will let his stare linger like a magnifying glass used to start a fire.

"All right, men," he begins.

It is here that the head coach will revisit the message of the week. For each week in the season presents a new chapter, and a coach will offer a theme depending on the ebb and flow of his team.

For example, if the team is playing extremely well and enters Sunday a big favorite, the coach may devalue earlier accomplishments to keep his players humble and hungry. In typical coach-speak, he will harp on the hardiness of the opponent, the way he did to the media all week.

Meanwhile, at the same moment, in another hotel across town, the coach of the opponent will preach something very different.

A Saturday Night in 1998

Before Reid coached the Eagles, an emotionally charged man by the name of Ray Rhodes did.

Six weeks into the 1998 season, disaster already loomed for the team. Philadelphia entered a home matchup with the division-rival Redskins at 0–5, following a spiritless 41–16 loss at Denver the week before. Before that, the Eagles were drubbed 38–0 by the Seahawks at home in of all games the opener, and vultures circled Rhodes.

In Rhodes's first year, in 1995, his team started 1–3 and later scored 58 points in a playoff victory over the Lions, and he won the NFL Coach of the Year award. But things steadily declined from there for Rhodes, known for his winding pregame harangues.

So he stood in a similar spot to where Reid stands now, in a softly lit hotel ballroom, trying to peer into his players' football souls. Eyes bulging and bloodshot, he challenged their manhood during a dia-tribe that former linebacker Ike Reese will never forget. Reese, then a rookie for the Eagles, swayed back and forth the way Rhodes did on that night and recited what he heard:

> It's like y'all are letting these motherfuckers in your house. Your home field. They want to beat your ass tomorrow. It's like they broke into your house. Big husky motherfuckers. And they got your wife tied up. That's what you got to imagine. Motherfuckers tied up your wife. They tied up your kids. They pissed on your good drapes. They pissed over all of your furniture. Then you come home. They grab your ass. They got you all tied up. And this motherfucker pulls his dick out and rubs it all over your wife's lips. And they force you to watch. And there's nothing you can do about it. You gonna let that happen?

The Eagles beat the Redskins the next day, but finished the season 3–13, and Rhodes was fired.

Saturday, 8:58 p.m.
Player Snack

Andy Reid concludes this Saturday night talk in a much tamer fashion.

"Let me buy you guys a hamburger," he says.

Reid refers to the snack listed on the players' itinerary. Hardly a bag of chips or an apple, the word "snack" is used the way it is on a luxury cruise ship. A section of the Grand Ballroom has been curtained off and converted into a finely catered cafeteria featuring a wide selection of comfort foods, including the hamburgers, chicken wings, pizza, French fries, cookies, and ice cream with every imaginable topping.

Players move in quickly, without reticence, their plates overflowing with food. Most are indiscriminate with their choices, reaching, it seems, for a little of everything, placing the excess—and a couple bottles of water or Gatorade—somewhere on their person for the journey back to the room.

Saturday, 11:15 p.m.
Bed Check

Bed check is under way on the seventh floor, and it feels something like lockdown.

With pay-per-view.

No other guests are permitted to stay on the team's two floors, with the rooms blocked out well in advance. Team security personnel diligently watch for civilians on the players' floor, particularly females, and curfew is at 11 p.m. sharp. "It actually compares somewhat to witness protection," said a former FBI agent now working in NFL team security.

Several retired FBI agents find employment in the league, as well as former police officers and other law enforcement officials, like Anthony Buchanico, the director of security for the Eagles.

A former mounted Philadelphia cop who reached sergeant and then chief of security for the mayor's office under Ed Rendell, now the Pennsylvania governor, Buchanico answers to a protagonist's name: Butch.

He's one-syllable blunt, too, the way all fixers operate. He knows what the owner doesn't want to know, the way the owner prefers it. Young men who play a violent game for many dollars will sometimes find the trouble of young men, and it's Butch's job to protect the many more dollars at stake. He lives in a gray world, sleeping next to his cell phone, and should it, dammit, ring in the middle of the night with bummer news he knows who to call—and more importantly, he has who to call's phone number on one-touch dial.

By the way, he's a father of four and a grandfather many times over, and this was supposed to be his retirement job.

Handsome and gentlemanly trim, especially for a man in his sixties, with thick graying hair, a matching mustache, and hooded eyes that continually dart from side to side, always sneaking a peek at something, Butch grew up the son of a numbers writer in an Old World neighborhood he never left. He doesn't really speak, rather he simmers in sequence, buoyed by boundless charisma, words leaping from him, often spiced by a blue tongue, trying to keep pace with his wild gesturing, and he brims with wilder tales he only tells to make a point. The one about the cop who was two-timing his wife with women on his beat comes to mind. How the cop's wife grew so sick of his cheating that she heated lye in the macaroni pot and sprinkled in some grits and when the cop fell asleep she dumped it right there on his privates.

Grits make the lye stick to the skin, he assures.

It's a good story to tell young men so maybe they won't find the trouble of young men.

They won't when he's around, he also assures, like right now as he makes rounds for bed check with a member of the hotel's security staff with a master key. They cover half the rooms, while two assistant coaches and another keyholder from the hotel handle the rest.

The hotel security guard opens the door, while Butch offers a rapid series of loud warning knocks and enters the room seeking two bodies. There are two players per room, with a few exceptions for some veterans with lengthy service time or star players who prefer their privacy.

"Yo?" he barks into the darkened room.

Already asleep, one of the players offers an inaudible response.

"Butch?" the other beckons.

"Yes?"

"Tell me a story?"

"Good night, babycakes."

Butch exits to laughter and moves to the next room. He raps on the door and walks into the space. Once again, the lights are out.

"Police," he booms. "Who's here?"

"Me," a voice answers, sounding rather awake.

"Any broads in here?"

"I wish. Just my man over there."

"Get a good night's sleep, you hear?"

"Night, Butch."

"Sweet dreams," he says, slipping out of the room for the next one.

The scene bears the innocence of summer camp, a welcome moment of sentry duty for Butch, who recalls one night before a playoff game in San Francisco the year he started the job in 1996 when a group of players rented a limousine and cruised a seedy section of town dubbed "Ho Road," picked up two prostitutes, and brought them back to the team hotel.

What ensued was one of those nights every young man succumbing to temptation fears in the light of day, when one colossally poor decision leaves a very good life hanging in the wind. When the young man curses himself for being so ridiculously foolhardy and curses God for not supplying a rewind button. Hugging his chest, he rocks back and forth in the chair. He feels like he's going to be sick.

Following a squabble over payment, one of the prostitutes claimed she had been raped.

For the record, I do not know how the players felt during their moment of reckoning, only that, according to Butch, the night was terribly long after he was jarred awake by the ringing of the phone in his room, and how he arrived to a scandalous scene in the lobby, and how the prostitute urged him to speak to her pimp and the pimp mentioned something about money and alerting the media, and how the police were called, and how the woman gave investigators a fake name and address, and how in the end the two local detectives found little evidence to support the prostitute's allegation, and how none of the players were charged with a crime, and how the team was trounced the next day by the 49ers.

Sunday, 7:01 a.m.
Wake-up Call

The morning brings forth luminous sunshine, the sun perched higher it seems than yesterday, a mark of northern autumn, and so the light cascades down in neat folds and warms the clean, chilled air.

During football season, inside the game and for those who love the game, Sunday morning feels like Christmas morning. Sunday morning represents why football is the perfect game, the anticipation from a week of wait now heightened. It's the wonderful spacing of the games, enough to have you panting between them, thus it can never grow desultory. Because unlike other sports, a football season offers no dog days.

It's a sprint of a season, and today marks the sixth of sixteen legs.

Sunday, 8:08 a.m.
Religious Services

Back on the subfloor of the hotel, two of the meeting rooms have been converted to the Lord's house.

Sunday morning beckons the believers, mostly born-again Christians and Catholics. Some teams will hold nondenominational services as well, but most other sects are absent.

Here in one room, a handful of players, maybe a dozen, mostly black defenders, listen intently as a preacher recites Jeremiah's Parable of the Potter.

> Go down at once to the potter's house; there I will reveal My words to you. So I went down to the potter's house, and there he was, working away at the wheel. But the jar that he was making from the clay became flawed in the potter's hand, so he made it into another jar, as it seemed right for him to do.
>
> The word of the LORD came to me: "House of Israel, can I not treat you as this potter treats his clay?"
>
> And this is the LORD's declaration. "Just like clay in the potter's hand, so are you in My hand, house of Israel."

The preacher's voice rises. "Yes," he directs to the players, "you are the clay and God is the potter who shapes you."

One player near the front of the room—the middle linebacker with the strong neck—nods his head. He loves this parable. In some ways, he delivers the message, in the way of a namesake.

"Amen," whispers Jeremiah Trotter.

Sunday, 8:29 a.m.
Breakfast

Down Ballroom Hall, back in the Grand Ballroom, supersized men crowd the breakfast line panting, with famished faces after a full night's sleep.

They brandish plates and silverware like weaponry and their eyes follow each steaming buffet bin of food: bright yellow scrambled eggs, shavings of hash brown potatoes, plump sausages, long wisps of glistening bacon, giant perfectly squared waffles, half-inch-thick spongy pancakes browned on one side. Breakfast in the National Football League reminds you of a sumptuous Mother's Day brunch without the linen. Next to the bins sits an array of fresh grains, a variety of sliced breads, bagels and muffins, and mini cereals, and then a table of fruits and a drink station with pitchers of fresh juice and water and milk and thermoses of coffee, and then an omelet station and a pasta station with heaping folds of fettuccine Alfredo and linguini with chicken, and over to the right some more is a carving station with hunks of roast beef and a huge tray of filet mignon swimming in its juices.

The menu feels all-encompassing, but it's purposefully planned by the strength coach, who consults a nutritionist. Most football players eat breakfast. The body craves carbs and protein, lifeblood for a taxing day.

Watching the eaters, this feast isn't celebratory. It's also not leisurely. And while the food may taste pleasing, it's not viewed by the players as pleasurable as much as just simply fuel. In other words: What do I need to ingest to burn for sustainable energy? Which of the contents inside the many chafing dishes of this orgiastic buffet give me the best results? After a day of pounding on the body, heightened stress, and pregame nerves, the body's will steadily burns, like a candle.

Sunday, 9:24 a.m.
Stadium Departure

Across town, downtown in the shadow of city hall, two oversized motor coach buses—the kind used to transport touring rock bands, with soft, extrawide seating and individual climate control settings—sit parked along the city's main thoroughfare, Broad Street, in front of the elegant hotel. Engines humming, they take on their passengers.

A smattering of New York Giants players and personnel wind through the hotel's revolving doors that lead to wide marble steps and down to the curb. They will await the hiss of the bus doors opening, file inside, and soon depart on a thirteen-minute ride due south to Lincoln Financial Field accompanied by a police escort.

The buses make two runs, departing this morning at 9:30 and 10:30. The rule is players must arrive at the stadium two hours prior to kickoff. Those players in need of treatment must be on the first bus to see the trainer, a busy fellow on game day.

On the bus, like on the plane, players always sit in the back, a safe distance from the coaches and staff members. They carefully guard their space, pinching an eye at a potential interloper. For sure, the unoccupied seat is taken.

In the case of the Eagles, the defense man the very back, the farther back the more boisterous the player. When he played, Hugh Douglas held that last row, which led to Andy Reid's one major rule: Douglas had to ride in the other bus.

Douglas's constant yammering annoyed him.

Meanwhile, back at the hotel by the airport, players for the home team drive themselves to the stadium.

In Philadelphia, it's a brief trip past the D and E terminals to the exit road heading east to a two-lane over a truss bridge that overlooks the unflattering innards of the city, a Sun Oil refinery, once the Gulf Oil refinery, where in 1975 a raging fire broke out in a tank being filled with Venezuelan crude oil and resulted in the deaths of eight firemen.

You make a soft right off the George C. Platt Bridge, not far from where a menacing housing project once stood, and wind through a pop-up residential neighborhood until facing you is a city park, a public golf course, and a man-made lake—home of a creature called the Frankenfish, a toothy snakehead fish rooted in Asia that spawned two B horror movies.

Here you turn left onto a wide, tree-lined street called Pattison Avenue, and head straight, past the Eagles' sprawling team headquarters and a series of gated practice fields on your left and through the main intersection of Broad Street. Herein lies the old home of this part of "Sports Philadelphia," once flanked by the recently demolished Spectrum arena and Veterans Stadium, a brickless, colorless, impersonal multipurpose monolith. Born unto a time in America when modernism was viewed as being first and foremost functional, forsaking all style and taste, given the spreading rash of suburbanism, strip malls, silver Christmas trees, and Astroturf, the buildings, without enough suites, signage, and savoir faire, outlived their usefulness, became parking lots, and gave way to the nearby Wachovia Center for the basketball and hockey teams and a divorce for the baseball and football teams. A couple of blocks in the distance, on the north side of Pattison, stands a lovely throwback baseball park, one of those lyrical little knockoffs that combine the charm of the past and the revenue generators of today.

Meanwhile, your destination, positioned directly across the street at 1020 Pattison Avenue, offers homage to the present, because pro football is now. Like the sport it houses, Lincoln Financial Field dominates the landscape.

The Eagles' home is a capacious place, tastefully dressed and, except for the once swaying ramps on the second deck, since buttressed, constructed from an impeccable design, with its 172 luxury suites and 10,828 club seats and two club lounges some 40,000 square feet apiece and 308 concession points and 22 novelty locations and one men's restroom for every 58 fans. Lamely dubbed "The Linc," the place reminds you of every other stadium that opened this century, which means it offers the charm of a Best Buy. Only the quantity of creature comforts and the size of the whizbang differs from stadium to stadium, with Jerry Jones's rising above them all like the Burj Dubai.

The question begs to be asked. Is the difference between the Linc and Cowboys Stadium really worth the extra half billion dollars it cost Jones? Even if that number shrinks after factoring in inflation from a six-year construction gap between the two projects, what could possibly make it *that* much better an experience? In the last ten years, nearly half the cities in the league built new stadiums, and they're all basically the same, give or take a retractable roof and a grass or RealGrass Matrix playing surface.

Because pro football is now, the way baseball was then, when all of those hallowed parks—Fenway, Wrigley, the old Tiger Stadium—were just beginning to compile lore. Though you wonder whether a place like Heinz Field, even after already playing home to two Super Bowl winners, or an M&T Bank Stadium in Baltimore, or any of the faceless others with their stiff corporate names—Reliant Stadium, Qwest Field, Lucas Oil Stadium, University of Phoenix Stadium, Gillette Stadium—could ever become ballpark-storied.

Another reason stems from a dearth of big games in them, which deems a place legendary. Since the biggest game of the season is held essentially offsite for every team, stadiums struggle to fill with lore. The Super Bowl might as well be held in a conference center somewhere.

The notion of storied buildings likely becomes obsolete anyway the farther we travel forward in time—with luxury trumping literary, a fact not worth hissing about, especially now in pro football's golden age. Much of anything pre-1970s, and certainly pre–Super Bowl, might as well be the Dark Ages, the leatherheads playing the Frisians in NFL history, Student Body Right as crude a weapon as the arbalest.

Unlike, say, college football, pro football keeps its past confined to one place: Lambeau Field. Typical pro football, everything so orderly. Even the ghosts are compartmentalized. A delightful town, Green Bay represents the league's lone link to the past, and it works that way.

The game is barely recognizable from the days of Title Town—which now seems like a fictitious place—with the players and play-books swelling into entirely different forms.

"People always say in sports, the game is not what it used to be," remarks former coach Dick Vermeil, whose career in the game spanned almost forty years. "I'll never say that about football. The players are bigger, stronger, faster, more athletic. When I first became a head coach, the strongest player on our team was Roman Gabriel—and he was the quarterback. They don't work an off-season job, instead taking care of their bodies. They're smarter now. They spend more time studying, and the coaches just give them more and more. There's no off season anymore. There's just a time when they don't play games."

Vermeil shields his eyes, the way only a coach does, and gestures toward the practice field during an afternoon session at training camp. He is a visitor on this day, taking a break from making his boutique wine in Napa Valley and coming east to see old football friends.

"My second go-around, with the Rams," he says, "I saw the volume [of plays] of my offensive coordinator and said to myself, 'We can't coach all this stuff.' But you can. The players are brighter. And they invest more time. They have a lot more to gain by doing it right. Therefore, the game has evolved. Football has never been better than it is right now."

Sunday, 9:31 a.m.
A Coach's Arrival

In his colorless Sunday suit, the man could be going to services, if not for the police escort that surrounds his Denali all the way to the entrance of the heavily guarded parking lot.

The man climbs out of the SUV that will be stationed by security in one of four papal parking spots inside the stadium—next to that of the team owner, the owner's wife, and the team president—and confers briefly with the attendant, who dutifully asks, "Need anything?"

"I'm fine," grunts the coach, awash in Sunday reflection and Sunday sternness. He's been up for hours, and it's not enough. Now he's thinking about how quickly he can reach his office and resume last-minute preparations, though he never stops thinking, preparing, hatching scenarios, fishing for the outcome. He's consumed by it, consumed the way a stalker is. A big man with squinty eyes, he shrinks the corridor with his presence, the rimple in his pink brow spelling Do Not Disturb.

Sunday, 9:59 a.m.
A Superstar's Arrival

The other man's arrival at the stadium engenders a similar stir: crackling exchanges on security walkie-talkies and distant ripples from the "it's him" crowd that has gathered on the stadium's veranda high above the lot. It's him, of course. The out-of-state license plates of the BMW 745 with the crunk rims that hypnotize howl it: EIGHTONE.

That man parks on the outside, the first spot next to the tunnel opening, next to the emergency vehicle. He's much thinner up close, especially the legs that resemble chopsticks, and he's also rather muted for a guy who goes by initials, down to his very collegiate dress: checkered shirt under a burgundy sweater, collar out, jeans, white sneakers, throwback baseball cap backward. He wheels a piece of luggage behind him the way a flight attendant does and heads to the locker room, where he'll sit by himself draped in his own aura, offering little interaction with the room, and later with the field, where he'll stand on the outskirts of the pregame makeshift mosh pit comprised of his new mates, absorbing the scene, detached from the group the way the elite always are.

You know the man. Sort of, which is to say you know of him, though he'll say that you only know of his portrayal. "You'd think I was a felon the way they talk about me," he'll say. The "they" he speaks of speak of the incidents that accompany his mad skills, and it's never an occurrence or happening with the man but always an incident: verbal jousting in the press with his former quarterback in San Francisco, calling him gay, feuding with his former quarterback in Philadelphia, welling up with affection for his former quarterback in Dallas—"That's my teammates," he sniffled, "that's my quarter-back"—only to later accuse that quarterback of side deals with the tight end to get him the ball, helping blow up the Cowboys of 2008 years after stomping on the star at Texas Stadium, the overdose in Dallas, the Sharpie in San Francisco, the reality show, the shuffle to Buffalo.

He'll feign a deaf ear, pondering of his infamy, "Only got my family and a few friends, and that's all who matters in this world."

On this pregame Sunday, the man with all the troubles flashes a toothy smile that makes him seem so very endearing.

Terrell Eldorado Owens counts his touchdowns. "I'm getting three today. Write that down right now. You my witness."

Sunday, 10:09 a.m.
Time to Get Numb

The training room, a sanctuary for players, their hiding spot away from the coaches, the front office, the media, begins to fill up with bodies on tables, like slabs on a butcher block.

Those players in need of treatment because of lingering injuries must arrive earlier than two hours before kickoff. The body beckons.

Now, let's debunk a myth here, the totally skewed cinematic portrayal of treatment, as though players are the men on benches in Needle Park sticking their own veins to stop feeling. It's not seedy or sensational, with players huddled together in a bathroom stall, one playing lookout, sticking each other amid a cacophony of animal noises, or others gulping down painkillers like breath mints.

Numbing the pain is a real thing, done by medical people with the precaution of medical people in the sterile environs of the training room. It is a necessary ritual to trick the body and mask the effects of all that punishment, particularly during the middle of the season when minor injuries and nicks and bumps and bruises multiply like teenage acne. It is necessary to divert the mind's attention from the constant harangue of reminder pain, and necessary sometimes not to feel to play.

"Show me a guy who hasn't taken painkillers, and I'll call him a liar," former offensive tackle Kyle Turley pointed out. "Mondays are brutal. You're gonna wake up, and your body feels like shit. That's the way it should feel. I would give everything I had. I was jacked up from pregame to the end of the game. I would be near passed out on the tarmac at the airport after games. In Carolina, I once passed out on the tarmac. Trainers had to come get me and bring me back.

"By the end of the year, you're going Sunday to Sunday. You don't feel right until the adrenaline hits you the next Sunday. [Painkillers] shut down the pain receptors so you're ready to go."

Said Chris Samuels, the former wonderful offensive tackle for the Redskins, "In a preseason game once I sprained my ankle really bad and tore some stuff in there and played all year long on a bad wheel. I would take the shots of cortisone and Toradol before the games. It reduces the swelling enough to let you perform. Cortisone shots in all of your joints before the game just to cover up the pain. All kinds of crap goes on in that locker room pregame. Guys are getting their fingers injected, their shoulders injected, getting shots just so they can get out there and play."

Toradol, a powerful anti-inflammatory drug commonly used after major surgery, feels like WD-40 going through you. Totally takes the edge off. Takes your mind off the pain. Suddenly it doesn't hurt that bad. Think about somebody who has average aches and pains and takes Advil and feels better. Now here's them. Football players.

"I was popping Vioxx every day when they were legal," Ike Reese said. "My last four years I couldn't practice without a Vioxx pill. I didn't take one on Friday because it was a light day. Then every Sunday morning I'd get a shot of Toradol right in the buttocks. Out of fifty-three players, I estimate that at least twenty of us were taking shit."

"It's a tough job," Tampa Bay tight end Anthony Becht said. "We could be doing it for twenty-four straight weeks with preseason and the playoffs. You have to have a mentally strong mind-set. Some guys can take it. Others take painkillers."

There are whispers before a game. Former offensive lineman Spencer Folau knew what Brian Cox meant when he asked him that one Sunday, "Got any?"

"Sure, I knew what he was talking about," he said. "I didn't have any on me that day. But that was common before the game. After the game. [Offensive lineman] Jerry Fontenot bagged six to eight pills after every game. You don't understand what your body feels like. You did whatever you could just to get through those games. Before every game, Toradol shots; after every game, pills."

Meanwhile, amphetamines have been a quiet problem in all sports for years, including baseball, where a retired player who played in the 1990s told me of guys taking "beans" on a daily basis before the game and how there were two jugs of coffee in the clubhouse: leaded or unleaded, meaning coffee laced with amphetamines or regular coffee.

"Drug testing got worse or better depending on how you look at it," said Kevin Gogan, who toughed out fourteen seasons in the NFL, from 1987 through 2000. "They were all over you for uppers and downers. It was always a grind. You go to a doctor and you know it hurts but you want to tell them that it doesn't. And there's always residual pain."

And then there was Romanowski, a self-proclaimed amateur pharmacist who aimed not only to kill the pain but to reach what he called a football state. "I used to hand out the uppers," he said. "I'd try to get everyone in the zone. I used everything from ginseng to ephedrine to different medications that were legal to take. I had all kinds of different cocktails that I had herbologists put together to help keep my teammates. Meanwhile, I went to that dark place. I went to a quieter, more concentrated place, compared to that jacked-up place. I had to concentrate on getting to that dark place."

Sunday, 11:02 a.m.
The Morning of a Rematch

The room is the size of an airplane hangar, though more lounge than locker room. There is plush carpeting and wood finish on the stalls, which provide ample space, even for the extra-large men who dress here. Yet it feels rather close with the noise, a cacophony of music, hollering, talking, singing, belching. The noise is what you notice first, before you see anything, ahead of a game between the Eagles and Panthers in 2004, a rematch of the 2003 NFC Championship Game won by Carolina.

Hugh Douglas cats around, carrying on, saying one thing, then breaking into song without warning. Old-school Rick James bleats—his "best of" CD—and Douglas wails, "Cold—blood-ed, holy smokes and . . ."

In the middle of a song, he stops and blathers about the game, which on this day comes after a bye week. "Gotta shake that rust off," he brays. "Choo-choo! Gotta catch that train to work! Choo-choo, c'mon, catch that train. Y'all runnin' 'round the city tellin' everybody you play for the Philadelphia Eagles. Tellin' them hos that you love 'em. C'mon now, let's go to work. You too, T.O., be ready."

Owens dresses without a peep. Today's game centers around Owens versus cornerback Ricky Manning Jr., who had manhandled Eagle wideouts in the title game and picked off Donovan McNabb three times.

"That young boy wants a piece of you, T.O.," Douglas continues. "Be ready now."

Douglas's words seem to fall before reaching Owens, who dresses silently in front of his locker lost in thought. A forever subplot to any game, preening for the cameras, doing the pose, part Narcissus, part Leon from the old Bud commercials, Owens is barely noticeable.

A year later, however, Owens would have words for Douglas, who was then working for the team in the capacity of "ambassador"—self-dubbed the *badassador*. Owens became moody and disruptive. No longer was he the jovial character offering gifts to everyone, like he did his first season in Philadelphia. One day he came in with dozens of the latest gaming system and handed them out to the team like Halloween candy. Now he sulked over his contract and bickered with Donovan McNabb, and one day he snapped at Douglas in the training room. Douglas fired back. The exchange became heated and Douglas tackled him across a training table.

When the men were separated, a frazzled and emotional Owens turned toward the bystanders and said, "Anybody else want a piece of me?"

His gaze turned toward McNabb. "What are you looking at?" he snapped.

McNabb ignored him.

"Let's go." He continued staring around the room. "Anybody else want me?"

Soon Owens was suspended for the second time for a different transgression, this time for the rest of the 2005 season. The good times, as they often do with the ultimate misunderstood heartbreaker, turned sour, and he moved on to Dallas, where history repeated itself again.

Sunday, 11:04 a.m.
Hot Tub, Cold Tub

The ritual begins for many of them back here in the tubs, especially the ones still sore from the week, especially the hulking ones with cranky backs.

First they enter the cold tub, a very cold tub, where the water temperature dips into the forties and you're in up to your neck. Some players wear ski caps to lock in as much body heat as possible. Doesn't help much. The initial shock is torturous. Forgive the pun, everything seems to stop cold. Your mind freezes. After an initial gasp, you can't feel yourself breathe. The moment rivals an out-of-body experience, the only noise you hear that of your own teeth chattering uncontrollably.

If you can stand fifteen minutes in a fifteen-by-ten-foot pool of really cool, according to many players and backed by league trainers, a soak helps reduce inflammation and rid soreness in the muscles.

"It's like the fountain of youth," Anthony Becht said.

For most of the body.

"Let me tell you," former linebacker Jeremiah Trotter cracked, "shrinkage does exist. At least that's what I hear."

"Some guys will put towels down there," Titans cornerback Cary Williams told the *Tennessean*.

Some guys will soak in the hot tub directly after the cold tub, and repeat the process twice for the hot/cold contrast. The hot tub—usually set around 115 degrees—helps loosen the muscles and promote blood flow. The Steelers' Hines Ward is a huge devotee of the hot tub. At home, he will soak in Epsom salts.

Following a soak, players may get adjusted by the chiropractor or go through a series of elaborate stretching exercises. Then they will get taped and begin slipping on their pads, though Ray Rice, the Ravens' dynamic young running back, must first cover himself with oil and body lotion. "I can't put my pads on without it," Rice said. "It feels like an extra layer on my body."

Former Eagles linebacker Nate Wayne used to spray his knees with WD-40. "Crazy, ain't it?" his teammate Ike Reese remarked. "Some of these cats, the things they do before a game."

Sunday, 11:14 a.m.
Special Teams Head to the Field

The special teamers hit the field first before the game, led by the kicker and punter, who will assess the weather conditions and direction of the wind and the playing surface. Is the field slick? Meaning condensation, rather than the obvious rain or snow. How's the footing for the plant foot? If the game is away, how does the field play? Sometimes at a road stadium a kicker will identify landmarks to be used as aiming points, and pregame marks the time to align on various spots of the field.

A kicker will also judge his leg within the conditions so he can report back to his coach the edges of his range. So he'll try many long kicks pregame to figure out how far out his comfort zone lies.

Sunday, 11:30 a.m.
Pregame Caucus

A same-page meeting between the head coach and two officials occurs about now in every stadium across the league. It's a useful tool for the referees. Here they will get a lead on possible things to watch for during a game, like trick plays or exotic formations a coach may employ in the game, so they don't make a mistake with a possible penalty call. Or the coach may detect something studying the opponent on tape during the week, say, a blocking technique by the right tackle, and alert officials to look for the possible transgression during the game.

"That's illegal," the coach will say.

The head official pacifies him with a nod.

"Keep an eye out for it, okay?"

"You got it."

They talk about the time frame for the rest of pregame, and everyone in the room—which also includes the team's general manager, director of security, and director of media relations—synchronizes their watches.

"Flag?" the official asks.

The coach retrieves the red challenge flag from his pocket and holds it up.

"You know the drill. Make sure you get our attention."

The coach nods knowingly and changes the conversation. "Sixty-eight," he says.

"What do you mean?"

"Number 68. Watch him, you know?"

"Oh . . . right. Good luck, Coach."

Sunday, 11:32 a.m.
Warm-ups

Players wander to the field in packs designated by positions, sort of like a portrayal of Noah's Ark. Three, four, five at a time, they emerge from the tunnel for warm-ups, the quarterbacks, then the running backs, then the wide receivers, and so forth.

89 Minutes to Kickoff
Super Bowl XLIII: Arizona vs. Pittsburgh

The field is busy—but relaxed all the same. It feels almost like a city park. A catch here, a practice kick there. Old friends wearing opposing helmets deep in conversation. Stadium personnel resemble power walkers, with their purposeful strides. Cheerleaders practice their routines. They could be a dance troupe. And it's the same even before the biggest of games, except the number of interlopers swells. They all seem to be officials of some sort—league officials? network officials? stadium officials? team officials?—their matching color-coded field passes purposely visible on a rope-chain swaying from around the neck.

Near a cluster of more officials, all clad in dark expensive suits with matching power ties splashed with color, right there on the visitor's sideline, near midfield on the playing field of Raymond James Stadium in buzzing Tampa, two-time MVP Kurt Warner of the Cardinals approaches opposing quarterback Ben Roethlisberger of the Steelers from behind.

"Hey, Ben," Warner says.

"Yo, Kurt!"

"Do you know why I started wearing gloves when I play?"

"No," says Roethlisberger, "why's that, man?"

"Everyone thinks it was because I was having trouble holding on to the ball. But it was because I saw you do it and I figured, why not?"

Roethlisberger beams at the notion of the accomplished quarterback ten years his senior copying him. Him. Ben. Not Big Ben. Next to Warner, he's just Ben. "Get out of here, man. No way! That's crazy!"

"No, seriously," says Warner. "That's why. Learn something from anybody."

"Wow."

"Good luck to ya today," Warner says.

Roethlisberger nods. "You too."

"Can I say a prayer with you?" asks Warner.

"Sure."

And in an honest moment, tucked deep inside Super Bowl hoopla and production, the two men who would trade hero status throughout the game bowed their heads and prayed.

84 Minutes to Kickoff
2009 Opener: Tennessee at Pittsburgh

Ben Roethlisberger stopped abruptly inside the tunnel that leads to the field, the noise growing louder with each step, which is something this early on game day, even for Pittsburgh. From where he stood without a full view of the seats, accompanied by his fellow Steeler quarterbacks, you could feel the place filling rapidly, the tailgate breakdown over in RV city—across the street on the back side of the stadium, next to the Carnegie Science Center—long since under way. Most everyone extinguished their coals and sealed their chip bags early on this highly anticipated Thursday evening that kicked off the 2009 season.

Most everyone in town had cut out of work early, if they even went in at all, and hacked their way down to the water. They did lunch and noon beers at Station Square and then boarded the Gateway Clipper Fleet riverboat for the quick scoot across the Monongahela and Ohio to the North Shore right at Heinz Field.

This opener was even more special than usual, even for Pittsburgh, where football represents identity. Without the Steelers, Pittsburgh would be relegated to third-city status, no different from Wichita, Plano, or Toledo, only with a richer history, the town having peaked in 1911 when it produced nearly half of the nation's steel.

Because Pittsburgh won it again in 2008 and henceforth became Sixburgh, on this September night before the first game everyone would revel in what happened the previous February, and look down on the rest of Football America from the hilly perch of the NFL's winningest city.

So Roethlisberger turned to his fellow quarterbacks, veteran backup Charlie Batch and second-year man Dennis Dixon, a University of Oregon man, and said, "Boys, if you ain't ready for this, then there's something wrong. Let's go."

And the three quarterbacks lightly jogged out of the tunnel and onto the field, past the dignitaries, including NFL commissioner Roger Goodell and national anthem performer Harry Connick Jr., and the surviving families of those who perished in the nearby crash of United Airlines Flight 93.

It's always interesting to Steeler-watch during pregame warm-ups, if only because you can see the evolution of a successful franchise, the current players direct descendants of the dynasty team of the 1970s, winning just another trait passed down to them, no different from eye color in a family.

Because it's not a coincidence that those in the black and gold act differently than do, say, Arizona players before their first game since the Super Bowl.

"There's something bred in players in franchises like those," said then Cardinals tight end Anthony Becht. "Everybody wants to win. But in places like Pittsburgh, it's like a birthright. It's something you're forced to live up to. Like going to school at a place like Harvard or Yale when your father went there and your grandfather went there. There's something expected of you and so you act that way."

For one, they embrace the colors and the meaning of them, which is the butt of another man's joke. Because nowadays it's corny to revere anything, and cornier still to move away from the contemporary and honor the past. Because a jaded man can't appreciate something as good as this scene, throwback innocent, when God, family, and football wasn't a political notion too right—or too left. And the Steeler players are Steeler serious, moving about without silliness, whereas rewind back to a scene, say, in Philadelphia in 2004. Donovan McNabb emerges from the tunnel bumping butts with ample defensive tackle Hollis Thomas and says later about that locker room, "All that's missing are cocktail waitresses."

One man's looseness is another man's chicanery.

Now here's Roethlisberger, having finished throwing fade passes to Hines Ward and Santonio Holmes and tossing the ball with Batch, literally seeking out every player in a Steeler jersey on the field and whispering, he said later, something about being a champion and something about being a Steeler.

Sunday, 12:22 p.m.
Time to Purge

"Ever hear of a bulimic football player?" one NFL player asked one day, irrespective of nothing.

"No."

"Well, there are plenty of them."

"What do you mean?"

"Guys throw up all the time. Some guys don't want anything in their stomach. They want to get it all out of there. Mostly, it's the nervousness before the game. That's why I stay out of the bathroom. You hear guys throwing up in the stall. You hear them throwing up in the trash cans. I hate hearing it. You know when you hear it, how it makes you gag? You hear the splatter and then you feel like you're going to do it. Or worse, you smell it. And then you have to hold your breath and suppress that feeling."

Mark Schlereth, now a wonderful sportscaster on ESPN, described the scene that used to take place in the corner of the Broncos' locker room where the offensive linemen presided. There were twelve of them altogether, six men on either side, their own garbage basket in the middle.

"Somebody," he said, "usually myself or Tommy Nalen, would start heaving and it would be a chain reaction. Next thing you know, four or five guys are puking over the trash can.

"When I was with the Broncos, we were vomiters. Before every game, myself included. It's nerves. It gets you. You constantly have to pee. All pregame, you're back and forth to the bathroom. Four and a half hours before a game you're at the stadium. Then game time approaches and the nerves hit you. My stomach is upset right now as I talk about it."

In San Francisco, the honors were designated for the defensive linemen. "Larry Roberts seemed to be a guy who always would throw up," Romanowski said. "Kevin Fagan also did a little bit here and there. So did Pierce Holt. For me, I threw up after games from concussions."

Each team, it seems, has designated pukers. "I've seen Donovan [McNabb] throw up before games," former Eagle Jason Short said.

"When I was with the Giants," Brian Mitchell said, "it was Rich Seubert. He would throw up before every game like clockwork. I'm in there talking about what we're doing after the game, what I'm going to eat for dinner, shit like that, and Rich was in the bathroom puking. The whole team didn't feel good until he threw up."

Tiki Barber told the story of Seubert's harrowing injury back on October 19, 2003, against the Eagles, and how he threw up after N. D. Kalu stepped on the back of his right leg and broke his fibula, tibia, and ankle. "They gave me a shot of something," Seubert said. "I don't remember much of what happened. Except the pain. I remember the pain."

"I used to throw up before games for my first five years in the league," said former Colts defensive tackle Montae Reagor. "All the nerves and anxiety got to me. After three plays I would hyperventilate, and then after that I'd be fine. I could cope with it. Now, some guys would take three or four—or even five—craps before the game."

Linebacker Takeo Spikes laughed about the comparison of the pregame to the medicine hawked by pitchwoman Jamie Lee Curtis. He shared, most personally, "I take a shit once every two days [during the off season]. On game day, I'd get three in."

Preparation and More Preparation

Sixteen games comprise a season. Unlike the other professional sports, where games are plentiful and the rhythm of a long season dulls the meaning of each contest, football offers little opportunity for redemption. Each game is paramount.

Preparation is endless and relentless. The player endures minicamp (or the proper term, OTA, Organized Team Activities) and training camp. Two-a-days and practice and walk-throughs. Hours on the field and hours on the training table. Hours in the weight room and hours in the film room.

Hours talking about it. Sunday. The game. And by the way it's always Sunday, even if the game is Sunday night or Monday night or Saturday or Thursday, except Thanksgiving Thursday, when it's just Thanksgiving.

Elsewhere, the week happens. Six full days of life before the afghan comes out and Sunday beckons. For them, Sunday is omnipresent. In the elevator of their building with the neighbor inside. At the convenience store. The kid's school. On the phone with their brother. And when the phone is passed to their mother. It's Sunday or late Saturday afternoon when they check into the hotel on the road or in their home city.

And then finally it really is Sunday, and they arrive on the great day of rest for everyone else to a parking lot already jammed with eager onlookers with their grills and their beer and their fanatic ways. They see a stadium fill before their very eyes and they just know that no matter what position they play or what ranking they hold on the team, it will somehow come down to what they do on this day, Sunday.

They don't discuss pressure out loud. They feel it deep in the belly. That churning, where their insides feel like they are reorganizing. Such a terrible motility. And though intellectually they know it will eventually subside once they get out there on the field and do what they've always done, what they know, it's getting there that consumes them now.

They wish away the clock. Pleading for kickoff.

Then they hear a moonlighting cop or whoever is their Paul Revere give the early distant warning.

Two minutes!!!

"You'll be somewhat fine and then all of a sudden you get that two-minute warning until game time," kicker David Akers said. "Out of nowhere it feels like you have to take a huge dump. It's the anxiety. You think about the people watching, the possibility of you letting your team down. So many things go through your mind. It's why Pepto-Bismol is so popular before the game. I take it all the time."

"Before the game," longtime quarterback Jeff Garcia said, "I have to continuously pee. The fluids go through you at such a fast rate."

"Yeah," agreed cornerback Rod Hood, "you see a lot of guys throwing up, but it's like two minutes before the game I gotta pee again. And then again. I'm constantly going back and forth between my locker and the bathroom. I know a lot of guys that pee themselves on the field and on the sidelines. That was never me, though. That's nasty. I would be in that tent pissing in empty bottles all game long, though."

Mark Schlereth's nickname is Stink, which is short for Stinkman, which came from a dish the Eskimos of southwest Alaska would eat called "stinkhead." One day, Schlereth, a native Alaskan, is regaling his teammates with stories about stinkhead. How it's made from the whole head of a king salmon, which is somewhat larger than a football, and how it's prepared by wrapping the head in the long grasses that grow along the rivers and streams and burying it in a moss-lined pit in the ground for four to six weeks, where it rots. Just rots, with the bones softening up until the whole head has a consistency similar to mashed potatoes. The Eskimos then dig up the fish head—and presumably hold their nose because the smell is absolutely rancid—and eat it.

"I was telling them about stinkhead the meal and it just so happened I regularly peed my pants," Schlereth said. "Pretty much every game I did. I was already drenched in sweat so it was no real difference to me. So later the nickname got shortened to just Stink. Hey—I was miserable anyhow out on the field, I wasn't going to hold it in and become even more miserable."

Garcia said, "I've been on the field and had to go underneath the stands or figure out a way to take a leak. For a fact, it became a problem because it was affecting the way I threw the ball. I've always said there needs to be a Porta Potty for guys on the sidelines who can't leave the field."

Think about it. For players with a nervous bladder, they can't keep going back to the locker room, especially if it's a longer walk. So what's a player with a nervous bladder to do? Kevin Donnelly, formerly of the Titans, had a unique solution.

"He used to piss right there on the sidelines," a former teammate said. "He'd sit on the bench and stuff a towel down his pants. Piss in the towel. Then throw it away. Back in Houston, at the Astrodome, it was a quarter-mile walk to get back to the bathroom. So you can't keep going back and forth. It actually works. You cram it down your pants and just go.

"Koy Detmer used to piss in a bottle in the ice shanty right on the field. Everybody gets it. Nervous bladder. It's just like anything else. As soon as you start to do something you have to go to the bathroom."

Said Garcia, "My first year in the league, I tried the towel thing. It was in a preseason game. Second half. I figured, 'Well, I'll try it with a towel. Just pee into the towel.' I had to go pretty bad. As soon as I felt the warm pee touch my leg, I shut it down. I said, 'I can't do this.' It's just nasty. I couldn't follow through with it. Players try all sorts of tricks to relieve themselves out there. My teammate in Tampa would just pee his pants and say it's not going to make a difference because of all the sweat."

Former fullback Jon Ritchie agreed with Garcia's teammate. "You're drenched in sweat anyway," he said. "What does it matter? By the time warm-ups are over, you're overhydrating and you're drenched. It's clear. It's not urine. What's the big deal?"

That was Ritchie's thing. Hydrating. He obsessed over hydrating. Fearing a cramp or pulled muscle, he would drink gallon after gallon. Water. Electrolyte drinks. Sports drinks. He had this duffel bag that he carried everywhere—his water bag—and he constantly replenished it. As a result, he would gain as much as eight pounds in fluid weight at a time.

"Seven bottles of water in it at all times," he said. "I took it with me everywhere. I was always completely bloated. Always sloshing around in my stomach. I heard somewhere that was when your body was in peak condition. I think everyone is obsessive about something. I just didn't want to pull something blocking a guy. Guys do it all the time. They pull their calf muscle and it just shreds. If you get hurt like that during the game, that's one thing. But if you're not properly hydrated? Then you're not prepared and it's your fault."

For Saints linebacker Mark Simoneau, that sensation goes beyond hydration. It's a product of Sunday, no matter what's in his system. "I gotta pee like every three or four minutes it seems like," he said. "I don't know if it's the nerves or adrenaline or if it's something where you know you're going into battle and want to get it all out of you."

Nervous bladder is bad. But not the worst attack of nerves. "Imagine," one player said, "your hands are all taped up, your gloves are on, and you have to take a crap. How do you wipe your ass? Enter the sacrificial towel. You use a whole towel and throw it away. Gotta protect that hand. Sometimes it works and sometimes it doesn't."

Perhaps the most embarrassing attack of nerves was from Titans offensive lineman Kevin Long. "It was a fat nasty lineman thing," he said. "I thought it was a fart, but it turned out to be a 'shart.' It was my first preseason game in the league. My first game with my new teammates. Of course we had to be in our white pants. Someone told me I sat on something and I looked down and said, 'Ahhh, shit.' I had to run into the toilet and I had to scrub my britches. Welcome to the NFL, kid."

Said Simoneau, "This past year against Carolina, some guy for the Panthers, I can't remember his name, had crapped his pants. You could see from the sidelines this brown streak under his bright white pants. He played the entire second quarter with the brown-stained pants. We were having a good time with it, yelling at the ref, 'Get this guy off the field! He shit his pants!'

"The second half started, and sure enough he had brand-new pants on. I give him credit, though, for being able to play through that. That's the length some guys go to stay on the field."

Sunday, 12:44 p.m.
"Somebody's Got to Slap Me"

The players have settled back in the locker room following pregame warm-ups, and look to find a new mental state.

Game state.

Aggression is a football player's fuel. Many look to summon it now with contact. Feel the pain and you won't feel the fear. Punch, hit, wallop it away. Spike the adrenaline.

"Funny, I didn't do anything crazy," Brian Mitchell said. "I'd eat my pregame meal—eggs and bacon. Had to have my eggs and bacon. I'd wear the same pads on the same legs, same socks on the same foot. I was good about matching all that stuff up. I made my own knee pads and doctored my thigh pads. I made it worse by taking padding away. That was me. Then I would see these linemen punching and slapping each other in the face and I'm like, 'What the hell are these guys doing? We're about to go to war for three hours and they're in here beating each other up.' "

The Eagles were playing the Redskins at FedExField, and inside the cramped visitor's locker room before the game, defensive tackle Paul Grasmanis needed someone to slap him. Grasmanis, a typical Notre Dame lineman, who stood 6-foot-3, 298 pounds, paced the room in an adrenaline fit and yelled to no one in particular, "Somebody's got to slap me! Somebody's got to hit me!"

Line mate Brandon Whiting had heard enough. "Fuck it," he said. "Gras, I'll hit you."

"Then come on and hit me."

Whiting slapped him three times in the face. But it did not suffice. Grasmanis needed more.

"Hit me harder! Hit me again!"

Whiting unleashed a flurry this time, slapping and punching Grasmanis in the face and side of the head. All the while, Grasmanis hooted and hollered, scrunching his face, grinding his teeth. The sound of the beating was so loud that coach Andy Reid, whose office was adjacent to the locker room, rushed into the room and screamed, "What's going on in here?"

Following the game, Grasmanis rolled into the trainer's room and said, "Somebody's gotta check my ear. I haven't been able to hear since Whiting slapped me."

That incident hardly deterred him from his violent pregame ritual. Years later, he implored rookie Jason Short to do the same thing.

"Come on, Short! Slap me!"

Short recalled, "We were slapping each other around pretty good. He got me pretty damn good and suddenly everything went black for a minute. I shook it off and then I got him back real good."

Former Eagle Rod Hood also recalled that scene. "I would watch these guys slap each other around and I would try not to laugh because they're doing what they have to do to get ready," he said. "They're getting into their characters. But man, watching these guys get ready was pretty amusing to me.

"Then there was Brian Dawkins. He would be humble. Real light talking all week long. Then right before the game we would get that two-minute warning and something would go off and Dawk would just snap. He was Idiotman. It was like a cartoon changing into a character.

Peter Parker transforming into Spider-Man. Just crazy, crazy stuff. To watch him change right before your eyes was amazing to me."

Adrenaline spike. That's what they feel. What begets the froth.

And so there is Takeo Spikes back in pregame Buffalo, a typically numbing Buffalo Sunday in late November, and he's eyeing the Miami sideline from nearby on the playing field. He looks like he's counting as he paces from the 35 to the 40 and back to the 35. He's pointing. And now he's yelling at someone on the Dolphins.

"I like to pick one guy," Spikes said, "go out in pregame, look at him, and let him know that he's about to get that ass-whupping."

Meanwhile, former offensive lineman Mark Schlereth said he "didn't need false bravado to go out there. I was already scared to go out there. I could have been convinced your little sister was the best player ever and I had to play against her."

The locker room is a fascinating study of people. Often cliquish, just like every workplace, where you can see clusters of sameness, often divided by position or race or even religion. In baseball, for instance, the two most pronounced groups in the clubhouse were the Latin players and the born-again Christians, dubbed "God squaders" by some of the other ballplayers.

Here's Short and Grasmanis smacking each other, while not far away, Chad Lewis reads the Bible. "David and Goliath story all the time," he said. "I took a lot of comfort in that story. I would say my prayers. That helped me get my mind and my heart right."

With their coach a devout Mormon, Reid converting to the faith after meeting his future wife, Tammy, at Brigham Young University, the Eagles have had a significant number of religious players on the team through the years.

And while Lewis would ask Short to fist-pound him on the shoulder pads before the game—three times, always three times—and Dawkins is a devout Christian, which has no bearing on his wild histrionics, however PG, the difference in pregame behavior between openly religious players and nonreligious players seems fairly distinct, the most obvious being use of language.

"I listen to gospel music in my locker and prepare myself for the situation," Montae Reagor said. "I'm a mild-mannered guy as I've played ten years. I'd settle my mind and go over my notes. I always take notes and get myself in the mind-set that I'm ready to play. Meanwhile, you got guys around you doing a bunch of hollering, but I don't know what they're saying. They're just screaming and hollering."

Screaming and hollering Orlando Brown was notorious for working over his teammates in Baltimore. "I would call the huddle before the game and punch all of my fellow O-linemen in the face," he said. "I'd get them pissed off enough to want to fight me, and only then would they be ready to play a game.

"Coaches told me, 'Zeus, you have to calm down.' I was giving guys stitches before the game even started. The coaches wouldn't let me punch Kyle Boller. He was so fucking scared of me. He needed a punch to get fired up. I had fun with that shit."

Mark Simoneau, meanwhile, punches himself. "I like to hit my head to get myself going," he said. "It's hard to find someone that will hit you back sometimes. I've seen guys like [Saints defensive end] Charles Grant smack his head up against some teammates. You were wondering if this guy is going to get a concussion because he's hitting his head so hard."

Be ready to fistfight. That's what Kyle Turley would tell his teammates. "We'd be at a visiting team stadium and people would be somber," he said, "so I would go around and pick up tables and throw them around. I'd throw around water coolers. I'd say, 'Fuck these guys,' and all that. Then everybody would be ready for a gang fight. That's what it should be. They've really calmed the game down. The last two years have been a little weird for me. I'm too old to be doing that stuff now. Hopefully, these young guys get after it. Otherwise the era of the slayer mentality is gone."

Sunday, 12:51 p.m.
The Long Wait

A quick scan shows the orderly composition of a locker room, the players separated by stalls, separated by position, separated by units. Defense is stationed in the back, the linebackers deep in the corner, rolling forward with the defensive backs on one side and defensive linemen on the other, then blurring into the offense with the tight ends, receivers, kicker, punter, and quarterbacks manning the near side wall. Along the other side, traveling to the front of the room, the running backs beget the offensive linemen—who by nature exist unto themselves, a big man's trait that usually has something to do with their super size as young men.

They all, however, appear preoccupied, perched on their stools. Some don earphones, eyes closed, concentrating deeply on the music. Some have a towel draped over their face, while others just stare blankly ahead. There is no talking among them. It is a reflective period, wholly individual, marked by a grave quiet, sixty or so players and team attendants in a warehouse of a room alone with their thoughts in the company of men.

Jon Runyan holds the end stall and bears the stare of a prison guard. It seems at this moment Runyan was born to make grown men feel uncomfortable. At 6-foot-7, 340 pounds, as sturdy—and cuddly—as an oak-veneer coffin, Runyan reeks of that dark place, particularly with the unnerving calmness that he exhibits. He sits without fidgeting, without leg-bouncing, finger-cracking, neck-rolling. He is bronze-bust still.

This time is unimportant to him. Two hours ago, Runyan performed his pregame ritual of lounging flat on his back at the 50-yard line, a Styrofoam cup of coffee next to him. He stretched a little. Breathed deeply—a little. Just lay there, intermittently sitting up and sipping his coffee.

As usual, his thoughts were varying and disjointed, whizzing by: The color of the seats. His children. Michael Strahan. A plane over top. To where? The contrail it leaves. Like a Sharpie in the sky. The sinking sun into dusk. Dinner tomorrow. The sounds of a filling stadium.

While others summoned their inner beast, he gulped more coffee, oblivious to movement all around him.

Seconds tick away before the call to action with only faint noise. Someone clears his throat. A foot taps on the floor. Silence in a room with so many people huddled together grows tension.

The sound of waiting breaks suddenly when a security staffer and moonlighting Philly cop by the name of Butch Buchanico Jr.—son of the security chief—barrels through the heavy steel doors and booms, "Two minutes. *Two minutes!* Let's go. Twooooo minuuuuutes!"

The room begins to stir immediately. Players rise and fumble for their helmets.

The head coach will enter the locker room about now. He had been in his office scanning the game plan one last time, perhaps accompanied by a trusted assistant or two, the rest of the coaching staff cornered away elsewhere. Perhaps he will make one last tweak to the plan or with personnel, usually based on hunch.

Andy Reid clears his throat and summons the players to gather around for the Last Words.

Sunday, 12:53 p.m.
The Sunday Sermon

Head coach Jon Gruden lived for this moment, and it came naturally to him. Certainly he knew he could inspire them with a look—some contorted face, a raised eyebrow or pursed lip—just as the great performers of the stage could evoke emotion from their audience. Because of the honesty. To will something in others one must first feel the message deep inside *his* being.

And he always felt it. A week's work on the line, the very purpose of the calling about to play out on a larger stage, now just twenty-two minutes away. The peak of the rush, between the busyness of preparation and execution, is now.

One last time to inspire. So he paced the room and looked his men dead in the eye, as many as he could in such a brief period of time.

"I need thirty seconds of your mind," Gruden would say to his team of Tampa Bay Buccaneers on one particular Sunday morning. "Zoom in. Thirty seconds. That stage out there, man. That stage . . . is the most beautiful stage of all. Way I see it—it's the most beautiful woodshed I've ever seen. The most beautiful woodshed. You take this team to the shed now. Do what you're here to do. Not a guy in this room feels any pressure. You apply it. Sixty minutes of speed and precision. That's a big beautiful woodshed. Are we clear? Protect the ball!"

Quarterback Jeff Garcia found himself riveted by Gruden's talks during his time in Tampa. "To listen to a guy like Gruden and his energy really creates an excitement within the team," Garcia said. "You and your teammates are able to play above and beyond what you would normally expect from yourselves. It allows us to play the game and play at an emotional high. If you don't play this game at a certain level, you're gonna get your ass kicked. You need ways to bring yourself to an emotional high, and Jon was able to bring that out of me."

A coach's final address to his team is the Cliffs Notes version of his main message for the week, and while the Gruden types in the NFL provide wonderful dramatic inspiration and also spawn the likes of Al Pacino's meretricious Coach Tony D'Amato in *Any Given Sunday*, they aren't two-page soliloquies on a script. Some may produce spittle, but many are succinct and impassive.

For instance, the most successful coach in the league operates Gipper-free. New England's Bill Belichick offers only basic reminders before games. According to former Patriots cornerback Ellis Hobbs, Belichick is a relative stranger to his players. All boss. He's discerning—thus his nickname, the Brain—and detached. Tight-lipped, even curmudgeonly, Belichick wouldn't resonate as a fiery Gruden to his players.

"He's like a stern stepdad," Hobbs said.

Belichick says his parting words usually come as game day nears and "we see really where our team is and maybe what the most important issues are at that point.

"During the course of the week sometimes things fluctuate a little bit and you want to make sure your team is focused on a particular area going into the game," he said. "Sometimes you know what that's going to be at the beginning of the week, but sometimes you don't, and sometimes it depends on how the week goes."

Seeking some rah, Belichick for years often had charismatic veteran Junior Seau address the team after he spoke. But even Belichick shed his manteau on one noted occasion. Before Super Bowl XXXVIII against Carolina, perturbed by all of the glowing talk surrounding the Panthers, Belichick told his team:

> Everybody's talking about how the Panthers are similar to us. It's a bunch of bullshit. They're not what we are. They can't be what we are. We are what we are. They're not us. They'll never be fucking us. They'll never be champions. We're the fucking champions and the trophy is coming back where it belongs.

In the book *Patriot Reign*, Michael Holley's terrific account of the New England dynasty, injured offensive lineman Damien Woody said he was moved by Belichick's impassioned words. "This is going to sound weird because it was a bunch of expletives, but it was touching," he said. "We saw a different side of him. We had never seen him that emotional before. He got me ready. I felt like going out there, strapping it on, and playing on one leg."

Legendary coach Joe Gibbs took a similarly reserved approach before games. "Joe wasn't a loud person, but he had respect," said former Redskin Brian Mitchell. "He said what he had to say and treated us like the men we were supposed to be. We knew what we had to do. He was just like he was always. He was cool. That was his thing. He only yelled when he had to. He never got rattled. And you don't know what that means to a player, because a team will always reflect its coach."

Meanwhile, Reid—who comes from the Mike Holmgren coaching tree that also includes Gruden—believes in consistency. In other words, if by nature you're not a booming individual then you cannot suddenly transform into Coach Hyde moments before kickoff and come across as believable.

"You don't want big highs and big lows," he said. "You don't want to be a screamer and a yeller. People turn that off. You don't want to be a rah-rah guy because people turn that off. If you just shoot 'em straight, people accept that—whether it's football players, other coaches, or your wife."

Mitchell, who also played for Reid from 2000 through 2002, adds, "If your coach is rattled, you're gonna get rattled. Players look at a coach's face. If it's droopy, well, we think, 'Damn, how am I gonna make that play?' Or, 'Damn, how we gonna win this game?' If the coach doesn't believe it's gonna happen, then how are we supposed to believe it's gonna happen?"

When it comes to conveying belief, few are better than former Steelers coach Bill Cowher. He invokes an almost cultish following. Consider 1995, when the Steelers played the Cowboys in the Super Bowl. Pittsburgh stood at 3–4 following a disheartening 27–9 loss at home to the Cincinnati Bengals. The next week against Jacksonville, Cowher let loose with a wild all-jaw diatribe before the game. Then team trainer Rick Burkholder recalls that Cowher ended his speech by declaring, "You guys will win all nine games we have left."

The Steelers routed the Jaguars that day and went on to win eight in a row, losing only the season finale against Green Bay in what amounted to a meaningless game because they had the division already clinched.

Talk to those around Cowher, and they swear by what he says. They talk of a gift he has to reach each individual player while addressing the masses and will results. "He could get you to do anything," said former Steeler linebacker Levon Kirkland.

In a key division game in 1997, the Steelers trailed the Ravens 24–7 at halftime following three interceptions thrown by Kordell Stewart. During intermission, Cowher told his team, "We're gonna take the opening kickoff so deep in their territory. Then we're gonna score. Then we're gonna get a three-and-out. Then we're gonna get the ball back and score again. And we're gonna win this game. Yes we are! We're gonna win this game!"

Will Blackwell faked a reverse on the second-half kickoff and raced 97 yards for a Pittsburgh touchdown and the defense held Baltimore on a three-and-out in the next series. A touchdown pass by Stewart later in the third quarter brought the Steelers to within three points— and they went on to win the game 42–34.

"He was like a prophet," Burkholder said. "You believed in him. You believed in what he said."

Linebacker Joey Porter, who embodied the Steelers' ferocious play for years, said the entire team looked forward to Cowher's pregame musings. "I needed to see that jaw going," he said. "Got us going real good. We were ready when we saw his jaw going up and down and all of the spit flyin'."

Following the game, Cowher was so emotionally charged that he often couldn't pray with the team because he'd catch himself cursing. "You could be dead flat right before you went out, but Cowher would get you fired up," Burkholder said. "Everyone fed off his energy. He was so emotional. You'd never want to miss one of his pregame talks. It wasn't anything unique. But it was just something. He talked about passion. He talked about the Pittsburgh Steelers. How hard you work. How much it meant to be on that field.

"Most coaches do their pregame speech based on the week. Bill would start his rhetoric on Monday. This one time, he talked to the team about when you were a kid and you used to go to the amusement park and your older brother told you about the roller coaster. How big the hill was. How you remember standing in line and feeling the butterflies, looking up at the cars coming down. Every day he'd talk about being in that line.

"Then right before the game, he said, 'The bar has just hit you in the legs. You are now locked in. We're going up there together. We're going to take that hill. Over the next three hours it will be like a roller coaster—you'll have the ups and downs—but you'll defeat that hill.'" He boomed those words before the opener of the 1995 season.

Cowher's approach doesn't always yield Cowher results. Take the case of Ray Rhodes, the career assistant who took over as head coach of the Eagles in 1995. After having initial success, culminating in a 58–37 playoff victory over the Lions that season, the fiery Rhodes—known for his provocative pregame speeches—quickly faltered as a one-trick magician. While his players genuinely liked and cared about him, all of the rah-rah rhetoric couldn't disguise the reality that Rhodes—another Holmgren disciple—was a coordinator with a head coach's title.

He could only invoke the intruder scenario so many times before his words hit deaf ears and disappeared into rolling eyes and yawns. "I'm like, I know this cat is not serious," Ike Reese recalled thinking after one of his infamous diatribes.

Rhodes was fired at the end of that disastrous 3–13 season in 1998, and after landing in Green Bay the following year, he made it through only one season as head coach with the Packers.

In hindsight, Rhodes's downfall stemmed from a close relationship with his players, a tactic that works better from a coordinator level. He cultivated them on a personal level and enjoyed one-on-one discourse. Many who played for him will admit that the team took advantage of his familial ways.

Reese talked of his first training camp in the summer of 1998, when he and fellow rookie roommate Jeremiah Trotter received an unexpected visit to their dorm room from their head coach. Rhodes sat down on the bed sniffing ammonia tablets—his way of staying wide-eyed and alert—and said, "Reese, keep doing what you're doing. I don't expect much from you."

Rhodes turned toward Trotter, the middle linebacker, and said, "Trotter, you ain't shit. You're supposed to be tough. You ain't tough."

Then he winked at them and asked if they had any beer in the room.

Meanwhile, Garcia joked that Gruden borrowed some of Rhodes's material. He too appealed to the inner Hun of his players. "He would depict a scene of rape and pillaging," he said. "The opponent slashing your throat. And when we were visiting another team, it was take their women and all that stuff—do whatever it takes to be victorious."

Takeo Spikes played in Buffalo for Gregg Williams, who rose through the coaching ranks through defense and who exuded defense and spoke the howl of defense. Spikes loved Williams, and he especially loved Williams's pregame tirades when he used to say, "[He's] gonna line up in front of you, that fucker, and it's a street fight. Play like your dick is hard."

Pregame speeches often work because players want to go there. From afar, from a civilized place like the home with a child's drawings posted to the refrigerator with a magnet from the local pizza shop, they sound cartoonish and overwrought. But it's about context, and the reality of football is anything but civil. Besides the work aspect, such as meetings and final preparation, and the camaraderie, the reason teams stay at a hotel that Saturday night is to begin the journey to that dark place. It won't work how most men go to work, kissing the wife or girlfriend goodbye, newspaper under the arm, briefcase in hand.

Like Spikes, most players need to go there. It's their predisposition. "I felt like if I threw a punch out there he'd be right behind me," Spikes said of Williams.

Tom Coughlin, who coached the Giants to an implausible Super Bowl victory over Belichick's Patriots, had to alter his approach from when he was in Jacksonville and known as a firespitter who was so strict that he forced players to keep both feet on the ground during team meetings.

"He's been controlling himself very well this year," cornerback Sam Madison said Super Bowl week. "Just hearing the different stories from Boston College to Jacksonville, I don't see it. There's been a huge change with him. We have a very young football team at positions that are demanding. He's the man they trust and we're going to the Super Bowl because of the things he's done and instilled in each and every one of these players."

When linebacker Antonio Pierce was asked at the Super Bowl about the evolution of Coughlin's pregame speech, he said, "He's getting better, I can tell you that. The ones before were kind of like bedtime stories. There was too much going on. Half the guys couldn't relate to it. Now he's getting up to date, to the 2000 era. He's been doing a lot of things different each and every week. We've had special people [come] in there and talk, and he's had honorary captains. So he's done things very differently. Of course he says things to fire guys up. He knows what buttons to push with certain guys on our team and I think he understands out mentality."

Whoever the coach, he must remain true to himself. "You can spot a fake motivator a million miles away," former tight end Chad Lewis said. Now, John Harbaugh, head coach of the Baltimore Ravens, Lewis added, "is a leader of warriors. Quite a motivator."

"If you're a great coach," longtime Packers safety LeRoy Butler said, "your players will believe what you say as gospel. You've got to make sure you say the right things to push the right buttons to get guys ready to play. You would think that as professionals, you shouldn't need a speech to get ready to play, but it can never hurt."

It can't hurt, if they actually hear it, that is. When Marshall Faulk was asked whether Coach Dick Vermeil deserved his reputation as the best pregame speaker, he replied that he didn't know because he didn't listen. Instead, his focus was on reading defenses and his own preparation for the game.

"Yeah man, for me I never listened to a coach's pregame speech," said Kyle Turley. "I was always in my locker, towel over my head, ammonia caps in a cup sniffing those, getting lit, playing Slayer and Pantera, blasting them as loud as my headphones would go. I had my mix. Right before we went out I'd explode out of my locker, throw everything off, and run out."

A Monday Night in 2002
Locker Room Exit

We fly back in time to the final days of a stadium, doomed and even then overrun by stray cats. It's Monday Night, back before it was usurped by Sunday Night.

Outside the home locker room, at the base of a stairwell in Philadelphia's Veterans Stadium, three men in long overcoats speak of the day you couldn't get warm under an afghan and how the frozen Astroturf felt like a slab of moon rock. Yes, one man harrumphs, more unforgiving, that turf, than a scorned woman.

So cold it was that day that one man sealed chemical heat packs to his body, and on the first play from scrimmage he got railed so hard in the chest by the Cowboys' Randy White on a play-action pass that one of the heat packs ruptured. Chemicals blistered the skin on his belly. Ron Jaworski kept rubbing that wound while in the huddle, and he remembered how much it had irritated him before the next play, the one in which he handed the ball to Wilbert Montgomery on the greatest play in Eagles franchise history.

Jaworski knew Montgomery would score on that play because the Cowboys were in nickel defense and Dick Vermeil had told them the previous Wednesday that Montgomery could run for a mile against the Cowboys' nickel defense. Montgomery ran 42 yards for the touchdown to clinch the NFC Championship for the Eagles on that cold January day in 1981.

"Yes," agrees then middle linebacker Bill Bergey, "cold as the dickens that day was." And yes, agrees Bergey, the Eagles had game-planned the Cowboys forever. Their aim that season of 1980 was not to play the Raiders in the Super Bowl, which they did. On the night before training camp opened in July, Vermeil established their goal.

"Men," he deadpanned, "we have to find a way to beat the Cowboys."

Both men swear on this night of reminiscing that their team was going to win that day. "We didn't upset the Cowboys," Jaworksi recalls. "We set them up. We were laying in the grass for America's Team. We ambushed them."

"Coming down the tunnel, we were so focused," Bergey says. "There was no doubt we were going to the Super Bowl. We pulverized Danny White. We annihilated them in every phase of the game. It was 20–7, and they were so lucky to get off that easy."

Then on the ride from the stadium to a dinner party, after all the whooping in the locker room and owner Leonard Tose telling them to drink the Dom Perignon, don't spray it, because it's the real thing, Bergey remembers the girl driving in front of him. Every time their cars pulled even, she took off another piece of clothing. When she stripped to her bra, Bergey figured to hell with dinner, and followed her car.

Jaworski, the preeminent analyst in the game, especially following John Madden's retirement in 2009, draws a crowd. While the players await their call of duty, through the two black steel doors and past a dirty red carpet that leads to the stairwell, two security guards, a cop, two sportswriters, and a local TV anchor wander over to listen to Jaworski spin yarn. He's describing the milieu of thirty years ago. How trainer Otho Davis cooked chili for the players and players ate footlong hoagies—complimentary—from Vince's Deli every Wednesday and players huddled in mood rooms and always fought over whose turn it was in the new Jacuzzi.

How the weight room was a converted storage area and Vermeil called the DiMatteo brothers from South Jersey to do the job at cost and they really did it up nice, using the good wall paneling. Really looks wood, one of the brothers said.

How the budget was so tight most of the equipment was donated— like the stationary bike in the corner and some of the plates, the lighter ones, of course. The heaviest ones the team had to order. Not many people were doing seventy-five-pound plates on either side as a base back then.

How the baseball Phillies clubhouse was adjacent to the Eagles locker room and they had to share the showers and bathroom stalls. "I think Pete Rose spent more time in our locker room than with the Phillies," Jaworski says, grinning. "I think he was looking for a tip which way to go on the game."

Bergey's nostalgia wanes when the subject invariably becomes the doomed stadium, and it was just two months from this night, before the knee replacement surgery, that it seemed to take forever to climb the stairs—one step, left leg, right leg, rest. Repeat.

He can still see the wince on his son Jake's face. Jake's eyes said, "Whoa, Dad, you look old."

A grizzled orthopedic surgeon told Bergey it was the second worst knee he had ever seen in his career, the worst one stemming from a motorcycle injury. The inside of his knee had turned into mashed potatoes.

"For the first time I can remember I'm not in pain," Bergey says. "I don't have a limp, though I still have a hobble—because my brain taught me to walk this way for so long. Vermeil hated the turf so bad he didn't let us practice on it. He didn't even like us to go there for the Saturday light warm-up. It wasn't the injury factor. It was just so hard it took too much out of your legs. It was like laying a thin carpet on I-95. So let's just say I don't think I'll cry when they close the place. I could see it deteriorate year by year. I remember lifting weights in 1977 and I see this big ol' river rat run across the floor and into a hole. Then another. I remember thinking, 'Here I am in the NFL?'"

Herein lies football's legacy at Veterans Stadium. Turf by Thanatos. Critters and leaky pipes and paint chips. Peeping players and exploding tendons. Leather-lunged locos in the 700 Level who revel in a fallen man's agony. It doesn't have to be the sheer aesthetics of Flotsam Field, either, not with Buddy Ryan, the swaggering Svengali who ordered Randall Cunningham to fake-knee the Cowboys to run up the score for misdeeds done by Dallas scab players during the strike of 1987, who held a press conference in the coach's office to announce the signing of Keith Jackson without informing management, and who gave the tight end a game ball the following week for a two-catch game "just to shove it up the Guy in France's ass," referring to then owner Norman Braman, who gave the NFL the Bounty Bowl and the Pork Chop Bowl.

Late in that stadium's life, two former Eagles cheerleaders filed a lawsuit contending visiting football players spied on them while they changed in the adjacent locker room, and two other former cheerleaders told of an adjacent door that had to be painted black because players would huddle around it and peep on the women. They scraped off some of the paint, before finally drilling peepholes into the walls. The women heard men giggling through the wafer-thin walls. Some would be extra bold with lewd remarks and requests for dates.

More embarrassing, however, was the night they canceled a preseason football game because the new turf mimicked the old turf, splitting up at the seams of the bases for baseball. It began when Baltimore Ravens coach Brian Billick stumbled during his ritual of inspecting the field in the pregame. Soon he was mimicking a DUI test, walking one foot in front of the other around the second-base cutout, all the while dodging the paint compressor. Soon stadium workers were frantically trying to fix the dents and divots, but the soggy earth underneath wouldn't take to the carpet, and heads nodded and faces frowned. The teams waited for a call from the league office in New York to okay postponement and eventual cancellation. All the while, the cameras from HBO kept rolling. The show was called *Hard Knocks*, a behind-the-scenes look at the Super Bowl champions in training camp, and boy did they have good fodder. For those familiar with the Vet, however, it was familiar fodder. The only fresh news was that a game was finally called because of the harrowing field conditions. In fact, three times in the building's last five seasons officials from opposing teams threatened not to play regular-season games, the most serious coming in December 1998 from Arizona Cardinals owner Bill Bidwill, who was finally pacified by a last-minute touch-up to the infected areas.

Sometimes there was a wedge so big when the pitcher's mound was removed that you could fit three fingers in the crevice. Seams bulged and popped like buttons on the suit of a man who swears he hasn't gained a pound in ten years, and it cost former Bears wide receiver Wendell Davis his career after he shredded both knees on the same play.

"Worst conditions in the history of the game," Billick recalled recently. "I feared for my players' livelihood."

But after the Eagles moved to their new plush digs, Hugh Douglas said the team lost some of its home-field advantage. "That place was real, man," Douglas said. "It was ghetto. And ghetto is good in football."

Ghetto was the coating of gunk on the turf, the cat droppings and the seagull droppings, the shoal of worms that slithered from the dirt bottom through the concrete porous for drainage, summoned by the peanut shells and dried tobacco juice. "Sometimes the field looks like it's moving," an old stadium worker said.

Former Eagle Troy Vincent described an eerie sight of hundreds of cats crawling in the stands during one of the team's Saturday walk-through practices in an otherwise empty stadium. "Look," he told another player, "they're watching us."

One starving cat fell from a drop ceiling into the office of Eagles offensive line coach Juan Castillo and spent a week locked in there while he was at training camp. The office left in shambles, it was still better than the rat that fell through the ceiling of another Eagles employee's office, the rodent clinging to the sides of a panel directly above the worker as he talked on the phone.

Back inside the two black steel doors of the locker room, players encircle their coach. Near the end of the locker stall, taped to a concrete wall with peeling paint, an unattributed quote from Magellan reads:

The sea is dangerous and its storms terrible, but these obstacles have never been sufficient reason to remain ashore. Unlike the mediocre, intrepid spirits seek victory over those things that seem impossible. It is with an iron will that they embark on the most daring of all endeavors to meet the shadowy future without fear and conquer the unknown.

Andy Reid talks first about the basics of the sport, blocking and tackling, and winning the turnover battle. "All right, men," he says, "you know what you have to do. Let your personality show. Let's have fun. But remember who you are. You have earned the right to have three Monday Night Football games. You did. This is your time."

Reid pauses. "Hugh? Where's Hugh?"

He's looking for Hugh Douglas, the Pro Bowl defensive end, then the team's most vocal player.

"I believe. I believe. I believe," Douglas responds. He says it so fast it sounds like, "Ah-bel-lee, ah-bel-lee, ah-bel-lee."

"Okay, y'all," Douglas says to the group. "Let's do it for the big girls. We crazy! It's not gut-check time, it's nut-check time. Balls out. Das right! Balls out. On three."

One.

Two.

Three.

The team spits in unison.

"Balls out!"

While Douglas gathers his team in a circle, ordering hands atop hands atop hands, Reid bustles out the door, past security guards, and positions himself along an iron railing facing the locker room entrance.

12 Minutes to Kickoff
Inside the Tunnel

The players exit, one, two at a time. They move upright, helmets fastened, shoulder pads protruding, cleats clomping against the cement ramp in rhythmic patter, looking like Roman soldiers. As they trumpet by, Reid bumps his fist with theirs, slaps their hands, their shoulder pads, offering words of encouragement.

"C'mon, big boy."

Farther into the tunnel, at the foot of the spout, the defense gathers. Players jump in place, led by Douglas, helmet cradled to his side.
His hair in braided locks, spraying out like snakes, he doesn't stop
talking.

"I'm turning green. Like the Hulk."

From inside the pack of players, someone yells, "Whole world's
watchin'."

The tunnel leads to the giant inflatable football helmet on the field,
a sort of pregame weigh station from which each player springs when
his name is boomed to the frenzied crowd. We are deep inside the
show, heavy on the frill. Pregame is orchestrated like a musical. Sound
effects. Fog machine. Production people.

Follow the sound of football players through the tunnel. Howls.
Heavy breathing. Flatulence.

The words of Brian Mitchell come to mind. "Football is primal," he
said.

The figure swaying back and forth through the fake fog is safety
Brian Dawkins, talking to himself now. "Calm down, dawg. You good.
You real good."

Hands balled into fists, he begins to pace inside the helmet. His
name is the last to be announced to the crowd, now at ascendancy.
Dawkins offers a wail from deep inside his own wilderness and shoots
through the opening of the helmet, dropping to the ground and belly-
ing like a worm between a catena of cheerleaders.

"There's this click," Dawkins explained it. "It's like something hits
me in the head. That's when the man inside me starts peeking out.
I find the transformation. I cross that door."

The Dark Place

Most speak of it, a figurative door that leads out to the playing field.
A sort of gateway to the game. And at that gateway, each man must
check his life at the curb. He is no longer husband or father, friend or
former teammate, and he must shed those basic things he was taught
so very long ago to navigate the ordinary day. The simple etiquette of
our world does not exist in this one.

Clemency will render him weak. The game is cold.

Even the few axioms of professional competition go gray. Sportsman-ship is an idealistic notion in this game. Coaches preach it for appear-ance. To appease the outsiders, so easily outraged.

The game is one giant mixed message with a subjective line that's always moving. The notion that Bill Romanowski would say he went to a place before the game where he "was ready to kill people" says so.

Romanowski talked about the dark place one day with Alden Mills, the former Navy SEAL commander who developed the perfect push-up. "Now, they literally were killing a person," he said. "That's a darker place than where I went, but that's the kind of place I went to. It's not something that's talked about. Hurting people. Knocking people out. Trust me, there's nothing more motivating for a team than to knock someone out of a game. It's not talked about. The coaches don't tell you to do it. It's talked about but not talked about. You can't say it in the papers. But your goal was to knock the quarterback out. Chances are you have a better chance to win the game against the backup. So you try to hurt the quarterback."

Doing so through the grayness of the game, protected by the cloak of, say, falling a certain way on another man's locked knee. Understanding that it is not personal, only practical.

And believing it. A man who performs unpure deeds must rational-ize it first. Trick his own ethical code. Travel to a mind-set.

It's why Dawkins thinks he's the comic hero Wolverine, a greater do-gooder where the end justifies the means. And by the way, it's not really the God-fearing man Brian Dawkins out there visibly punch-ing that wide receiver in the kidneys after he catches the football and grinding him to the ground, but the superhero safety.

"I'd start the night before the game," said former Ravens tackle Orlando Brown. "I would dream about how I was going to fuck the other team up. I would be doing that *Waterboy* shit. I would make up names for players—call them 'Mikey' or whatever else I made up. Then the next day I'd say, 'Mikey, you're gonna be my bitch today.'"

Hugh Douglas summoned bitterness from his school days. He attended Central State University, a small, historically black college located in Wilberforce, Ohio, known more for its nationally recognized chorus than its football team. He resented players from big schools,

ballyhooed players who landed lingering looks and extra breaks
because of big-school bias. Trust-fund players.

Douglas had to work harder than they did. His road to the NFL
from his home in rural Mansfield, Ohio, and then Central State was
always so cumbersome. Even after he was selected in the first round
by the Jets with the sixteenth overall pick in the 1995 draft, he never
drew the benefit of the doubt.

The Jets fans hissed. Who's Hugh? Central what? In his first training camp, the veterans mocked him. You played where?

"That was my motivation going into a game," Douglas said. "That they
disrespected me and my tiny little black school. Like I hated that
[Marc] Columbo who played for the Bears. Couldn't stand him.
He was from a big school [Boston College]. He was supposed to be
number one in the draft. I told him he sucked. All those cats—[John]
Tait [BYU] from Kansas City, another guy who sucked. I couldn't
stand 'em."

Douglas would draw on anything to get into a foul mood on game
day. "Defensive players are hunters," he said. "I needed to be in a
hunter's state of mind. I used to try to get pissed. I'd go to work and
take whatever I could that was buggin' me. I would be pissed that
I couldn't find a good parking space at the stadium and I'd take that anger
out on the field."

Sunday, 12:58 p.m.
Kansas City, 2003

The color of blood surrounds you inside Arrowhead Stadium. It drips
from the fixtures of the place and from the seats in the stands and most
especially from the people who occupy them on game day—splashed
on their Chiefs coats and Chiefs caps and Chiefs jerseys. It feels like
you're in the deep end of a pool of red, and isn't red the perfect color
for a football team? The color that's associated with energy, courage,
war, danger, strength, power, determination, and passion? The color
that sparks emotion? That enhances our metabolism and raises our
blood pressure? That's used in several national flags because of its connotation of fierce pride?

And how appropriate that the team plays in Kansas City, where the slaughterhouses once ruled—the remnants of that time reduced to expertly carved cuts of red richness, belly-up in the refrigerated window of the West Bottoms steakhouse with the mural of the Cowman covering the south wall of the bar, four original sets of oxen yokes, including one in the banquet room that traveled the Oregon Trail from Westport, Missouri, to Oregon in 1843, and a set of longhorn steer horns, nearly seven and a half feet in width, once loaned from the Kansas City Stockyards Company to the Hoof & Horns Club.

Long ago, here in the West Bottoms, located west of downtown Kansas City at the confluence of the Missouri and Kansas rivers, the Kansas City Livestock Exchange flourished, ranking second only to the stockyards of Chicago. A now suddenly hip industrial neighborhood with artists' lofts and warehouse cafés once catered to the bloody-hands men of the bustling stockyards, offering cheap hotel lodging and a pool hall, a barbershop and a whorehouse. At its heyday, in 1923, over two and a half million cattle were received at the stockyards, along with an equal number of hogs, over a million sheep, and nearly fifty thousand horses and mules. The roaring business, however, perished abruptly in the Great Flood of 1951, low-lying areas washed away, along with so much of the airport that it had to be relocated to Platte County. Residents of nearby Armourdale had water all the way to their roofs, and back in the aptly named Bottoms, where the nightclubs of Genesee Street now stand, water rushed through like a biblical wrath devastating the Kansas City stockyards.

And so right now outside of Arrowhead Stadium, much of the meat comes from elsewhere. But the idea of Kansas City barbecue still thrives, and so many of the grills that literally turn a gray sky atop 1 Arrowhead Drive grayer with their smoke have been burning since late Friday night, when the people arrived here and parked the Winnebago next to the other Winnebago and so forth, until it looked like a sepa-rate city, like, say, Winnebago City, the environs fun and football-lov-ing, marked by harmony. So far removed from the days leading up to the Civil War, a period called Bleeding Kansas, because the entire region was so bitterly divided over the issue of slavery.

And inside their place of pilgrimage, an older white man in a red windbreaker, who would years later wind up making wine in Napa

Valley, stood in the middle of mostly young black men and led a battle cry.

"It so well defined what we have to do today," Dick Vermeil howled. "We gotta go to work.

"All right. Offense?"

"Go to work!" the players say in unison.

"Defense?" asks Vermeil.

"Go to work!"

"Special teams?"

"Go to work!"

"Coaches?" follows Vermeil.

"Go to work!"

"Let's go," Vermeil urged. "Let's go. Huddle up."

Sunday, 12:59 p.m.
The Last, Last, Last Words

In Baltimore, the Ravens prepare to play the hated Steelers. Ray Lewis summons his unit to meet him in the end zone, and they follow dutifully because everyone here knows whose unit it is.

Earlier he made his way through the entire team. He found center Matt Birk and they clenched at the shoulder pads and butted heads six . . . seven . . . eight times.

Now, pacing the inner circle of his defense, Lewis reached his usual pregame lather.

"Those of you right here," he shrieks. "You have to make up your minds right now! Those who wear purple have to rise up and defend our house. No one comes into our house and embarrasses us. Make up your minds right now. If you're wearing purple, make up your minds to protect your house! We are a team and we do this together. Leave everything on the field."

The others on defense pay close attention to him.

"One mind! One body! One spirit!" he begins to chant. "One spirit! One spirit!" His teammates join in. Oh, how they love this part. Gladiator shit. They'd follow Ray Lewis right to hell about now and kick the devil's ass.

"This is our house and they want to take it from us," he says. "You know that ain't gonna happen. Dig deep. I want you to dig deep! Find that inner nasty shit."

Lewis pounds his chest and moves down the line of his teammates looking them deep in the eye.

"Are you with me?" he says before going to the next player. "Are you with me?"

2

Training Camp

Postcard from Wichita Falls, 1998

It seems too early for it to be this hot. The sun hangs low on the horizon, just having made it in from Arkansas and Louisiana, and the day has already been cooked lazy. There's something far worse about prairie heat—breezeless, with a maddening stillness, the kind that beckons tornadoes. The air just hovers, like a nosy neighbor. That's the first thing you notice here in northeast Texas, fifteen miles from the Oklahoma border: how the air feels, as heavy as an afghan, and it goes down like wool.

Such is life in early August in a place called Wichita Falls, the kind of place that begs the question of why the Choctaw Indians settled in these here parts in the first place. Even its name is somewhat misleading, in that the falls on the Wichita River are fake, man-made only a few years back. The original falls were destroyed by a flood in 1886, and a hundred years later the city built a fifty-four-foot-high artificial waterfall beside the river in Lucy Park.

Now there are Dallas Cowboys here for their annual training camp, which seems entirely too cruel, even if this is the buckle of the Bible Belt. Sinners and football players beware of what be–Wichita Falls you in the dead of summer. Donning full pads and going full tilt in drills all afternoon on a sunbaked field that would turn Cleveland brown in a day if it wasn't watered twice a day is absolutely hellish—and somewhat unnecessary seeing that the Cowboys once upon a time trained in Thousand Oaks, California, named for the plethora of stately oak trees that keep camp days airy and manageable.

In 1990, the Cowboys left California Lutheran College and lovely Thousand Oaks after twenty-six years, for Austin, Texas, and now eight years later have migrated north for a sweeter deal in Wichita Falls. Though the players have said they like Wichita Falls better than the state capital, mostly due to Midwestern State's new state-of-the-art facilities and dorm rooms, a much better home than dreary St. Edward's U in Austin, they feel like they're on a spit by afternoon as the temperature reaches 106 degrees.

Mercifully, second-year coach Chan Gailey rarely holds two-a-days. Camp Chan, however, is usually held in one lengthy session, marked more by its painstaking tediousness than physical pain. Gailey will start a segment of practice over again three, four, five times to eliminate mental mistakes. Here in the grueling heat, it's hard to think. Concentrating becomes a dizzying act. By late afternoon the body is dehydrated and players go through IV bags like beer at a rib joint.

And this being Wichita Falls, a town of a hundred thousand that doesn't have a downtown with, say, the entertainment of Austin's renowned Sixth Street, supper boils down to the Bar L Drive-In for some curbside barbecue and a cool but spicy Red Draw, a cocktail that combines beer, two ounces of tomato juice, two Spanish queen olives, a lime wedge, and a dash of salt.

Except right around dinnertime the swarm rolls through Wichita Falls like a thunderstorm. The sky is filled with locusts, sending people rushing for cover. They wave their arms frantically as millions of winged insects buzz about their mouths and ears, their hair and skin crawling with them. Cars sit pulled over to the side of the road because the windshield wipers cannot move fast enough to clear the diving locusts. The town falls silent, the way a surprise blizzard drains life from the street.

The invasion lasts a little more than an hour, leaving behind a thick coating of tiny brown-and-pink-colored bodies on the sidewalk and street and parked cars, a sort of apocalyptic residue. Walking outside afterward brings forth a sickening crunch at your feet.

Tomorrow brings only another practice.
Wish you were here.

Let us travel far back for a moment, away from the panoply of pre-game, well before the honorary captains give way to the playing captains and the ball is placed delicately on the tee. Before back-to-school season and the first wisps of cool air drape the Midwest and the moon threatens shorter days. Before Sundays offer any anticipation, folks' minds focus squarely on extending vacation.

Football training camp represents baseball's spring training turned inside out, innards-ugly, like everything in the world that is turned inside out, peeled and harsh to the eyes.

Spring training connotes rebirth, sealed with a Florida holiday, and blooming Florida as well, the only time that it's really divine. For northerners, Florida in February is early parole, when sixty degrees feels like seventy and seventy feels heavenly, before the bugs and the regular five o'clock showers and the air that coagulates.

Same thing goes in Arizona, where summer humid becomes summer arid—but with the sun supercharged and blinding, unlike the six weeks before spring, when it's friendly and nourishing. Spectacularly crisp, nightfall in the desert arrives quickly during that time of the year, offering a dramatic temperature dip that acts like a cleansing of the palate against sun-swept skin.

And so throughout these charming little towns in South Florida and Arizona under the perfect powdered skies there are these little complexes that offer baseball in this concentrated form that should be sickeningly sweet but isn't. The infield dirt is the color of the Grand Canyon in a postcard and the lush outfield grass feels like fur, and you have an uncontrollable urge just to lie down in center field in front of the fence emblazoned with garish ads that surprisingly don't seem to bother you all that much.

While covering the Mets more than a few springs back, I heeded the advice of my then sports editor and napped one quiet afternoon at that very spot inside the sweet, petite Single-A ballpark in Port St. Lucie. A throwback New York newspaperman by the name of Greg Gallo, he would ask me every morning if I had smelled the grass that day and promptly spout the weather report from up north. I always did, except when the winds blew east carrying the overpowering aroma of orange blossoms.

During games, the ballpark smelled like popcorn and suntan lotion and was filled with frivolity. Spring training games offer an intimacy to the game that goes unmatched in any other sport. It's almost familial between the players and the fans in their matching caps. Autographs and well-wishes on the season exchange honestly and unforced, like the mustachioed ballplayer who used to write his phone number on a baseball and underhand toss it to the groupies by the third base line.

Two weeks into spring training, the players with their sun-reddened faces appeared healthier and more refreshed than when they first arrived. During that period prior to the games, they ventured into the clubhouse a little after 7 a.m. for a schedule that went like this:

Stretching. Light jogging. Fielding practice for position players. Scheduled throwing for pitchers, either pitch count or long toss. Pickoff plays. Bunt drills. Batting practice. Massage. Golf by two. Nap. Supper with teammates at that new spot on the beach. Nightcap, if so inclined.

It's all so very whimsical, busting with metaphors about recycled life and hope that feels fresh and cynic-free.

In keeping with the mien of the sport, the other camp offers the succor of a skinned knee. Morning practice. Afternoon practice. Dehydration. Film study in the evening. Cafeteria meals. Sore bones. Nightly bed check. Awakened at 5 a.m. and escorted to a bathroom in another building to pee in a cup for drug testing.

Football training camp borders basically basic training. Precise and unrelenting, excusing no one, no matter his condition, it's subsisting at the harshest time of the year—Incorrigible August—in nowhere towns with terrible-sounding names like Pittsfield, Platteville, Clarksville, and Mankato, hardly comparable to baseball's Clearwater, Kissimmee, and Lake Lulu.

"I would be playing golf in June and suddenly get a wretched feeling in my stomach, recalled former offensive lineman Kevin Long. "It was that 'Oh shit, camp is starting in two weeks' feeling."

One year, I visited nineteen training camps, including Wichita Falls and the five teams that constituted Wisconsin's Cheese League, including the Bears at UW-Platteville, a school that specializes in farming education. The dorm rooms were cutouts, many with no air-conditioning, at least those that housed the media. The ones for the players weren't much better, lacking the amenities of a roadside trucker motel.

Except for Green Bay, where it's typically Packer prepossessing, with the kids still carrying the players' helmets back from practice to Lambeau Field, the rest of the Cheese League was exactly what you would imagine. Depressingly hot and boring, though Kyle Turley thought it Elysium compared to Thibodeaux, Louisiana, home of Nicholls State, where the Saints had moved their training camp.

"Our brilliant owner [Tom Benson] brings us back to Louisiana, and puts us as close to the Gulf as he possibly could," Turley snapped. "Real genius. The heat index was 105 in Minnesota when Korey Stringer died. We decided to ask our trainers what the heat index here was. They told us it was 135 degrees. The news was saying to bring your dogs and cats inside and make sure that you drink plenty of water. We're in the thick of the sun in this heat with twenty pounds of gear on. Four guys went down with full body cramps. Guys' organs were shutting down. It was nasty. One of our coaches had to be helicoptered to a hospital from the heat.

"So then our great union comes down. We begged them to not let them do this to us. We play in an air-conditioned dome. The owner's answer was to build a luxury box next to the field for all of the owner's cronies. I wished I was a quarterback so bad so that I could chuck a ball at that damn tent. I tried to pay the quarterbacks every day to throw the ball over in that owner's tent."

Meanwhile, on the opposite end of the earth from the sticky bayou, in sublime Northern California, on the edge of wine country, the Oakland Raiders held their camp in idyllic circumstances. Each morning, the players left their spacious rooms at the Napa Valley Marriott Hotel, walked outside into a perfect sixty-three degrees under overcast skies, and traveled about twenty feet through a parking lot to a lush, fenced-in practice field.

"I didn't realize how good we had it," mused fullback Jon Ritchie, a former Oakland fullback. "We had a lot more sleep time. We had clean rooms and fresh linens every day. We didn't have to look for parking at the facility. It was the perfect setup."

Ritchie's wife visited him one year and they spent a day off from practice on a wine tour and dining at a fabulous restaurant. "Very romantic," he said. "Football and wine should definitely be mutually exclusive."

Ritchie could certainly joke that taking football camp from Napa to anywhere else in the land turns wine into whine.

Let us do that, shall we?

Let us travel inside life at football camp.

Arrival Day, Late Afternoon
Wednesday, July 22, 2009

The Philadelphia Eagles train at Lehigh University in the Lehigh Valley—a cluster of rugged old towns, Allentown, Easton, and Bethlehem, built on rolling hills in between Blue Mountain to the north and Old South Mountain to the south. Rookies and inexperienced types, the future foundation guys, long-shot hopefuls and desperate job seekers, arrived here a few days back, but this sort of freshman orientation ends today with the appearance of the veterans.

As the day grows long, a bustle of activity suddenly begins by the dorm facilities, tucked into the woods three levels up a winding mountain road overlooking the town of Bethlehem—so named on Christmas Eve 1741 by Count Nicholas Ludwig von Zinzendorf while visiting a small group of Moravians who had settled here on the banks of the Lehigh River near the Monocacy Creek. Those early settlers belonged to the oldest Protestant denomination in the world, the Unity of the Brethren, and fled a bloody Moravia and Bohemia, now the Czech Republic, for the religious freedom of the New World.

The quiet of a summer campus breaks with their arrival. The roar of big engines and bass-heavy music that pounds through closed windows begets a procession of luxury cars and SUVs into the parking lot. They motor by slowly in a metallic rainbow of colors, most of the vehicles freshly cleaned and waxed so they shimmer in the late-day sun.

A local police officer guarding the entrance to the dorm buildings appears to play a game of recognition:

That's Broderick Bunkley, the terrific defensive tackle from Florida State. Who's that who plays next to him?

Patterson, Mike. Right, right, from Southern Cal . . .

Yes, there's cornerback Asante Samuel. The dreads a dead giveaway. Same with the weird orange 'fro-hawk. Only Shawn

Andrews—the massive, eccentric offensive lineman—would sport that thing.

Who are those two? Hmmm. Must be O-line, too. 'Cause they're massive and they're white. Next guy is easy . . . Brian Westbrook. Helluva player, Westbrook. Real underrated back. What's he carrying? Looks like a microwave . . .

The cop's eyes widen when he spies Donovan McNabb climbing out of his SUV. This marks the eleventh training camp for number 5, and he suddenly looks fatherly. It's not just that his wife, Roxy, is pregnant with the couple's fourth child back home in South Jersey, or that he has eleven years on his top receiver (DeSean Jackson) and twelve on the other starter (Jeremy Maclin) and nine on his tight end (Brent Celek), or that he has now spent one-third of his life as a quarterback in the NFL.

One day you report to camp and the faces appear strangely soft. That's the thing about youth. It can't be disguised by size, pose, or soul patch. Meanwhile, the other guys have all disappeared, the final two your bookend tackles (Tra Thomas and Jon Runyan) who treated you like the little brother.

The locker room bears no buffers, Senator. Just the coach.

In fact, the 2009 season marked the eleventh year for the duo of Donovan McNabb and Andy Reid, tying Marv Levy and Jim Kelly, Don Shula and Bob Griese, and Tom Landry and Roger Staubach as third longest coach-quarterback combination in the history of the league. Chuck Noll and Terry Bradshaw were together in Pittsburgh for fourteen seasons, while Hank Stram and Len Dawson manned the Chiefs and Texans for thirteen years.

Tag, says time, you're the guy.

McNabb has always been the guy because of the position. But it's different now. "I'm like the lone wolf," he would say later in the season.

Donovan McNabb hasn't changed much through the years, which is to say he still checks the ground more than he does his hair—if he didn't shave his head clean now, probably partly to disguise his receding hairline.

Way back in his second year in the league we dined together at a Philadelphia restaurant and I recall how he ordered a Shirley Temple before dinner and how the face of chef/owner Pietro begged, "Wouldn't you prefer to see my wine list?"

And how McNabb's face begged back, "I know my request might seem a tad anomalous, but I can go for a little ginger ale and three parts grenadine over ice about now." Our host returned shortly with a pelican-shaped glass, the contents the color of a prom dress, and handed it to the football player who didn't give a damn that Dick Butkus, I presume, wouldn't drink a Shirley Temple if it tasted like Jack Daniel's.

I recall how McNabb giggled so innocently when Pietro read off the specials for the evening and he thought Pietro's veal Gianna sounded like veal vagina.

Look at Ron Artest, McNabb said over dinner that night, "He has his own barber, his own tailor, his own chef, his financial guy, his marketing guy. He has a lot of people on his team he has to pay. You know who's on my team? My mother, my father, my brother, my dog, and Roxy. I do have a barber. I've known him eight years. I like him a lot and he comes to the games, but he's not on my payroll.

"I know a lot of guys, they go buy big houses. They go buy cars. They change their wardrobe. Next thing you know, they have $100,000 left. Then they have to sell everything off for dirt cheap."

We spoke at length about money. I told him the quote an athlete once told me: "I treat it like a whore—because then I won't miss it when it goes away."

I told him an Allen Iverson story. How the Sixers were playing Monopoly with real money while waiting for a flight and Iverson left behind two KFC bags—one filled with chicken scraps and the other with $19,000. An attendant cleaning up the room discovered the contents and returned the money to Iverson just before the plane took off.

McNabb told me he spent a summer in high school working at Chicago's Mercantile Exchange and Stock Exchange and copped to his reputation of being cheap. "Anytime you look at something," he said with a grin, "and say, 'I can buy that so I'll just buy it,' you don't really need it. It's a waste. A lot of people waste a lot of money. I'm very protective of my money."

I swore then, he was your father's quarterback, consumed by the electric bill. The year before, McNabb's rookie season, I met him outside at a Friday's for lunch and nodded toward his car, a burgundy Chrysler, a dealer's car, and he sprang to defend it. "What did you expect? A Benz? I like this car. It's a nice car." I shrugged. I had also thought it to be a nice car.

That day we hung at a back table, along with a teammate buddy, a tight end by the name of Luther Broughton, and had a bar food feast—buffalo wings, chicken fingers, potato skins, mozzarella sticks. He wildly dipped everything in ranch dressing, and anointed it "the bomb, especially when you run out of mayonnaise."

The year before that I met him for the first time in his parents' family room of their split-level in the southern burbs of Chicago, the smell of Wilma McNabb's hotcakes wafting in the summer morning. I found him to be unsullied and attributed it to upbringing and playing his college ball at Syracuse, way up north, imprisoned by the murky Finger Lakes and a dreary, endless winter, but close enough to swill Canadian perspective.

A graybeard now, he's still relatively the same, despite Rush Limbaugh and falling short of winning a Super Bowl, the only thing that keeps him from joining the circle of Peyton Manning and Tom Brady.

Maybe it's all about wearing your older brother Sean's hand-me-downs, being raised with just enough, no more, under the watchful eye of two sturdy parents, in a simple home on a simple street, located in a leafy suburban sprawl like Dolton, forty-five minutes south of Chicago's Loop. Maybe it's the fact that he grew up so ordinary, starkly different from, say, his good friend Barry Gardner, a linebacker who played in the NFL years ago and came from neighboring Harvey, Illinois, where he once held the hand of his dying friend riddled by stray bullets from a gangland shooting. Maybe it's going to an all-boys Catholic, sports-crazed school of about eight hundred kids like Mount Carmel and living on a street like Diekman Court, the archetype of middle class, proof that ordinary ol' America works.

McNabb grabs a box from the trunk. Another veteran watches him and suggests that he have a rookie unload the rest of his belongings.

Arrival day feels a lot like college in this respect. Most NFL training camps take place at universities, but it's the gathering of men in the company of only men for a significant block of time that brings forth the hierarchy and the pranks and that corridor of Macho Row.

Observing the collection of vehicles still filing into the parking lot, yes, college, most definitely college, but with real money, with the exception of the no-bonus boys. They represent camp fillers who have no real hope to make the team but fancy a chance. Perhaps they'll be the one who inspires the next film based on a true story.

One of those players who thickens the roster makes a quick run to the nearby Kmart to buy a small television for the room that he will be sharing with two other players. While other rooms will resemble a penthouse suite at a casino with flat screens and video games and all sorts of creature comforts, theirs will seem bare.

A once great defensive end not far removed from the league, Hugh Douglas watches the movement and becomes wistful. He played with some of these guys.

This, he says, is what he misses.

Hell, he says, training camp sucks.

Sucks big time.

He couldn't handle the physical part ever again. He mutters something about the ragin', motherfuckin' sun and the terrible aches and how the older you get and you're still playing? You better be married, son.

Married?

Yeah, married, he says. Because when you get home and you start playing in those games, you need someone to take care of your ass.

But *this*, he says, watching the players unload their belongings like they're going to a shore house.

This, you miss.

The company of men talking football and everything else. Men making fun of other men while playing video games all night. That's fun. Especially when your ass is married and you spent the off season checking off items from a list in their handwriting and it's your turn to watch the baby and your wife admonishes you because you never *watch* your own baby.

With no disrespect to his wife or any of the wives, come July he couldn't wait for that first whistle with a bunch of disgusting men.

Good times, he says.

Then he tells a story of Hollis Thomas, the 6-foot-5, 350–360ish-pound defensive tackle.

"Most guys bring their video games or music," Douglas says. "Not Hollis. He brings his porno—movies, magazines, you name it. He'd say, 'We're away for a long time, sometimes you gotta take care of business.'"

Training Camp Day 1, the Fitness Test
Thursday, July 23, 2009

The first day of camp brings forth a knot of dread in most players because it then brings the conditioning test: the gasser.

Run the width of a football field, 53.5 yards, back and forth without stopping. Most teams employ the half-gasser.

The Eagles hold one of the toughest fitness tests in the game. The players are split up into three groups—small guys (defensive backs, wide receivers), medium-size guys (linebackers, running backs), and big guys (offensive and defensive linemen)—and they must run sixteen half-gassers in an allotted time.

Run.

Rest.

(It works out to be about forty seconds of rest while the other two groups run.)

Repeat.

Sixteen times.

"It's the quickest forty seconds of your life," linebacker Chris Gocong said. "You reach the sideline and in a blink you have to start running again. The worst is when you lose count. You think you're at thirteen–fourteen and you find out you're only at eleven–twelve. You just want to give up but you know you can't."

And that's precisely why Andy Reid makes them run all of those half-gassers. Beyond the obvious, like who's in shape and who's not, it's who's mentally tough and who's not. Who mysteriously suffers a sore back four half-gassers in and walks off the field. And who pushes through the knots of pain that arise in various body parts with each half-gasser.

Trainers watch the half-gasser test closely, looking for those who overheat and wilt. Some become tingly and lightheaded. Some others are doubled over, having already vomited.

Now, it used to be even worse on this day. Before OTAs in the off season, the first day would also include a physical, which is more like an auto inspection.

Each player is given a sheet that's basically an exceptionally long checklist of body parts. Imagine the scene of eighty men shuffling from station to station with sheets in hand for the doctors to sign upon completion of the exam. First to the podiatrist. Then to the internist. Knee doctor. Optometrist. Undergo an EKG. Have blood drawn. Have hips checked. Dentist, for a personal mouth guard. And down the line they go, moving as prized cattle.

Rise for Morning Session, 6:30 a.m.

The days of training camp begin early, and they begin in earnest. So the players begin with a short walk to the cafeteria, where the breakfast food is plentiful and the chocolate milk tastes especially good.

Sleep having been eaten away, they wind their way to camp headquarters amid the buzz of the morning insects. Their faces droop, their mood one of dread.

"Every morning before practice, it's like a funeral in there, especially at the beginning of camp," remarks Chris Patrick, a deep-depth-chart offensive lineman. "Because everybody knows what's coming."

The rookies head to the practice fields first to stretch, followed fifteen minutes later by the veterans. How important it is to prepare the body for the grueling day in the heat, where fatigue and dehydration threaten tendons and muscles and perhaps a season and a career.

The Morning Session, 8:15 a.m.

The work whistle blows like the one in a factory, a long, piercing tweet that demands attention, which makes it highly obnoxious. The offensive linemen were already working, as they usually do. They're always the first ones sweating and the last to leave the field. Their individual time with their coach comes before practice and afterward, working on things like hand placement and foot technique for pass blocking.

At Eagles camp, they go live every day, which means contact. The nine-on-seven drills open team practice, and those plays benefit the defense because everyone knows it's a run. So the defenders fly off the ball, without fear of deception, filling their gaps, homing missiles crashing into the line.

Then it's on to blitz pickup. The offensive linemen will have to concentrate harder now, listening for the center's call, watching the body language of the defender. Is he tipping anything? Will he spike inside?

The voices of camp fill the morning, a cacophony of coach-speak—emanating from both sides of the ball, from inside both units—mixed with howls and grunts, the crunching of pads, and short rapid-fire whistles.

"Come on, now! Watch him. Waaaatch heeeem!"

"Head up. I said head up!"

"Look out! Look out! Look out! Look out!"

"Square! Square! You know how we do it. Square! Square!"

The deeper into practice, as the sun rises a little higher, the more physical the play, especially when the team moves to one-on-one pass rush, another loaded drill for the defense. Defensive ends versus offensive tackles, the whistle blows, and they shuffle, ends on attack.

It's not until they move into team that it evens out for the offensive linemen. In team, the play is run or pass, and it's on the defense to sniff out the call. Here is the longest block of practice, and the part that is the most physical.

Cornelius Ingram, the hulking tight end from Florida who presented President Barack Obama with a Gators jersey during the team's post–national championship trip to the White House early in 2009, learned quickly the difference between college football and the NFL. On one crushing collision, Trent Cole knocked both contacts out of Ingram's eyes.

"That was a 'Welcome to the NFL, kid' shot," Ingram would say afterward. "I was out there blind after that play."

The Desperate Bloke with Fresh Legs, 9:12 a.m.

Eleven days into training camp, with a dearth of pass rushers, the Eagles invite former first-round pick Jason Babin for a look-see. A hybrid end/linebacker, Babin never reached his potential after being picked twenty-seventh overall in the 2004 draft by the Houston Texans, the reasoning, according to one personnel man, partly size, partly scheme, partly bad team.

So Babin, a Michigan boy, out of Paw Paw High School in Kalamazoo, became another NFL wanderer. The Texans traded him to the Seahawks for safety Michael Boulware just prior to the 2007 season and he barely played. Seattle released Babin after week 1 of the 2008 season to make room for a wide receiver on the roster, and Kansas City picked him up in November of that year after a rash of injuries at defensive end.

The Chiefs were 1–9 at the time. Nothing worse than trying to rehab your career on a terrible team with the locker room split and ready to quit and the head coach about to be fired. So he's here now with a chance at redemption and he's active, and the offensive linemen do not appreciate the new guy with the springy legs.

Chris Patrick, one of those camp hopefuls who fills out the deep depth chart at both guard and tackle, squared off with Babin in the first of their three skirmishes for the day.

"[Babin] is fresh as hell," Patrick would explain later. "He shows after we've been killing ourselves and we're beat up, and he's flying off the ball. My legs were dead. I went to play slide protection and he tried bull-rushing me. The right guard whacked him and he fell down to the ground."

And Babin rose, swinging at Patrick, who already was building a donnybrook dossier—four in the second week of camp alone. So he started swinging those big paws at Babin, and the fight went down as most football fights do, with heavy blows that make a loud thud bouncing harmlessly off the combatants' pads. Punches turn to grappling and lots of cursing before the others break it up.

"It's hot and everybody's tired," Patrick said. "People don't want to take shit. Perfect environment for fighting."

Coaches encourage fighting, sort of, and obviously they can't say so, because it would be frowned on by the outside world—which knows little about training camp life and the desperation of physical men for a livelihood and the need for desperate physical men, particularly in the fourth quarter of a game with playoff ramifications in December subzero windchill.

The outside world can't comprehend what transpires in the pile on steamy, buggy days in August. And by golly, certainly what is said between desperate men, which would rake the ears of the guests at the owner's Saturday night cocktail party.

"Coaches want to see who's mentally the roughest guy out there," Patrick said. "They want to see who gives up. Who says, 'Fuck it. That's it.' Fights are going to happen. We're really competitive guys. Nobody wants to lose."

Anatomy of a Training Camp Fight

The breaking point usually occurs two weeks into camp. Achy and homesick, bored and heat-broiled, weary of cafeteria food and strange beds and nightly bed checks and being tucked away from the rest of the world at a tiny college in some godforsaken town, veteran players become irritable.

Their college experience is a distant memory, replaced by wives and children and stays at five-star resorts. And worse than dorm life is the monotony of camp life, marked by long, exhausting days of too-familiar drills. When you know something so well the routine becomes mind-numbing.

On this particular day in August 2000 at this particular Eagles camp, now two weeks old, Jon Runyan is an irritable veteran performing mixed player drills—which consists of a blend of first-teamers, second-teamers, and deep reserves, a fact important to the story because of the sprightly undrafted rookie playing opposite Runyan at defensive end, apparently playing a little too sprightly.

A faceless player, merely, in fact, a live body to absorb the August grind, the rookie free agent pushed extra hard at Runyan. You could hardly blame him. In many ways, it's the only way to get the number on the back of the jersey noticed by the coaches.

But Runyan, in his first camp with the Eagles, having signed that off season as a free agent, was quickly losing patience, and finally during one play drove the young player into the ground like a golf tee well behind the quarterback. Then, while he squatted on his hands and knees, Runyan kicked him square in the rear end with the side of his foot.

The side of the foot is dismissive. Shoo piece from a veteran.

Wise up, young man.

But defensive players are pack players. So now Jeremiah Trotter sprints in from the sideline and attacks Runyan low at the knees from behind. He tries to pick the bigger man up and body-slam him to the ground. But Runyan's girth is too much and the two men collapse to the ground.

Fight.

Heavyweight fight.

Trotter stands 6-foot-2, 270 pounds, but he looks small next to the 6-foot-7, 330-pound Runyan.

They wrestle on the ground, exchanging blows from in tight. Offensive players and defensive players collapse toward the men and begin jostling with one another. The practice field becomes a battle-field hosting a huge scrum. Head coach Andy Reid jumps into the middle of the combatants trying to separate them. Offensive line coach Juan Castillo rushes to his side.

They finally peel off the bodies, and Reid emerges with his hand dangling in the air. Zoom in and you see the ring finger forked in a most painful, unnatural way. The coach hooked Trotter's face mask by accident and ended up dislocating the finger.

Years later, Trotter, Runyan, and two witnesses recalled the altercation:

Trotter: "The heat is getting to you. You're ornery. I was young and he was younger, and your testosterone levels are built up. We got into it, and yeah it was something. It's something now we look back on and laugh. As you get older you tend not to worry about that stuff. You let the young guys beat each other up.

"I gotta say I came out on top. I ran up on him. I tried to scoop him and he dropped all of his weight on me. Once you get a big man on the ground it's easy because they can't move around as easy. I got on top of him. It was hard to punch with people jumping in. I was trying to choke him. Then we had had each other's face masks."

Runyan: "I remember that one. It was my first year in Philadelphia. I got into it with somebody. The kid was being a dick. I turned around and kicked him in the ass. I had ran the guy seven, eight yards past the quarterback and Trotter comes out from the back. Takes me right at the knees. So I latch on to him and start pounding on him in the rib cage. I'm on top of him and then Juan tried to jump in the thing. When we watched the film, you could see [offensive lineman John]

Welbourn almost take Juan's head off. Welbourn had no intention of getting in the fight. He just wanted to hit Juan."

Bystander 1: "I was on the field on defense. The kid was going extra hard and Runyan got irritated with it. It was one of those, 'You're trying to go too hard on fresh legs.' Runyan was probably in a bad mood. He said, 'I'll slow your ass down.' And he did. He slammed him down hard. He didn't use proper technique. Then he kicked him in the ass.

"Trot come in from the sidelines yelling, 'Who you think you is? You think you swolled up? I'm gonna get you, motherfucker.' He tried to body-slam Runyan. But he couldn't lift him. Then it became a damn free-for-all out there. That's what happens in training camp.

"When Runyan first got here, he was fighting twice a week. Brandon Whiting, Derrick Burgess, any young defensive end. If Runyan thought the guy was practicing too hard or Runyan was tired of practice, he'd pick a fight."

Bystander 2: "You had two very tough men who are stubborn guys. They were in a fight to the death. Then two minutes later I heard on the walkie-talkie that Reid is in center field with his finger all screwed up. Reid's a big man, too."

Following practice that day, Jeff Thomasen and Mike Bartrum, two classic grunts, a third-string tight end and a long snapper, trudged up the hill back to the locker room. Exhausted from practice, feeling miserable, the two walked in silence until Thomasen finally spoke.

Thomasen: "So how 'bout that fight?"

Bartrum: "I've never seen anything like it."

Thomasen: "Yeah, we just saw a gorilla fight a polar bear."

Singers, Talkers, and Ballbreakers, 9:40 a.m.

Big guys fight, small guys talk.

Herein lies a truism of the football field, and so it's no surprise that the biggest trash talker of practice now is Pro Bowl cornerback Asante Samuel. He ignores the wide receivers who run against him and talks directly to the coaches.

"You can't throw the ball over here," he snaps between plays. "Man, I shut down half of the field today by myself. Can you get a receiver who can beat me?"

Back at the line of scrimmage, one offensive lineman shakes his head in disgust. "Those little guys are so annoying," he would say later.

But the good ones act as the lifeblood of a lockdown defense. They'll set the tone of camp. Cornerbacks like Trenton-bred, Trenton-tough Troy Vincent, who played fourteen seasons in the NFL for the Dolphins, Eagles, Bills, and Redskins and made five Pro Bowls, the tall and rangy Bobby Taylor, who shut down Michael Irvin just about every time, and super nickel back later turned longtime starter Al Harris, known for the dreadlocks flowing out the back of his helmet.

They lived for battering their wide receiver counterparts, especially the ones with the empty swagger. Guys like Freddie Mitchell, a first-round pick from UCLA in 2001 who fancied himself a hotshot.

One day at camp, Mitchell called out Vincent, jabbering to the coaches about how much he wanted to face the leader of the secondary during one-on-one drills.

According to one player within earshot, Vincent shot back to the coaches, "Tell Freddie Mitchell not to come out here until he gets off the line against Al [Harris]. If he can actually get off the line he can come get embarrassed by me."

So Mitchell squared up against Harris, who by now was in a foul mood and eager to silence him once and for all. Most of the defense didn't particularly care for Mitchell's act, the incessant talking and space-chewing bluster without merit. That's the thing with attention seekers, you know, the code among players says *you better be that good*.

Or else it goes down the way it did between Harris and Mitchell. Here's one eyewitness account: "Al held Freddie at the line of scrimmage for like eight seconds. Just wouldn't let him free. Totally bitched him. Freddie tried this swim move and hit Al on the ear of the helmet. So Al grabbed Freddie by the jersey and took him all the way past the sidelines and threw him in the bushes. Literally threw him in the bushes. They had to stop one-on-one drills."

It was worse for the wideouts at Falcons camp in steamy Suwanee, Georgia, where cornerback DeAngelo Hall and linebacker Keith Brooking beat up wide receivers for sport.

"They pounded guys left and right," recalls former linebacker Ike Reese. "Poor Greg Jennings got laid out flat one day by DeAngelo, and that Brooking has a screw loose. One day, he beat up two guys and got kicked out of practice."

Fan Interaction, 9:55 a.m.

The nature and flow of the sport breeds it for bigness. Part show, it naturally works the masses best on television. Replays and rapid cutaways make the game feel whole, even though it's played in quick, short bursts. Television fills and then smoothes the gaps, and that's why camp—even controlled scrimmages that are more gamelike than practice—feels so foreign to fans.

But it's a good foreign. Unlike, say, watching how they make sausage, watching training camp live is being invited through the side door of the inner sanctum. It's watching a rock band rehearse in an empty arena.

It also works the other way around. See, players don't really hear catcalls during a game, outside of the rare interaction by the bench area of the sideline and the first row of seats, depending on the proximity. They'll tell you they hear this white noise. At best, they'll discern between applause and groans, cheers and boos.

It's entirely different at training camp, where sound bleeds over the steamy summer morning at the fields. Whistles. Singing cicadas. Barking coaches.

And forked-tongued fans.

One player, new this year to the Philadelphia Eagles, grew fascinated by the fans. It's one of the things that struck him first about this training camp. How many fans actually show up for practice. In other places, members of the media outnumber the onlookers. Here the number easily goes deep into the thousands on a daily basis, and they're vocal.

The player finds these fans especially entertaining. He listens to a few of them howl at backup running back Lorenzo Booker—who had been a major disappointment since coming over from the Dolphins for a second-round pick—after rookie LeSean McCoy makes a good run on a screen play.

"You see that, Booker?" one snaps. "You see that? That's a real running back. That's the guy who gonna take your job."

Moments later, former Eagles wide receiver turned coaching intern Todd Pinkston walks by the crowd. Slowly they gain recognition and begin pointing at him. Pinkston was a pariah in Football Philadelphia—which should be recast Physicaldelphia. Pipe-cleaner thin, avoiding contact like a germophobe, Pinkston is forever known for that deep pass attempt in Washington where he shied away from the ball with the late safety Sean Taylor bearing down on him.

The play prompted former ESPN analyst Joe Theismann to say, "I've heard of alligator arms before, but that was alligator body."

So a fan fires away. "Hey, Pinkston! What are *you* going to teach the wide receivers? How not to go across the middle?"

Insults begin to rain down on him, becoming more and more crude.

"Pinkston the pussy!"

The player's eyes widen. "Man, those fans are not afraid to say anything," he would say later. "They'll go anywhere, you know?"

You haven't heard anything, he is told.

Mercifully, Practice Ends, 10:20 a.m.

On the first day of full contact, whistles blow in cadence with many short loud bursts, signaling the end of practice. The players gather around their head coach, and he tells them it was one heckuva practice.

"That's good work," Andy Reid says. "Real good work."

He pauses.

"But that's only one, you know?"

He reminds them of the grind, and how the days will get longer and their body will hit that dead period and it will be hell on wheels, yes sir, hell on wheels. For now, though, good job. Get a bite and a bit of rest, and be ready for the afternoon session.

Some of the young offensive linemen stay behind to work an extra fifteen minutes with their position coach, a serious fellow by the name of Juan Castillo. Castillo represents a rare breed of position coaches, one who was able to jump to a new regime after his head coach got fired. Most new head coaches fill their staffs with coaches with whom they have a kinship.

So when Castillo learned that Packers quarterbacks coach Andy Reid had won the Philadelphia job, he was determined to meet Ray Rhodes's successor before any decisions were final on the new staff. It was January. Green Bay was still alive in the playoffs. Castillo just had to meet Reid. He loved this job. He couldn't be on the street again. He had to take a shot. He had to let the new guy know what he stood for as a football coach. Maybe, just maybe, he could survive.

So Castillo drove from Philadelphia to Green Bay overnight, much of the way through a driving snowstorm. He arrived at Lambeau Field a little after five in the morning. Reid was already in his office.

A security guard alerted Reid that a man was here to see him: "Juan something. Some crazy guy who drove here in the snow from out east. Says he's a coach."

While he knew the name, Reid had never met Castillo before that early morning. Reid told Castillo that he couldn't promise anything, only that he'd give him fair consideration. Deep down, however, Reid couldn't help but give the guy a leg up on the job. A man who would drive halfway across the country in perilous winter conditions is the kind of man you'd want on your staff.

And that man would be a loyal man, the most important ingredient for an assistant coach.

Postpractice Recovery, Part I, 10:39 a.m.

Still dripping with sweat, fullback Leonard Weaver repeats the question. "How do you feel after [a training camp practice]?"

Weaver sloshes when he walks, he's so drenched.

"See that?" He nods toward a browning, shriveled orange peel that lies on the edge of the grass by the curb near the entrance to the team facility. "That's how you feel."

Arizona tight end Anthony Becht asks, "You ever jump into the pool with your clothes on? When you climb out of the pool and you're standing there, sopping wet, your clothes heavy with water? That's how you feel at the end of the practice. That's how much you sweat."

Most of the other analogies are far less thoughtful. "Feel like dogshit," big offensive lineman Todd Herremans huffs.

They all paint the portrait of exhaustion. They're nauseous and lightheaded. They've lost as much as sixteen pounds of fluid no matter how much they hydrated before practice—and that's when you hydrate, according to that hydration expert Jon Ritchie.

If you're thirsty during practice, he reports, it's too late. You're dehydrated.

They'll tell you about now they just want to be floating heads. Bodiless.

You really want to know what it feels like? You want to ditch your body. Exchange it for a new one, right away, please. The quickest way to relief happens to be the cold tub. Now, the cold tub is only ever really crowded after a session of training camp, because the cold tub feels like the water beneath the hole in the ice when you're spearing sturgeon in Sheboygan.

But your body feels overheated, swollen and sweaty, smelly and itchy. Hot all over. Like it's burning from the inside out. The icy water provides immediate relief, and it's amazing how clarity coolly washes over you.

In fact, you didn't realize how loopy you felt. Terribly dizzy, off kilter.

Your muscles, now chill-packed in the tub, no longer throb. The movement—the rhythmic twitching of your heartbeat in several odd places on your body at the same time, which can be so pronounced it looks like a parlor trick—finally ends.

Ah, what a wonderful feeling when your body finally quiets down.

After fifteen minutes or so, you will pull yourself out of the cold tub and take a hot shower. Standing there, the heat now soothing, you will reflect on the morning, replaying the entire practice in your mind. The trick is to focus first on what you did right. Visualize it—and make it stick, applying a mental check mark. Because invariably, you will curse yourself for the mistakes you made.

Even if it's just one, however minor, it will haunt you in the immediate aftermath.

Until you rationalize it away.

You're good at rationalizing, and you have to be or you might as well not play. Because everyone misses an assignment, you know, turns the wrong way, doesn't square up, or drops a pass. Ask any coach. The success of any play usually hinges on which unit—offense or defense—makes the least number of mistakes.

So now you can wander over to the cafeteria and relive practice again with some of your teammates. The pasta bar calls your name today. Every shape and size of pasta and every type of sauce is before you. You choose the wheat pasta twirled in Alfredo sauce with bacon and peas.

Energy food.

And nap food.

Midday Musings, 12:42 p.m.

When you're finished eating, all you can think about now is retreating to the dorm room, closing the shades, cranking up the air conditioner, and closing your eyes. Pasta works quickly on the system, especially after a grueling workout, a cold soak, and a hot shower, especially when the suns moves higher in the sky, and it's this ungodly humid.

Feels like Laos.

The only good thing about the afternoon practice—besides the fact that it's usually shorter and less physical—is that your body feels looser later in the day, much better than in the morning, when you rise creaky and sore. Soreness in the muscles makes your body feel heavy, particularly the extremities, as though you need to pick up one leg at a time with your arms to make yourself walk. Of course, your arms feel weighted down too, dragging, it seems, all the way down to your ankles.

It's why football people aren't morning people, certainly the players in training camp.

"When you wake up in the morning and put the pads on, it's a terrible feeling," former linebacker Ike Reese said. "Once you're out in the weather for twenty, twenty-five minutes, your body gets used to it, you start to loosen up, then it's okay. But first thing in the morning, it can be unbearable. You're tired and you're sore, and worse—you know what lies ahead of you."

The Afternoon Session, 2:09 p.m.

The sports complex of Lehigh University is tucked in the hills and midday feels sleepy at the sunbaked practice fields. The first sign of life comes when two rookies, each carrying two sets of shoulder pads—undoubtedly rookie duties, lugging the equipment of a demanding veteran—make their way from the team's facility across a small access road to the spongy grass that leads to five massive fields, three of them football fields, two complete with goalposts, one a converted soccer field and the other a sort of grassy knoll where players will work with the trainer far removed—and safe—from the action.

Slowly, the main field begins to fill with the coaches and players, and the action moves from stretching to individual position work to special teams. The sun peaks now, and it's a good thing this afternoon session is a special teams practice in "shells," which means no pads and no hitting.

But lots of running. Special teams always means running.

Run to cover the punt. Run to cover the kick.

Unless he tells them, few people know Matt Bowen ever played in the NFL, let alone for seven years. He sweated out a career on smarts and mostly special teams with the Rams, Packers, Redskins, and Bills.

"Everybody sees the Sundays on TV," he offered. "That's the glory. Sundays are great. No one's watching Tuesday morning training camp practice. It's hard. It hurts. Think a guy like Brett Favre who's gonna be forty wants to live in a dorm for a month? No way. So he signs late with the Vikings. I don't blame him. Though I was never in that position. I had to be there every day. I remember being in Green Bay with nothing guaranteed. Covering kicks. Wondering if this practice was my last in the NFL. I was one of those other guys."

There are two types of guys in the NFL. Pro shop guys. The ones who sell jerseys in the pro shop. And those other guys. Hacks. Plodders. Grinds.

"You're not a pro shop guy, you're doing all of the special teams drills," Bowen explained. "Those aren't fun. You just did deep passing drills? Too bad. Now you're going to run into somebody and you know the whole way it's not going to feel good. You might vomit on the way back to the starting line, but you do it again."

Postpractice Recovery, Part II, 3:21 p.m.

A regimen only begins when you repeat your first loop, and so that means a second dip in the cold tub and a hot shower, followed by two hours of downtime in the dorm room and dinner back in the cafeteria.

More pasta. Plus two heaping portions of prime rib and some veggies.

There's just enough time to sneak in a phone call to your girlfriend or your brother before a much different test of will.

Meetings and More Meetings, 6:29 p.m.

Like most of your brethren, you begin meetings upright in the classroom, then slowly slide down in the chair until you're in a full-fledged slump. The workouts in the raging heat have you exhausted, and you're happy the first meeting centers on special teams, because those last only a half hour.

After going over the responsibilities on punt and kick coverage and then the return game and then the field goal unit, you follow the rest of the men into a larger room where you are joined by all of the men for the overall team meeting.

It feels even more like college, with the structure of class. The head coach stands before the team, so the mood is less jovial than the previous meeting—and certainly less than the one to follow that consists of just the individual position group, where everyone knows each other too well.

"Hey, men," the coach begins. "Good job today. Make sure you keep hydrated. Take care of yourselves. It's gonna get tough. It's gonna get harder. I'm gonna push you guys, so be mentally prepared. It's gonna be real tough."

NFL players gossip too. And now as the head coach wanders off and the players prepare for their unit meetings, those from other teams tell the ones who have only in their career experienced this team's camp just how hard it is by comparison.

A lot of teams go no pads, one player says, and they definitely wouldn't go live (with hitting) if too many guys were banged up. That player spoke nine days into this camp, after the Eagles lost their starting middle linebacker (Stewart Bradley) and their prized rookie tight end (Cornelius Ingram) to season-ending knee injuries.

"From the first day on, when those guys go down, Coach Reid didn't bring it back," one player remarked later. "Practice was just as intense. I was talking to one guy from the Colts. He said *most* of the time they don't go in pads—and they just about never go live. That it's one of the easiest training camps in the NFL."

For the record, one of the hardest days of the preseason occurred in the second week after the team had broken camp and returned to Philadelphia, following a desultory loss to those Colts in the second exhibition game.

"Coach Juan gets revved up at practice—well, this day he got on Coach's wrong side," that player said.

A few plays into practice, Andy Reid blew his whistle. According to the player, he snapped, "Since Coach is revved up, I'm gonna make this live. Like that, Juan? Like it? It's live. Let's go."

And so on a very hot August morning right outside its complex on one of the finely manicured fields, the team endured a grueling 140-play scrimmage.

Live.

"We're talkin' practice," the player said, imitating with irony the infamous Allen Iverson quote.

Scared Straight, 7:15 p.m.

There's another team meeting tonight, but this one centers around life off the field. The trappings of the life. Real life. The one only security director Butch Buchanico will address.

Women, guns, and money.

Haters, baiters, and prison biscuits.

Buchanico stands before the players like he does at the beginning of every training camp, just he and the players in the room. No coaches. Definitely no women.

He speaks to them in the language of men—which is seaman salty. If they're going to listen—and he prays that they do—the message needs to be delivered that way, reeking of realism and authenticity.

The following talk stems from tragedy and wasted lives.

How tenuous it all really is, the former cop with the scarred soul tries to convey to them. The examples are plentiful, and how sad is that? He doesn't need to go back in time, either. Just recite a list of the fallen from this calendar year alone—and these are the ones whom everybody knows, mind you:

- Steve McNair. Dead
- Donté Stallworth. In jail.
- Plaxico Burress. In jail.
- Michael Vick. Just released from jail. Bankrupt.
- Pacman Jones. Banished from the league.

So you want to be a football star?

How easy to attract the harlots, the parasites, the bedbugs, the social climbers, the swindlers and the charlatans, the ticket hounds and the memorabilia freaks. How easy to corrupt young men with swelled egos and raging libidos who wear the thin armor of invincibility.

How easy to lose it all over foolishness. Acting the fool or being the fool.

Butch is believable because Butch once lived in the underbelly of life. When he was a city cop and arrived home to his family early in the morning after the night shift, he changed out of his clothes right there on the porch because didn't want to bring the stench of that world into the house. Like after the time a hysterical woman flagged him down on the street and shrieked that her husband had gone berserk and chased her out of the house with a butcher knife and he escorted her back to their home and the place was in shambles, broken glass covering the floor and blood smeared on the walls and every piece of their life systematically smashed. The good china, glasses, ashtrays, lamps, dining room chairs, picture frames, the smiling faces now staring back at him through jagged cracks. And he tiptoed up the staircase with his gun drawn calling out the husband's name—he wasn't there—and begged the woman to stay with a relative before he left.

"Whatever you do, hon, don't go back into that house alone," he told her.

And later that night he was at the morgue and he opened the drawer with a body in it because that's what city cops on the night shift did to keep sane, and he pulled aside the slivered scalp bearing the long hair that veiled the corpse's identity and that woman's face stared back at him. The tears welled so quickly, and he screamed at her, "No, no, no, no, no, no. I told you not to go back in that house! Why didn't you listen to me? Why, goddammit, why?"

That's his greatest fear with the players before him now. He grows to love these boys, he says.

He begins his talk in a subtle way, explaining the landscape of Lehigh—how they are surrounded by three law enforcement agencies, Lehigh, Bethlehem, and Lower Saucon Valley, and if they get stopped by police make sure they hand over license, registration, and proof of insurance and immediately identify themselves as an athlete.

"Be polite! Speak to him in a yes-sir, no-sir fashion. And turn down the fucking music."

He becomes animated and starts to roll stream-of-consciousness through scenarios:

No means no with a woman! Respect women.

Respect kids. Respect animals. Respect our fans.

Be mindful when you go out. No gangster shit. Look out for one another.

All the electronic toys you have . . . fight no battles over the Internet. Don't get involved in any wars with people through the phone, text messages, Twitter, whatever. And stay off weird Web sites—even if you're just being inquisitive. Treat that stuff like nothing is ever erased—which it's not.

Okay, gambling. Casinos? You're allowed to go—but watch yourself. Anything with sports betting? Stay out!

Drinking. Use your fucking head. If you're going to go out and you're going to drink—and I know you are—get a fucking driver. Be smart. We have safe rides you can join. Always have a friend you can call. Have a designated driver.

Okay, nightclubs, bars, hotspots in the city. No matter where you go, always know there will be one or two law enforcement people there—state, local, federal, an informant. Wiseguys all go to the nicest places. The Russian mob controls a lot of the night-clubs and strip clubs.

You know what I'm talking about!

Gangsters all have nice women around them. Don't get invited to any private parties. Watch where you go. Never leave a drink.

Be mindful how much you're on camera—from the time you leave until the time you get home. Somebody's always watching. You're on a toll road? There's a camera. You're at a convenience store? There's a camera. You live in an apartment? There's cameras all over.

Guns! Guns don't go off by themselves! If you need a gun to go someplace, then you shouldn't go to that place. Plaxico had a Glock, and a Glock doesn't have an external safety on it. So it's basically a trigger within a trigger. You only need two and a half pounds of pressure to fire it. Want to shoot your johnson off?

Think that's cool?

If you really think you need a gun, come see me.

I asked Butch which story ripped from the headlines resonated most with the players.

"Oh, the big one this year?" He nodded. "Steve McNair. What a sin. Forget about all of the details, for a second. He died because he was dating somebody. A lot of these guys are young. They think they're immortal. All these guys say the same thing—it's not going happen to me. Meanwhile, happens to them. They are targets. They are bull's-eyes. I worry about them. I pray the phone doesn't ring in the middle of the night—like I did for my own son and daughters. I haven't lost a kid yet [to something very bad] and I pray to God I never do."

The other hot topic of the talk entered their lives unsuspectingly a few weeks later back in Philadelphia amid great hullabaloo.

Ten days after Michael Vick sat alongside Andy Reid, Tony Dungy, and Eagles owner Jeffrey Lurie at a news conference and spoke of regret and second chances and a deep desire to do the right thing, I had dinner with Butch at a restaurant on the river. Actually, I was an interloper with Butch's blessing at the large table tucked in the back of the dining room.

See, Butch thought it a fine gesture to invite Vick for a night outside of his hotel room, where he'd spent every waking moment outside of practice at the complex. The fallen quarterback, an A-list pariah, had been confined plenty in recent months, as you can imagine. Ever since he reported to prison for his part in operating and financing the Bad Newz Kennels dogfighting ring, all of his movements had been orchestrated, down to his release after twenty-three months and subsequent house arrest, and oddly, even more so in this strange city that offered a chance for redemption, because the public relations types were calling the shots now.

Whoever signed Michael Vick would have to withstand the initial public outcry, and protesters circled the gates outside the Eagles' practice facility the day of his news conference and outside Lincoln Financial Field for his first game with their signs—*How Low Could the NFL Go?*—and their chants—*Vick is sick! Vick is sick!*

Upon Vick's reinstatement to the NFL, no one figured on Philadelphia as his destination. The Eagles had their franchise quarterback (Donovan McNabb) and they had their future quarterback (Kevin Kolb), and they already had a mini quarterback controversy the year before in Baltimore when McNabb was benched at halftime during an ugly loss to the Ravens. But under further review, what a spectacularly perfect place for Vick to rehabilitate his life and resume his career, here under the cloak of the depth chart, with expectations low, playing for a forgiving man whose two sons had slipped into the ghastly world of drugs and institutions and programs and left him in a state of unremitting prayer. Yes, Andy Reid knew all too well how the news helicopters will hover over your house and beam your family's despair to the world.

Led by McNabb, the players, meanwhile, championed giving Vick a chance in Philadelphia. By the end of the year, he would make little impact on the field, but in the locker room his teammates voted him the winner of the team's Ed Block Courage Award.

Dinner is totally on the down-low, Butch said earlier that day. "Show up, I'll introduce you," he said.

So I showed up, not knowing what to expect, other than my own faraway perception of a man who could commit such a heinous crime.

And of course, he came across very different. Life is not art, where the bad guy offers such defined lines of evil. Man is a blend of good and evil, and it's impossible to know what resides in another man's heart. I can only say that Michael Vick seemed a weathered man just looking for peace. A night is merely a night, and on this one he acted gentlemanly and demure.

He said how horrific the past two years were for him and how he cried many a night and he couldn't believe how he made such a mess of such a wonderful life and how he thought about what he did and couldn't believe he really did it.

He said, "I think back and say, 'That wasn't really me, was it?'"

The conversation about the past didn't last long. The dinner conversation wasn't an interview. He knows he needs to remember but he really wants to forget. He so wants to lie low and rebuild his life, and any more details he preferred not to share.

Back at training camp, Butch was talking again about Steve McNair:

You don't want to lose your life over dating somebody. Dating somebody? Think about that. You get in a relationship with a woman, don't promise anything. A lot of girls are looking for a stairway to the stars. They see the big cars. They see the bling. They think that's their ticket. You don't want to be baby daddy. Wanna see your paycheck disappear? Get a paternity suit slapped on you.

When you're dealing with the public, wear your baseball cap right and save that jive shit for when you're hangin' with your buddies.

"I talk to them," Butch adds. "I don't preach to them. I talk to them straight from the street. They've been talked to . . . to death."

You like the money and the cars, right? You like being a celebrity? Don't give me any of that 'All I want to do is play football' bullshit. You want to be a football star? Well, it comes with a price.

Donovan McNabb has heard that speech more than ten times during his career. By his public conduct over the years, he could provide a handbook on how to handle NFL stardom. "Let me tell you," he said. "Guys in that room listen to Butch. He tells them the way it is without pulling punches. Let's just say he's pretty colorful."

So colorful that each year, one or two devoutly Christian players depart the room because of his storytelling. Brian Dawkins, the ferocious safety, protested Butch's language—but he knew why.

Just the same, Dawkins always left, like wide receiver Jason Avant did this year.

Meanwhile, players also must complete two one-hour life skill sessions during training camp and eight more during the regular season conducted for the Eagles by director of player development Harold Carmichael, a former four-time Pro Bowler with the team.

Inside a Unit Meeting, 8:35 p.m.

The projector might as well be spitting out somebody else's old home movies about now. A scan of the darkened makeshift classroom catches each contagious yawn, growing more frequent as the long day's work settles into their bodies. One man exercises his jaw and rounds his shoulders. Another gulps down an energy drink. Others sip coffee. Others chew tobacco and spit into a cup.

Stay awake, they tell themselves silently.

Concentrate, damn it.

Some of their eyes flicker, so they blink wildly.

The position coach in front of the room is not oblivious. Like a college professor, he's stood before many a class of players, and knows too well the last place they want to be is here. He begins to call out players by their name, though not in an accusatory tone.

"See that, Jackson?"

Jamal Jackson perks up.

The coach rewinds the film of today's practice again. Whizzes it back, then forward. Then back a smidgen, and again forward, and again back, repeating the process sometimes twenty-five times, sometimes thirty.

We're with in the room with the offensive linemen now and Coach Juan speaks of technique.

"You know, playing college and high school football is fun," lineman Chris Patrick says. "At this level, you have to work your ass off and rely on technique so much. In college, you can dominate on raw ability. Here it's imperative you keep your shoulder square and get off at the snap count. You don't do those two things, you're going to get exposed. You're late off the ball? You have no chance. I don't care how good an athlete you are."

The unit meeting lasts close to two hours, and then it's back to the cafeteria for a snack before bed. You fill the plate: two grilled chicken breasts, some fried shrimp, and a ham sandwich. Two more chocolate milks. Makes five total for the day.

Passing the Time, 9:38 p.m.

The sounds of men away from home being boys play in the distance.

Splat.

Splat.

Laughter.

"Dumbasses."

You laugh to yourself. Schoebel and Curtis must have gotten somebody good. You remind yourself to avoid the path below their room on the second floor.

Matt Schoebel, the tight end who'll turn thirty-one in November, and Kevin Curtis, the wide receiver who turned thirty-one earlier in July, like to drop water balloons on the unsuspecting passersby below.

Training Camp Mind Games

The biggest mistake former safety Matt Bowen made was the calendar. Why in the world did he tack that thing to the wall in his room? The third day he marked down the X, he looked at what remained of training camp and nearly panicked.

Thirty days.

The way he felt at that very moment, directly after a full day's work of nine-on-seven, seven-on-seven, live team scrimmage, it seemed like a life sentence in prison.

"I'm telling you, the mental part is just as hard as the physical," says Bowen. "It's like being in a car accident in the morning and then going to practice in the afternoon—and mentally preparing yourself to do that.

"Every time you hit someone it takes something out of you. But that's camp. It's necessary."

It's necessary, Bowen says, to hit someone—or something—forty times in a day and feel all torn up getting out of bed the next day and go do it again and feel worse the following day. It's necessary to do that for a week straight, and then the body suddenly responds and the legs come back and it still hurts bad, but the recovery is quicker and you do by golly feel a slight spring.

Then, of course, you trudge back to your dorm, and there's that calendar staring you in the face.

Twenty-six more days left.

Under the Terre Haute Sun

The Cowboys no longer hold their training camp in Wichita Falls. Dallas left after the 2002 preseason and last year announced a five-year deal with the Alamodome in San Antonio, which should at least ease the heat effects of training camp—though due to a scheduling conflict at the dome the team later returned to pleasant Oxnard, California, about sixty miles north of Los Angeles.

Following Korey Stringer's heat-related death in training camp in 2001, many teams altered their approach. For example, head coach Andy Reid will often either limit or cancel entirely the afternoon session during Eagles camp in Pennsylvania's Lehigh Valley.

The National Weather Service had issued heat advisories for Mankato, Minnesota, and the surrounding area during the first week of that fateful August, with temperatures in the upper nineties and stifling humidity. Stringer, a mammoth offensive tackle at 6-foot-4, 335 pounds, experienced awful cramping and retired early to the locker room the first day of camp. Adhering to the code of football, he vowed to return the next day and collapsed during practice.

Stringer was rushed to a nearby hospital, where he died in the early morning hours of August 2 due to complications from a heatstroke. When he arrived at the hospital, with Randy Moss and Cris Carter at his side, Stringer's body temperature was 108 degrees. He was twenty-eight years old.

Two other football players perished in heat-related deaths in the summer of 2001, including Florida freshman running back Eraste Autin and a high schooler. A year later, Northwestern's Rashidi Wheeler similarly died of heatstroke.

Though Stringer and J. V. Cain, a tight end for the St. Louis Cardinals who died in summer 1979, have been the only NFL training camp victims, some eighteen high school or college football players died from heat-related causes between the years 1995 and 2000 alone.

"Training camp probably took five, ten years off my career, and probably the same could be said for my life," Kyle Turley said. "Then you take the Broncos, who had two practices with pads the whole camp this past year. The rest was in soft shell pads in cool areas of Colorado."

Said former Bronco Mark Schlereth, "Especially as a veteran, [camp] does more damage than it does good. You know you have to work technique. Certainly, it's a necessary evil. Twice a day, every day, is really brutal."

Said veteran Montae Reagor, "I hate training camp. It's brutal. You're in the center of contact every day. Your knees are sore. Your fingernails are broken because your fingers are stepped on every day. Your head hurts. Playing on the offensive and defensive line you're in the middle of hell every play."

"Camp is brutal," Jason Short said. "It's awful, to be honest. Once I tore my feet up so bad, I was getting shot up with lidocaine before every practice. There were like two silver-dollar-size pieces of the bottom of my feet that would tear off every day. After practice my socks would be covered in blood. Every day they were like that.

"The thing about Lehigh that made it so brutal was that it was so hilly. Your legs are already dead to begin with, and everywhere you go it's all hills. You're walking as it is, but there it's up a hill, down a hill. Then it's upstairs to get to your meetings. Your legs really get abused during camp."

Schlereth agreed. "When you come back from an injury, your legs are fresh. Say you miss three weeks of camp. Guys would be saying, 'Fresh legs! Fresh legs out there!' In the film room you can see the fresh legs. There is such a noticeable difference because they don't have the wear and tear that the guys who have been playing the last three weeks have endured. You wonder why they don't scale it back. Some of it is that the establishment has done it this way for so long, people are resistant to change."

Say what you want about punters, and how they obviously don't endure the same punishment of position players, but Sean Landeta has attended nearly twenty NFL training camps and offers fascinating insight into the mental grind.

He said, "The two best days of the year for a player are the day he makes the team—everything you've worked for is validated—and the first day of the off season. You can then finally take a deep breath and relax. There is so much pressure throughout the year, even in practice. The toughest time of the year is the four to six weeks of camp. Basically you have to go out and your day covers from 7 a.m. to 9 p.m., six days a week, and you're competing for a job.

"You've got to stand next to very good players and compete for that job. Can you imagine how productive the working world would be if every secretary or pilot or lawyer had to prove themselves up against people that were recruited to do that job? That's something they can't measure. Because if they did identify the toll it takes, the U.S. government might outlaw football."

And Landeta doesn't want to hear about being only a punter. "They only keep one at my position," he said. "It's a tough job to get and that other guy you're standing next to, well, he's very good. The effects mentally are debilitating of your job constantly hanging in the balance, and that feeling doesn't end when the season starts. At any time you can be told you're not employed and you're not receiving a paycheck anymore. The mental stress and worry causes more problems than the physical. Everybody can see the physical. I had herniated discs, a torn ACL, a broken wrist, a torn calf. I've had those. I've recovered from those. You can see a scar and the result of the physical, but you can't see the worry and mental strain. If you could see it, it would be monstrous."

In the end, however, the body wilts. Two weeks into camp, players limp along drawn and weary.

"Training camp is the absolute worst on your body," Kevin Long said. "Of course, some oddballs like it."

Welcome back—surprise—Bill Romanowski.

"I loved it," Romanowski said. "I lived for it. I had to learn how to love it because everyone hated it. I used that as an advantage for me. Every day I would fly around saying, 'It's a great day to be alive.' I did that to fuck with people. Guys would be saying, 'What the hell is he taking? I am so sore and miserable and tired. How does he do it? He's thirty-seven!'

"That's just a mind-set I would get into when I went to camp. I felt just as bad as everyone else, if not worse. I just didn't want to let them know I felt that way."

Chided Schlereth, "Romo was a strange duck! That proves my statement that he actually enjoyed training camp."

"Camp is what you make of it," Brian Mitchell said. "The main point of camp is to get away from everything and all of the distractions, and build chemistry. For rookies and second-year guys, it's hell because you don't know what to expect. Veterans tell horror stories to the rookies all the time. Trying to get them real scared. You have to have fun with camp."

Until tempers flare. At training camp, tempers always flare.

Jostling for jobs, for positions, whether it's to start or simply make the team, players are in heat in training camp. They become edgy, downright ornery, especially when it's young versus veteran.

"I went to the Jets, and Matt Willy was this big tackle from USC," Hugh Douglas said. "So we're in practice at training camp and we have on shorts and helmets, and he was manhandling me. He's throwing me to the ground like, 'Who's this little guy?' I was a rookie and I was skinny. I looked like a linebacker playing defensive end. Well, the dude snatched me up again and drove me into the ground, and that was it. I had to prove myself. I got up to fight."

Douglas snapped to Willy, "I don't know who the fuck you think you are. You got the wrong one. I ain't no punk. Ain't no ho in me."

"He respected me after that," Douglas said.

"Fights would happen in camp all the time," Long said. "People are tired and hot and fighting for jobs. Coach Jeff Fisher did not take you out of practice if you got in a fight. You're playing the next play no matter what."

One of the legendary training camp fights occurred during a scrimmage between Kansas City and New Orleans at the Chiefs' site in River Falls, Wisconsin. The controlled scrimmage quickly turned uncontrollable as players from both teams squared off in a huge melee that became known as the Brawl at the Falls.

The Chiefs said Kyle Turley started it, and Turley doesn't dispute it. He was coming to the aid of a teammate in distress. "Every fight I've ever been in has been in defense of someone or something," he said.

Turley also doesn't regret the River Falls fracas, which ended any possible future scrimmages between the teams before the Saints moved back to Louisiana.

"It was full benches cleared," Turley said. "Like *Braveheart*, with everyone on both sides going at it. We were supposed to scrimmage them the next day, too, and they canceled that real quick. We're acting like we won the Super Bowl after that fight. I was fighting the whole day. It was a great camaraderie builder. Nowadays, you get fined. We set the new rules. We made a difference."

A Saints Haze, 1998

And so it happened on the final night of training camp in a stuffy room on the third floor of Sanford Hall at the University of Wisconsin–La Crosse, men with beer behaving like boys because men—at least most men, and particularly athletes—will forever have that boy trapped inside them, especially when there's beer and they are holed up together in close quarters for a period of time.

It happened for amusement and for the sake of hierarchy and for the code of team, which is not to excuse the actions of men with beer, as cruel as they were, but merely to point out that such a practice exists and why it exists.

The men with beer were veterans of the team, each having earned his own standing on the team in his own way, proud, proprietary men with something to lose, mostly their jobs. And they would certainly lose their jobs to the other men, if not now, then at some moment in the near future. For the sake of accuracy, let's acknowledge that they would lose their jobs to those like the other men, those who now had pillowcases fastened over their heads, younger men who looked like boys if you could see their faces.

Masking their faces masked the guilt inside the men with beer. To them, to their bloodshot eyes, the young men were just slabs of flesh, each of them no different from a fatted calf.

And why the hell not? Who did they think they were? Hotshots. They were all hotshots, with no respect of how it's done here.

Getting paid. Some of them more than the men with beer. Or at least some of them would over the course of their careers, once the insurgency was finally complete.

Regrettably, it got out of hand. And the cops came.

•   •   •

The New Orleans Saints moved their training camp site to La Crosse because, first, Louisiana in July and August resembles life on a griddle inside a sauna. Why subject your players to *Survivor: Thibodaux*? What do you really have to gain when you play at home in a dome? Like Kyle Turley said, "Some things don't make sense."

Residual health problems, Turley said, do not stem from just hits. "The temperatures we have to train under? And you have twenty pounds of gear on and every pore is closed by gloves and helmets and shoes so your sweat doesn't have anywhere to go? Then they wonder why a guy like Korey Stringer dies?"

At the very least, following the path of the French fur traders up the Mississippi River from Louisiana all the way to La Crosse in western Wisconsin offered the chance for bearable weather. At the time, the Saints were hopeful that just maybe the team would enter an upswing with the legendary coach beginning his second season.

Super Bowl Mike Ditka had become a legend not terribly far from La Crosse, down in Chicago, and he provided the cachet that had forever eluded the Saints. In his day he was one of those men with beer, the consummate man's man who smoked cigars and knew how to swear really good. The trick of a good curser is knowing what swear words to use, not unlike, say, ingredients in a dish at Ditka's Restaurant, aptly known for its roasted hunks of meat.

Iron Mike Ditka, born in 1939 in western Pennsylvania—Carnegie, to be exact—was a former football player turned football coach who pushed his players with a heavy paw of a hand until he hugged them. All of the great men's men and deep barkers possess a softness deep inside. It's why Ditka never could eviscerate Ricky Williams, even though trading his entire first-day draft for him hastened his demise in New Orleans.

It's important to the story that you get Ditka.

See, it makes sense the incident involving the men with beer happened on his watch, considering how much Colonel Nathan Jessup he had in him. Uncanny, too, how Ditka said publicly shortly thereafter that he had heard whispers about something happening on the final night of training camp. Like Jessup said on the witness stand, Ditka said to the press that he specifically warned the players against such behavior.

Who knows if deep down it really worried Coach Man's Man? After all, it could be said, men haze as cows graze.

Cue: you need Mike Ditka on those sidelines.

Kyle Turley, hotshot from San Diego State, selected seventh overall in the 1998 draft, was one of the five hooded players, who were forced to run through a line of approximately twenty teammates wielding clenched fists—a practice called the gauntlet, based on the former military punishment in which the offender is struck by two rows of men with clubs.

"All of the veterans came up to the rookies' floor and made us run the gauntlet," Turley said. "The floor was primarily concrete with a nice thin carpet layer. You could play basketball on these floors. So we ran the gauntlet while every veteran got to take a shot at us as we ran by."

The night grew ugly fast. Almost torturous. Certainly bloody.

One of the rookies, Jeff Danish, told the *New York Times* after he was cut from the team shortly thereafter that he was struck with a bag of coins, punched, and elbowed. Danish, who later sued the Saints and settled out of court for $650,000 in damages, needed thirteen stitches in his left arm in addition to suffering facial bruises. Cam Cleeland, a second-round pick that year, suffered the worst injury, a broken eye socket.

"One defensive lineman literally almost went through a window," Turley said. "The only thing that saved him was the waist-high bars in the windows. There was blood everywhere. I almost broke my knee-cap. Someone tripped me and I fell on those hard floors. Luckily it ended up just being a bruise. The cops ended up coming."

At first blush, campus police, followed by La Crosse police, entered a frightening scene. Hulking men with bruises the color of red wine grapes. Other hulking men with swollen knuckles. Blood smeared on the floor of a room that appeared ransacked.

"The whole thing was a mess," Turley said. "That ended hazing for the most part in the league. And by the way, we weren't very good that year."

The backlash brought forth an examination into hazing on all levels of all sports. Following the incident, head coaches clamped down on hazing during training camp, implementing harsh penalties.

The pendulum always swings too far in the opposite direction. The notion that begets hazing suddenly became dirty, disgraceful. But initiation in some form occurs in every workplace. It becomes demonstrative in sports because of the demonstrative nature of sports. The world of team needs the integration of youth and it needs to establish a pecking order, and all of the deeds breed a bond.

"It's a fun thing," Mitchell said. "I understand as a rookie you gotta bring breakfast and all that stuff, but there is nothing disrespectful about any of it."

"I would tell the young guys to have fun with it and look forward to it," Sean Landeta said. "This is one of the best ways to ingratiate yourself to the guys. Do it with a good attitude because the guys notice that. Football players are very perceptive people. The guys appreciate it. That can be one of the first times you're accepted by your teammates. If the veterans see a rookie coming up there with a skirt on or doing a funny poem, they enjoy it."

When they were rookies, before the Eagles built their state-of-the-art practice complex that includes a fine-dining cafeteria, linebackers Ike Reese and Jeremiah Trotter played errand boys. Their mission: twice-daily food runs for the veterans on the defense—Trotter for breakfast, Reese for lunch.

Trotter hated it. He debated an uprising. He'd fight any of those guys. Shoot, the young man from Texarkana, Texas, thought, they don't know me.

First, he'd talk to his position coach, then linebackers coach Joe Vitt. "They're trying to punk me, Coach. I ain't taking it anymore. I'm getting up too early."

Vitt pursed his lips in disappointment and shot back, "You pay your dues. Anything the veterans want you to do, you go do it. Hear me?"

The coach began to walk away and stopped as if in second thought. "Trotter?" he said with sudden empathy.

The rookie perked up. "Yes, Coach?"

"Bring me a bacon and egg sandwich with some onions tomorrow."

Trotter often tried to pay Reese to take his food run turn. Sometimes, especially since the rookie always buys for everyone out of his own pocket and it can grow pretty steep at times for a middle-round pick, Reese accepted.

When quarterback Matt Ryan first reported to the Atlanta Falcons, one veteran offensive lineman sidled up to him in the locker room.

"Hear that?"

Ryan shrugged. "No."

"You don't hear that?"

"No. What?"

"Listen closely."

Ryan strained to hear.

"Hear that?"

"No!"

"Exactly. This room needs a good stereo system."

And so that very day, following practice, Ryan dutifully went to the store and bought the best sound system he could find.

The hazing that occurs throughout every training camp is similarly benign, whether it involves rookies carrying the veterans' pads or having their eyebrows shaved, like what happened to Patriots running back Laurence Maroney.

Others will see their head shaved or shaped into a bad haircut, while most every rookie must sing his alma mater's fight song in the lunchroom or perform a skit in front of the team. One rookie got into serious trouble in the room a few years back when he mimed a skit about a veteran player rumored to be a steroid user shooting a needle into his arm and growing muscles. The laughter quickly turned to *oooooooohhh*s, and the veteran player had to be restrained from attacking the rookie.

"We've tied people up, shaved eyebrows, heads, innocent things that comes with guys being accepted," Mitchell said. "Like with Ray Horton, who used to play in the league, and became a coach when I was with Washington. I said, 'Hey, Ray, you're a rookie coach, so you're a rookie technically.' So we taped him up and put him in a laundry pail and poured ice water on him. We always got Norv Turner's son real good. He had a smart little mouth on him and he was always running around having a good time, and we would fuck with him a little bit."

Recalled former Falcon Mark Simoneau, "The fourth day of camp or so we got into a team meeting, and [head coach] Dan Reeves was late for the meeting. Well, Reeves walked in at the same time as I was getting up to sing so I thought I was safe. Then Dan said, 'Why don't you get up and sing for us?' So I sang my fight song—which I had learned for this special occasion."

"In Cleveland this past year," Jason Short said, "Brady Quinn and Joe Thomas had to shave their heads."

In 2006, on the final day of Carolina Panthers training camp in Spartanburg, South Carolina, veteran wide receivers Keyshawn Johnson and Steve Smith helped tape rookie wideouts Daniel Smith, Jovon Bouknight, Taye Biddle, Lynzell Jackson, and Justin McCullum to one goalpost. The rooks were then sprayed with water and sunscreen.

While that was happening, two rookie defensive linemen were being taped to another goalpost, and another was strapped to a chair and doused with Gatorade.

"I'm not exactly a hazing guy. I'm a supervisor hazer," veteran Chris Draft told the Associated Press thereafter. "Our guy James Anderson asked for more tape, like a good rookie should. We used regular tape, two-inch, stretch tape, and some good prewrap. He also asked for some Gatorade, because he felt a little dehydrated. Now he smells like strawberries."

The Plight of the Unheralded
July 23, 2009

The real stories of training camp originate from desperate men. You can spot them without looking at their jersey number. You don't even need to watch them but simply capture their movement. Desperate men move faster than everybody else. Whatever the drill, they churn like machine parts, and they can because desperate men report to camp already in football shape.

Meanwhile, the best players practice only with the purpose of losing a few extra pounds or becoming reacclimated with taking hits again. And the best players usually complain the loudest. It's why coaches love desperate men. Desperate men still believe in dreams and so they will study harder and practice harder and do exactly what the coaches say.

Anything, Coach, anything.

Desperate men compete for that last roster spot like it is food. Even if they hold no chance of making the team and know it, they practice for the opportunity to build a reel from a real NFL game so they can show another team and maybe secure that last job there.

Desperate men comprise the lifeblood of camp.

For a strapping young fellow named Chris Patrick, the quest begins when he sees the city in the rearview mirror of his black Dodge Ram start to blur from the heat. The row houses in the cramped neighborhood where he shares an apartment start to sway like a movie scene fading to flashback. A dramatic blend of old Italian ways and new immigrants from Mexico and all over Asia and hipsters seeking affordable urban living and beer pubs, South Philadelphia is a strange place for a farm boy from the center of Michigan's Lower Peninsula who played offensive line at the University of Nebraska to find himself, and even stranger is that he wants to stay here with all of his heart. It's not Green Bay—man, he loved it there—but this will do just fine, especially since he wandered into Mister Tony's place on the river and Mister Tony fed him for free because he says in broken English, "Number one, Chris is a nice kid. Very respectful. Number two, Chris is a foo-ball player—and I love American foo-ball. And number three, the poor kid doesn't make any money. He's plays foo-ball on the practice squad, which means he gets paid dirt. Less than me!"

And so Chris Patrick heads west on the highway out of the baked metropolis, following two of his teammates who know better the way to get to Lehigh University and Eagles training camp. Except they are driving like idiots, whizzing in and out of traffic, pushing it—speed freaks—and Chris is a bit paranoid. He keeps looking for cops. He doesn't need to get stopped, and with his luck he's the one who would get stopped. Not the other guys.

First, he can't afford the ticket. And how would it look to the team? Stopped by the police? Hardly a criminal act but certainly an immature one. Not that they would find out. But what if they did? What would they think? And even if the cop was a football fan—and just about every man, woman, and child is one in this football-crazy town—he probably wouldn't believe Chris Patrick drew a paycheck from the Eagles, however small for football it is.

If the guys weren't going so fast, he'd probably reflect on that awful drive a year and a half ago from Green Bay back home to Ithaca, Michigan. A workday's drive, eight hours, give or take a fast-food chicken sandwich that he wouldn't eat anyway because he wasn't hungry. He won't admit to crying. He would go as far as to say his eyes welled some, because there's no crying in football, either. But who would blame him if he had? Green Bay was going to be home. He just knew it. He would be a Packer, lay claim to a starting spot on the line in a year or two, then sign a real contract and buy a small house so Mom and Dad would have a place to stay when they drove down to watch his games.

The first two times he was released by NFL teams, however disappointing, he understood why. If he could do it all over again, he wouldn't have waited so long to declare eligibility following his junior season at Nebraska. Had he still not patched things up with Huskers coach Bill Callahan after their disagreement he'd rather not get into—and he undoubtedly would have tried harder to do so—he would have made up his mind in time to file for the real draft in April and a promising junior year in Lincoln in which he started twelve games at left tackle and helped the Huskers finish third in total offense in the Big 12 wouldn't have gone largely unnoticed.

The NFL Supplemental Draft is usually for hardship cases or troubled players who missed the January 15 filing deadline for the April draft because of academic or disciplinary matters. It is a draft of leftovers, a wasteland for traditionally wasted talent—that's if teams are even paying attention, since the event usually occurs in mid-July, when most of the NFL is away on a pre–training camp vacation.

The Supplemental Draft began in 1977, and as of 2009 only thirty-eight players had been selected. It's structured differently from the normal draft in that if a team covets a player it must submit a bid to the commissioner with the round in which it would select him. If no other team bids an earlier round then it wins the player and as compensation will forfeit a draft pick in the corresponding round of the following year's draft. If two or more teams bid the same round for a particular player then his rights would revert to the team with the lowest grouping (based on win total from the previous year).

Meanwhile, Chris Patrick was never selected. Following a private workout, he received interest from a couple teams, including the Patriots. But word soon came to him that New England would have to pass on drafting him because Bill Belichick was vacationing in Europe and the Patriots don't make a move without Bill Belichick.

Chris Patrick wound up signing with the Giants as an undrafted free agent, the NFL's version of cheap meat. Much as the railroad was built on the bodies of discarded men, those without any options who scaled death cliffs and cleared tunnels in the Sierra Nevada, the league churns on flesh that might as well be a separate line item titled "disposable cost-effective labor."

After all, not everyone in that room can carry the contract of the quarterback, let alone the status of him. First string equals first class. The back of the depth chart—where every undrafted free agent automatically begins—work for food. They donate their bodies to practice, especially training camp, where the carrot of making the team will inspire every player to work through exhaustion and play on injuries that could have long-term ramifications.

Coaches need sacrificial players out there for the framework of practice, and it's why one player told me that when his awkwardly positioned ankle collapsed under a colossal defensive tackle during a one-on-one blocking drill at training camp his rookie season, the team sent him for X-rays knowing that only an MRI would reveal any potential damage.

"My ankle popped," he said. "I got rolled up on. I knew it was messed up. But in my case, the X-ray looked fine. Of course it did! It's basic film. Soft tissue damage doesn't show in an X-ray. So I come back from the hospital and I can't even walk and they want me to practice."

The undrafted free agent is a guy on leave from the street, the contract he receives little more than an NFL lottery ticket. There are 6,000-plus players eligible for the draft and only 300 can be invited to the combine in Indianapolis. A little more than 200 are drafted and of those about 150 actually make a team. The rest are undrafted free agents—most of whom had good workouts during their senior year at college.

It's nearly impossible to give every player a fair and comprehensive appraisal. Somebody usually tells somebody about *this kid you just gotta see* and that somebody relays the tip with the same fervor without ever having watched the kid play to some scout who circles back for some tape and may or may not watch it after hearing the kid's raw stats—height, weight, and 40 time.

A few have made it big, most recently running backs Willie Parker, Priest Holmes, and Dominic Rhodes, tight end Antonio Gates, linebacker James Harrison, kicker Adam Vinatieri, and quarterbacks Tony Romo and Kurt Warner.

Everyone now knows well the Legend of Bagger Kurt, whose career arc looks like a financial chart from the first decade of this millennium. If every man will have three careers during a lifetime, Warner has had all three of his in the same profession. From obscurity to the Super Bowl he began, and then from MVP to shell-shocked shot, especially when he surfaced in New York and was awfully brittle and looked terribly skittish, especially in the face of a rush, so much so that the quarterback-desperate Giants traded for Eli Manning in the draft. And then he rose again in unlikely Arizona, all the way back to the Super Bowl, a scenario less plausible than how he landed a job in the NFL in the first place.

"The story of Kurt Warner will never happen again," his coach Dick Vermeil said. "I didn't know he'd be that kind of player. I thought he'd be a backup when I signed him to the World League. I brought him as a third quarterback."

In fact, when Trent Green went down in the preseason the year the Rams became the Greatest Show on Turf in 1999, Vermeil considered signing Jeff Hostetler, a graybeard at the time whom the coach thought could just manage the game, just like he did in Oakland and before that in New York, where he once Super Bowl subbed for Phil Simms.

"I figured Hostetler wouldn't get us beat," Vermeil said. "But he was pushing forty and we basically had no choice with Warner. What I saw was a guy who threw the ball accurately—very accurately—and had a great ability to slow the game down. It never, ever appeared too fast for him. It still amazes me. He goes from St. Louis Rams scout team player of the year to NFL player of the year. He played six minutes of football in the NFL before that season. Six!"

The path for long-term success is more unlikely for the grunts. For the skill players, like Warner, that one shot comes out in the open for everyone to see, the brush having been cleared and the land leveled. It's way more subjective for the grunt, who must battle stigma and agenda from the personnel executive down to the head coach and position coach. It sometimes takes years for the grunt to get established, and one hiccup, like a minor injury, can derail his future.

"I don't know if there's ever really a sense of comfort," offered Colts center Jeff Saturday, an undrafted free agent who was cut by the Ravens in 1998 and needed a close relationship with Peyton Manning for a team to really notice his ability. "You know, you have to keep your head on a swivel. You're always afraid they'll give a draft pick the nod over you."

Meanwhile, Chris Patrick didn't sign with the Giants until just prior to training camp and missed all of the Organized Team Activities during the off season. The OTAs have become especially critical for rookies from a learning standpoint regarding the playbook and assignment and verbiage.

For a rookie, the mandatory spring minicamp and the involuntary OTAs—which come with a "be there or else" wink for everyone except a star player—also ease the acclimation period with new teammates and life in a new city and inside the world of professional football.

For the record, the collective bargaining agreement of 2006 between the NFL Players Association and the league stipulates that teams may conduct "strictly voluntary" off-season programs such as weight room and training workouts and classroom instruction sessions for no more than fourteen weeks, with no more than four workouts per week for any individual player—and no weekends allowed.

Now, during the workout period, there can be up to fourteen days of organized team practice activity. The rules state a maximum of six hours per day and two hours out on the field. These are again strictly "wink, wink" voluntary. Each team may hold a maximum of one mandatory minicamp for veteran players, and may add two more voluntary ones if that team has hired a new head coach. The mandatory camp can last no more than three days—plus one day for physicals—and that one is suggested to be held over a weekend.

While helmets are permitted during team activities, pads aren't—except protective knee and elbow pads. And hitting is "expressly prohibited," according to the agreement, defined as "contact work (e.g., live blocking, tackling, pass rushing, bump-and-run)." Teams are allowed seven-on-seven, nine-on-seven, and eleven-on-eleven drills without contact.

No contact for a coach is like simulated sex, so of course they try to bend the rules. A violation of the rules can cost a team a week of their off-season program and a fourth-round pick for a second transgression.

By the way, as compensation, players participating in the off-season workout programs received $130 per day in 2009–2010—up from $110 in 2006—plus traveling and lodging expenses.

The collective bargaining agreement also states that during the ten days leading to the reporting date for training camp no veteran may participate in any team organized workout or engage in any football activity with any coach. It's why most of the NFL goes on vacation in the days prior to training camp.

So here's Chris Patrick showing up at Giants camp in Albany completely cold trying to learn the league and the New York offense and trying to block Justin Tuck before everyone knew about Justin Tuck, and Justin Tuck was just a promising defensive end who ran with the second team facing third-team offensive linemen.

"For anybody it's tough," he said. "Now here I am a week away from training camp and they throw me the playbook. I had no idea of the offense. I didn't know what to expect. I felt like everyone was going a hundred miles an hour and I was just standing there. I remember going against Tuck. That guy was a bitch to block. I didn't know what I was doing. Bad situation."

It's how players fall into a career abyss. Coaches have neither the time nor the inclination to see if a guy can play under optimum practice time and study time. In Patrick's case, he was also relatively new to the position. He went to Nebraska as a defensive end and didn't move to the offensive line until his redshirt freshman season. During his entire career in Lincoln, he started only fourteen games at tackle, and now here he was with a hungry Tuck snorting in front of him.

Patrick didn't give up any sacks in the Giants' first preseason game, but he made a couple mental errors. For example, he worked the wrong linebacker on one play in the blocking scheme. The next day, now about three weeks into training camp, someone in the personnel office walked up to him out on the field before practice.

"Are you Chris?" asked the man, who looked to be in his early thirties.

Patrick didn't recognize him, which is not uncommon with the personnel office overflowing with his types.

"There's fifty of those people running around," Patrick would say later. "Some asshole who played Division III football and was never good enough to play at a big program now trying to play God. Telling you, 'We know your weakness, we know your strength, we know everything about you.' They walk around with all the authority in the world."

The man pointed to Patrick. "Coach Coughlin wants to see you," he said. "Coach is over there."

He was confused. And in that split second, it all made sense. The Giants were going to cut him. He started to panic as he walked toward Coughlin. His stomach knotted up. This wasn't happening.

"Son," the coach began, "you did a good job for us, but we have to release you. Keep working hard. Keep your head up. Everything will work out for you."

Patrick felt flushed. "I didn't see it coming," he would say.

He wandered aimlessly back to the locker room, changed his clothes, and retrieved his paperwork—getting released is not unlike checking out of a hotel.

And he's in Albany.

He called his agent, Joe Linta, a Yale man with a good reputation around the league who founded JL Sports Agency and represents, among other Ravens, quarterback Joe Flacco.

"That's bullshit," Linta said. "You're a good prospect. They should have put you on the practice squad." Linta told him not to worry. He'd make some calls.

He'd land somewhere, the agent told him. Patrick believed him. He had no choice.

Linta knew well personally then Patriots vice president of player personnel Scott Pioli, and New England had expressed interest in Patrick leading up to the Supplemental Draft. The Patriots had him graded out as a fourth-rounder, and so it made sense that the first call was there, and they immediately brought Patrick to Foxboro for a look-see.

Of course, New England presented the same challenge for Patrick, except the learning curve was steeper. He had lost more time this time, and had arrived way late into camp. Patriots camp, mind you. *New England Patriots* camp.

When he got there, that nervous, new kid feeling went away instantly. He couldn't believe how cool the rest of the guys on the line were to him. He makes it clear that he's talking about the starters. Guys like Matt Light and Stephen Neal. And it took only a couple days and Tom Brady knew his name. He knows so because Brady called him by his name.

"Hey, Chris," Patrick would proudly reenact.

He liked it a whole lot better in New England than he did with the Giants. And he played better too. He showed some promise, and when he called home like he did every night to report on his day his mother told him about the story she'd read in *Sports Illustrated* about that Tom Brady.

"Do you know he bought every one of his offensive linemen a brand-new Escalade?" she told him.

And right there over the phone, mother and son, each with their own vision, began to muse about the possibility of Chris blocking for Tom Brady playing for the *New England Patriots*. Someday, of course. He knew it would take a wicked flu for him to play any this season, if, of course, he even made the team.

Patrick was shooting just to make practice squad for the season. Then he could learn the system. Learn from guys like Matt Light and Stephen Neal, and grow into a player who could play for the New England Patriots.

Looking over his shoulder the whole time, working as hard as he worried, he made it all the way to final cuts. The morning of final cuts he looked around the room that he had grown to like so much in this short time and quietly envied guys like Matt Light and Stephen Neal and the rest of the Brady Blockade. Not their ability, or what they had. They had worked to get that good and they had earned everything with sweat, down to that Escalade. But he hoped someday to feel what they felt now, which is to say nothing. Their future for the coming season was certain. They wouldn't think about final cuts until they got back in the room and someone was missing, someone they liked, like that new kid Chris Patrick.

"Scott Pioli was very nice about it," Patrick said. "He said they considered putting me on practice squad, but they came down with some injuries and didn't have the room. He wished me luck and told me to have my agent keep him updated on my progress."

He got in the car and drove west with one constant thought.

"Aw, fuck, I think I'm done."

What could he do? He could get into teaching and coaching like his older brother Phil. He could be a cop. He was a criminal justice major at Nebraska. Maybe the FBI. He could farm. He always thought about farming. Hard work. Honest and thankless work. Sort of like playing on the offensive line.

He would keep in shape, just in case. Give it a real shot next year. What really sucked—besides the bills he accrued at college that he had to pay now—was working out back at Gold's Gym and seeing all of those people again. Some haters at home in Ithaca. Small-town envy, really quite commonplace. In black neighborhoods, it's called crabs in a barrel. No different here. Some of the neighbors surely, quietly rooted against the Patrick boys. Why should that family have all the luck?

Phil played first at Michigan State, and when Coach Nick Saban came here to see him on a recruiting trip to the high school—the only high school—the town blew a gasket. Located in Gratiot County, the midpoint of the Highway 127 university corridor of Central Michigan University, Alma College, and Michigan State, the town of roughly twenty-five hundred residents—give or take the fruit selection at the farmer's market on the corner of Pine River and Center streets— definitely takes Sparty over the Wolverines of Michigan. So it's a big deal when one of the local boys plays on Saturdays.

And a few years later when Chris brought news that coach Frank Solich from Nebraska planned to visit him at the high school, one of his high school football coaches cracked, "Yeah, right, you're gonna play football at Nebraska."

Chris became only the second player from the state of Michigan ever to play for the Huskers.

"When you're at that small a school, you get really poor high school football coach," Patrick would say later. "Basically at that level, it's whoever wants to do it. Whenever I'd go back, couldn't wait to shove it up their ass."

Now back at Gold's Gym, they would smile to his face and say, "Aren't you that kid who played at Nebraska? Yeah, Patrick's your name, right? Chris, is it? What the hell happened? Did you leave Nebraska? Thought you were going to play in the pros?"

What could he say? He didn't know then that the two teams that cut him—New York and New England—would eventually play in the Super Bowl that year, and if he did, so what? He was still dreading having to explain why he was back in Ithaca.

A few weeks later, Linta called him with good news. Green Bay was flying him in for a workout, along with a few other linemen. Linta told him to kill it—and he did.

The Packers signed him to their practice squad for the remainder of the season—the *Green Bay Packers*—and suddenly he felt sorry for those people back in Ithaca. They didn't know any better, he reasoned. And, quite frankly, who cares? Funny how we all become so magnanimous when something good happens, and how something petty that bothered us right to the core then seems so insignificant.

For Chris Patrick, he now had his place to grow and a steady paycheck of $5,200 per week, the minimum for practice squad players. The number shrank after taxes, union dues, agent fees, and other assorted tappings. But he would earn more here over the rest of the season than doing anything in Ithaca, and this was always about creating a path to the playing field. The location provided an unexpected bonus as well, Green Bay more town than city, with an affinity for his passions of hunting and fishing, a mere eight-hour drive from back home. He could see himself settle for good in such a friendly place, right there in the shadows of unrivaled Lambeau Field.

He enjoyed his year in Green Bay, where he spent his weeks soaking up knowledge in meeting rooms and his home Sundays in the press box watching the game with all of the free food. He particularly enjoyed the tutelage of Packers offensive line coach James Campen, who long ago was Brett Favre's first center.

A sturdy, square-built man, Campen presented the epitome of a man's man. He had a knack for holding everyone's attention during those tedious and unremitting offensive line meetings in that darkened room.

One meeting, Patrick remembers, was priceless. The guys were seated like always, and Campen stood in the front of the makeshift classroom working the projector when a loud knock at the door interrupted him. At first he tried to ignore it. But there was another knock. Louder. And two quick ones in rapid succession. Agitated, Campen finally wandered over and opened the door.

Poised in the doorway to greet him was a man's bare buttocks.

"There was Brett Favre," Patrick said. "Pants down around his ankles. Giving us a full moon."

Mooned by Brett Favre, he repeated, musing as though it was a career highlight.

Patrick finished the story. How Campen flung the door shut and shouted to Favre, "You're fucking sick."

"That's how Favre acted—he was like a prankster," he said. "He was always joking around. One of things I remember about him was that he didn't change in the regular locker room. His locker was somewhere

else. I think with the coaches. I'm not sure. I just know he changed
someplace different. Then he'd just appear in the room. I thought it
was cool to be around him."

It was colder than usual in Green Bay the day of the NFC Championship Game that January against those darn Giants—which is like
saying the ocean feels abnormally wet. Patrick watched the game with
the rest of the practice squaders inside a toasty suite, chowing down on
bratwursts with the secret sauce, unaware that the overtime heave that
doomed the Packers would be Favre's last throw in the colors.

In the coming months, Favre's messy divorce with the Packers
would dominate the sporting landscape so much so that the Saga of a
Retiring, Unretiring American Quarterback had its own scroll on the
bottom of ESPN programming. Meanwhile, in the middle of Favre
central, the team issued a seven-word housekeeping item too small for
ESPN's regular score/update news scroll: The Green Bay Packers have
released Chris Patrick.

Patrick suffered a hamstring injury right before the off season, and
"you know," he said, "once you get hurt, you're out of these places.
I was devastated."

The day he received the news, Patrick also received a phone call
from Coach Campen asking him to stop by his office. He told him, "I
brought you here to tell you I was in your shoes when I played. I got
hurt. I know how it works. One of the biggest things I can tell you is
that [team personnel officials] play puppet masters. They sometimes
keep guys they shouldn't and release guys they should keep. You can
play in this league. Keep working your ass off."

"Don't bullshit me," Patrick said.

"I'm not bullshitting you. I'm telling you this for your own good."

"Can I really play football in the NFL?" persisted Patrick.

"Absofuckinglutely," Campen said.

Ghost Stories

If the Turk were here, he'd tell you that he is but a notion, the
embodiment of football fate. A real person in the flesh way higher on
the flow chart ultimately designs the grand plan with input from his
cronies.

The Turk? He's just a messenger boy. Might as well be riding a bike.

The Turk is emotionally detached, though most of the time deep down he genuinely feels badly for the guy. He has nothing personal against him. And by the way, it's the football players who dress him in a black cloak and place a sickle in his hand or a hockey stick. Like he's some Wes Craven character.

Depending on the team, he takes different forms. He may come from the personnel office or the coaching staff. He may be a faceless character, truly some little schmuck doing the emperor's bidding for a promotion, or it could be someone of importance in the organization.

Former offensive lineman Spencer Folau recalled seeking the man's identity during his first camp with the Ravens.

"The first couple of camps in Baltimore were really rough," he said. "I was in my room after the third preseason game and I hear this knock at the door—six in the morning type shit. I answer and the Turk walks in. But he's not here for me. He's here for my roommate."

Folau breathed a sigh of relief that early morning, and told his roommate, "Aw, dude, I'm really sorry."

Truthfully, it sucks being the Turk. Who wants to crush a man's dream?

But the league is Darwinian. Everyone knows that.

And Chris Patrick knew, too. Patrick begged for a permanent home. Philadelphia presented a real opportunity. He did the math many times in his head. For the offensive line, it would come down to two spots between three guys on who would make the team: himself, King Dunlap—the massive tackle (6-foot-8, 330 pounds), who represented a long-term project—and Mike McGlynn, a fourth-round pick from Pitt in 2008.

Patrick was the smallest of the three, and he knew he would be sweating it out until last cuts. He reminded himself how very well he played in that last preseason game against Jacksonville. He didn't make one mental mistake.

He sure as hell didn't expect that phone call on this night. It was still only August 31, a good ten days before final cuts. And if he did get cut, he would surely make it to the end of those cuts, following the last preseason game against the Jets.

"Chris?" the person began.

For a moment, Patrick couldn't hear anything except the voice inside his head pleading, "Not again. Not again."

He tried to concentrate on the voice on the other end of the phone. It was Howie Roseman, the Eagles' vice president of personnel.

"Listen, Chris," Roseman told him. "We're putting you on the waiver wire. You need to come in here tomorrow, get your physical, and sign your exit papers."

Before Roseman could say anything else, Patrick hung up the phone. He didn't want to hear any of the platitudes.

Not again.

The next day, he went to team headquarters and checked himself out of Philadelphia. But he had to know.

Everyone on the offensive line he asked said he for sure outplayed Dunlap. But Castillo told him Dunlap had a higher upside. That he and McGlynn were simply the better prospects.

Once again he found himself in the car for a long, disappointing drive with nothing to do but think and replay every damn second of the preseason. Every game he stayed square. He kicked ass. What killed him was, the first cut? Were they kidding? They cut him before those three rookies who have no shot at making the team?

"I'm the first fucking guy cut?" he would say later. "Seriously? I don't want to think this. But Coach Reid is a Mormon, right? That Tongan kid is a Mormon. The rookie [Fenuki Tupou]. Coach Reid played with his dad at BYU . . . I know I shouldn't make excuses. I know it's a really deep team. But come on? First fucking guy cut? I busted my ass every day."

Patrick talks as though he's pleading with God to supply him an answer that's palatable. "Guys like me grind our nuts off every day. I can't miss practice. I can pull a quad and I can't miss practice. Or I'm gone. Fuckin' gone. Meanwhile, the one starting tackle—Shawn Andrews—is a fucking whack job. He hurts his back running [gassers] and he still hasn't practiced. And the other guy—Jason Peters, the big-money free agent—doesn't even know the playbook. He missed a crucial blitz pickup in the Jacksonville game. Missed a slide protection call. He just let the guy go. Donovan [McNabb] had to get rid of the ball or he was toast."

It's harder than protecting the quarterback, sometimes, protecting yourself from bitterness.

Patrick Postscript
September 19, 2009

The 2009 NFL season kicked off with our subject working on the farm back in Michigan, praying the phone would ring again.

After being released by Philadelphia, he received one sniff before the season, working out for the Seahawks. But Seattle didn't sign him and he's back working out at Gold's Gym, and it's hardest for him on Sundays.

He sent a text message at 10:49 p.m., the night before the Eagles' second game of the season: "I might be done. Im sick of the politics of the nfl."

When asked about Patrick's skill level and subsequent future with the league, Eagles general manager Tom Heckert said, "He's legit. At the very least, he can play somewhere as a backup."

3

The Blessed Day

L et us travel out of the stadium for just a moment, away from the fast-coming fighter jets for the thunderous pregame flyover that completes the modern portrait of American sport, the way Norman Rockwell captured baseball during another era.

Let us move to the closest home with a flickering flat-screen and say that home delivers a Sunday couch potato, only he does not lie vertically but in fact sits upright, almost Marine-like, because that's the only way the laptop works and he needs to track his own mythical team that he constructed to go against his buddy's mythical team in their world of fantasy. Next to him, beside the bevy of refreshments advertised to him all week long in preparation for the weekly holiday, is the remote control for the television he just had to have for Sunday connected to the satellite dish that offers the package he just had to have to watch all of Sunday.

Sunday's first session includes nine games, and chances are he will navigate among all nine, focusing on his local team and the games that feature the players on his mythical team and his opponent's mythical team in the fantasy world. He will scroll down with the down arrow button and see the games about to start momentarily in North Jersey, Tampa Bay, St. Louis, Philadelphia, Foxboro, Massachusetts,

Minneapolis, Houston, Baltimore, and Detroit, the pictures strikingly similar, especially when the feeds come grouped together by network.

We celebrate kickoff together in America, orchestrated almost to the second. Scroll down the channels and it's like watching frame by frame, the only difference the setting. Players from the one team are lined up, spread wide across the field, awaiting direction from a little man with a big foot. The other team's players are dotted over the other half of the field, looking to defend and attack simultaneously, led by the little man's nemesis way, way back toeing the edge of the end zone.

The little man jogs toward the ball that sits upright on a tee in the middle of the field and kicks it with a whipping leg, signaling for his men to sprint down the field and crash into the other men.

The ball shoots high into the air amid a humming din from the stadium crowd that crescendoes until reaching its peak, in some cases prompting the building to shake in what resembles a giant sphere of moving energy.

Such a breathless beginning.

Is there a better way to start anything?

Face-off or tip-off, the ringing bell that begets a round of boxing or trumpets prior to a horse race, the waving flag that begins an auto race or the firing of a starter's pistol before a race of men—all make for unique traditions of start. But they are lightning flashes of time that can't hold the anticipation the way an arcing football does. Kickoff lasts just a little longer, and thus builds before you in a series of moments, playing to our life survival need to have something in which to look forward.

And sometimes it's accompanied by surprise.

Anatomy of a Trick Onside Kick

Andy Reid, then a young head coach of a young and rebuilding team, noticed something on film during his ridiculously intense study of his mighty division opponent over the summer leading up to the season opener.

Alone in his office at the stadium, in the wee hours of the morning, undoubtedly surrounded by fast-food wrappers, he rewound the tape again and again.

Hmm, there's a soft spot on the right side that shows up on every kickoff return. They check right through a possible onside kick.

So the young head coach told the special teams coach to keep it in the back of his mind and to make sure to pay special attention to onside kick recovery. As the game grew closer, Reid seemed more convinced than ever to try it, especially after the team executed it so well that Friday in practice.

That morning of the opener, John Harbaugh, the special teams coach, before he took over as head coach of the Baltimore Ravens, first mentioned the possibility to special teams captain Ike Reese and kicker David Akers, and told them that the young head coach was mulling it over, probably as they spoke.

Sure enough, an hour before the game, with the players out on the field, some on the ground stretching, others jogging in place with exaggerated leg movements, the young head coach wandered over to the captain of the special teams.

"What do you think? Surprise onside kick?"

"Yeah." Reese said. "Okay, uh, sure."

Now, years later, Reese told the story and copped to how he really felt. "I said yes," he said, "because you don't want the coach to think you don't believe in the damn play. Shit, at least thought enough of me to ask me about it. But I really thought it was too risky."

Back on the field for the second time, this time with kickoff looming, the special teamers huddled in their own group the way they always do, the rest of the team now off by the bench area of the sideline. Harbaugh told the unit to hold up for a moment because the head coach wanted to say something to them all.

Reid peeked inside the huddle of men, and said, "All right, we're going to run the surprise onside kick. What do you think?"

The question was rhetorical.

Meanwhile, Reese didn't realize he held an expression of doubt on his face. He never said a word, mind you. But he did have that oh-no look.

"What are you scared of?" the young head coach snapped at him. "You a pussy?"

"Hell, since you put it like that, Coach, let's do it! Let's run it!"

And so they ran it, and sure enough that right side proved soft and the special teams captain threw a key block and a teammate fell on the football and cradled it next to his body, shocking the wits out of the mighty opposition. The young and rebuilding team went on to score and actually went on to win the game.

"From that point on, we did it like three times after that," Reese said. "Whenever [the head coach] would step into the huddle and ask me, I gave him that same look and he'd say, 'You gotta quit being a pussy.'

"And he'd wink at me. He knew he could say that to me. He used me to get his message across to the rest of the guys."

The Kicker

Special teams is jailbreak. It's anarchy and controlled chaos.

And here's the kicker, diminutive in stature, wandering the field amid the water buffaloes.

"Think about it," said the Eagles' David Akers, one of the more physical kickers in the league. "I'm taller than Brian Westbrook and he weighs only twelve pounds more than me—but all of it is muscle. You have to be smart. You got trains going at each other out there. It could get pretty ugly. If it's me trying to make the tackle, I'm going to go low on most people and play the odds in my favor. Now, if I see Runyan coming at me, I'm going to avoid contact at all costs."

A kicker's job doesn't end at kickoff. He remains on the field, an easy target—and a fun one, because it's always fun to hit a smaller guy, especially when it's an unsuspecting block. Thus it's crucial for a kicker to be aware of his surroundings at all times and try to stay away from the opponent's sideline.

Akers took a beating one game after getting caught on the Giants sideline. Brandon Jacobs had pushed him in the back and he stumbled. Instinctively he saw the sideline and jumped to the side, except he ran right into hulking New York fullback Charles Way.

"I hit him and we kind of caught each other," he said. "All of a sudden we're standing there and Luke Petigout pulls me down from the back and three guys go to town on me, just whaling on me. I was getting worked over real good. [Giants kicker] Jay Feely saw what was going on and helped me out. Very few times I've got my butt whupped and lost five grand. "

For the personal foul Akers received on the play.

"I complained," he said. "The ref told me [Jacobs's hit] was too late to be called a block in the back and too early for personal foul."

Sean Landeta's career as a punter in professional football lasted nearly twenty-five years. After starting in the USFL, he punted for five different teams, including the Giants for part of ten seasons, returned to St. Louis three different times and Philadelphia twice. He amassed over 60,000 yards, won two Super Bowls, made two Pro Bowls, and never got hit the way he did back in 1989 when he got roughed on a punt playing against the notorious Buddy Ryan Eagles.

"The defender tried to block the kick and he hit me so hard—and the combination of being hit and the hard surface of Veterans Stadium—I felt like I was broken in half," Landeta recalled. "The searing pain enveloped my whole body. It's what they mean when they saying numbing pain. I could barely walk off the field.

"I have a great deal of respect for guys that hit like that on a continual basis. I wish fans could feel what that is like. To really know what it feels like. Imagine playing through constant pain the way some of these guys do."

Small man's revenge, however, is best served by surprise. It happens, Akers says, and he remembers each one of his kills.

The Falcons. Omar Lowe. It was a counter-return (where the returner takes the ball to the opposite sideline), where it's legal to push someone in the back. Everyone is fair game on a kickoff counter-return. Akers torpedoed Lowe right in the back and he went flying face first.

"He shot up, got in my face, and tried to get under me and take me down," Akers said. "The next kickoff he didn't even block his guy. I could see him coming right for me and he got me with an elbow right to the face mask. He was just pissed a kicker got a good shot on him. It's embarrassing for him. No one wants to get hit by a kicker because they'll hear about it in the film room."

Or immediately on the sideline, like what happened to Frank Murphy of Tampa Bay. Murphy broke into the clear along the sideline and eyed a big return with Akers the last line of defense for the Eagles.

"All I'm thinking is that I can't let him get by," Akers said. "More than anything I have to act as a speed bump and just slow him down a little so the rest of the guys in pursuit can catch up. I got to use the sidelines. I eye him. I was going right for his ribs. He cut back at the last minute but I still got him pretty good.

"Everybody on his sideline got pumped: 'Dude, a kicker just got you like that!'"

The Wedgebuster

Jason Short set up where he always did on the kickoff that October day in Cleveland, right next to the kicker, the hero's spot on special teams. It's those four spots in the middle of the formation, two on either side of the kicker, that are designated for a team's best cover guys, and the ones who are most fearless.

Their job is to read the return and infiltrate, usually sacrificing their bodies to open tackling lanes. Wedgebusters, they are called. Suicide tacklers. Loco players.

Read the wedge of blockers and bust it up by getting in the way. Along the way, they must watch for booby traps and blindside hits and street corner setups. If all goes well, they are braced right for what is more collision than contact.

Jason Short found the NFL because of this dirty job. It's his niche, because it's always been his niche, because he's always craved the brutality. Even back in Lake County, Ohio, where he and his older brother by eleven months fought in the backyard. Pat Short broke Jason Short's arm once and his jaw another time. Jason knocked Pat out another time.

Jason Short broke two vertebrae in his neck playing defense and kicks at Riverside High School, came back and played running back and averaged seven yards a carry. He played linebacker on defense and kicks at Eastern Michigan and fought teammates in practice and beat up a roommate in his dorm. He grew to 6-foot-4 and 250 pounds. Even though he was undisciplined at linebacker, always leaving his lane in search of flush contact, he was a special teams star and became a captain in his third year. Eventually, though, he was kicked out of school for fighting three of his linemen—to which he said, "I just pounded the shit out of them."

He loved it when they called him a psycho. He loved it so much that he played in the Arena Football League 2, the lowest rung of professional football, a step above parking lot football, earning $180 a week for the Peoria Pirates. He graduated to the Arena League the following year and then to NFL Europe because some scout forwarded tapes of his kick coverage to Barcelona coach Sam Rutigliano, the former long-time Browns coach.

Rutigliano had no real plans for Short. At the time, NFL teams allotted players to the European teams, which usually only picked up free agents for training camp bodies. But he made the team as a defensive end and made 27 tackles in half a season before being sent home with a bum shoulder. He played on kicks twice as the wedgebuster in Barcelona and both times made big hits, registering a knockout on one of them.

"He played a hundred miles an hour," Eagles general manager Tom Heckert said. "He made plays as a defensive end even though he was undersized. Plus, you knew he was tough. He would get into pushing and shoving matches all of the time. Then when you talk with him he was a guy that you know would do anything it took to make it."

Those two plays eventually landed him with the Eagles and his spot next to the kicker and another flat on his back asleep on his hometown stadium field that October day. He ran hard as usual, at full speed, just to the right of reckless, and he dove for the tackle headfirst and slammed the middle of his helmet into the knee of the returner. The helmet popped off on impact and settled a few feet from his motionless body.

Eagles trainer Rick Burkholder rushed to his side. Short was out cold and he was snoring.

"That's called getting knocked stiff," former Pro Bowl special teamer Ike Reese said. "I seen guys sleep before and that was one of them. We used to kill Short. He'd run down there and get himself knocked out all the time."

Short awoke bleeding from the nose and mouth, and in a foul mood. "He's speaking in tongues," Burkholder said. "He's bleeding. He's so furious. He's not talking in a normal language."

Meanwhile, Coach Andy Reid saw Short in the throes of a fit, walked over, and said clearly and sternly, "Shorty, you need to listen to the trainers and answer their questions."

"Yes, Coach," Short said in perfect English. Reid's tone of authority snapped him out of it—momentarily.

Because then the Browns' Ebenezer Ekuban started taunting Short, who quickly returned to his frothy spate. Short had a concussion but he didn't know it and wildly tried to reach Ekuban to fight him. The Browns bench then began to empty, and the Eagles training staff frantically sought out a referee to help restore order. Eventually, Short was put on a cart and whisked into the tunnel. As he left his hometown field, boos filled the stadium, directed at him. Short cursed the fans in the end zone and flipped his middle finger to the stands.

Since the game was in Cleveland, Short's parents had attended the game and rushed to the Eagles locker room to check on his status.

Short now plays for the Browns.

"They've forgiven me," he said.

Here is Short's recollection of the event:

When the trainers got out there, I was dead asleep and it took a while for it to come back to me. I had no idea what had happened. Watching the film, small parts start coming back to you. I still don't remember all that happened. I don't remember any of this, but apparently I was screaming at all the fans and giving everyone the finger. I guess Reid came over to where they were treating me and told me, "You be good to the trainers"—my first reaction when something like that happens is to get angry and start yelling at people. Apparently I was screaming at my own trainers and Reid was telling me to chill out. I guess I recognized his voice through all of the chaos because I don't remember talking to anyone else.

Once Reid was gone I would go back to screaming again. I didn't remember any of it. I was in the locker room while the game is still going on and didn't remember anything. They told me everything that had happened and I couldn't believe that I did that. I'm always trying to control what I say and do. I was surprised by my actions. I didn't know why my parents were in the locker room. I was so out of it. I had blood all over my face. I was a mess.

The Eagles tried to petition the league about Ekuban's actions, but the NFL denied it, ruling that Short "is clearly out of control." It didn't matter that he had a concussion.

"I'll never forget when the trainers came out on the field, they told me my helmet was off, there was blood all over my face, and I was snoring," Short said. "I tore the upper lining of my mouth and needed stitches on that. I was bleeding from everywhere. I almost broke my nose. I couldn't breathe out of my nose for weeks. I still have the tape of that game and watch it occasionally."

Short once made a list of the top ten most feared NFL players in a player poll taken by *Sports Illustrated*. The accompanying quote read, "He is so recklessly aggressive on kick coverage that offensive and defensive players alike stop to behold his violent collisions."

"I was labeled a headhunter from the start," Short said. "We were in Detroit and I knocked some guy in the wedge out cold. Two weeks before, I got knocked out. It became my thing—always looking to knock someone's head off and go full steam."

Short estimates that he's suffered six or seven concussions in the four years he's played in the NFL. Two of his seasons, by the way, were cut short by broken leg injuries.

"Special teams is where a lot of the nastiness comes out," said Tampa tight end Anthony Becht, "particularly in a rival game. Like with us, it was Atlanta. That was an after-the-whistle type of rivalry. On special teams, they were pushing off player piles with their foot on our throats. They'd have their foot right on our neck and push down to get up.

"There's always one team that gets a team all fired up. These two games are full-on 'Let's go!' Both teams hate each other. The coaches hate each other. There are individual wars. Last man standing is going to win the game. The coach is talking about these games all year. He's saying, 'This is why you're here. We brought you here for this game.' As a player you've known about these games all year and you couldn't be more pumped up and it comes out just nasty on special teams."

Reese played against Becht in those games for Atlanta. He recalls those bitter battles with the Buccaneers fondly. His worst experience on special teams, though, came against the Vikings.

Against the wedge.

Reese proved a deft wedgebuster in his career, one of the kamikazes in the middle trying to read the return. Know that spot on the wedge. Crash it.

It's 2006, the opening kickoff against Minnesota at the Georgia Dome. Reese is trying to read the blockers and determine who has him as an assignment. He gets down to the 30-yard line and he's not picked up by a single blocker.

It means one thing: the wedge is his.

He processes quickly the right strategy. What's the right angle to take on the wedge. What's the right speed. How to position his body.

"I feel it," Reese said. "I know it. I know something bad is going to happen. I'm like, 'Oh, shit.'"

He wanted to split the wedge by getting skinny and sliding through it. But he got caught in between. The Vikings blockers were tight. Too tight. And he didn't have the correct angle to brace himself right.

"They ran my ass right over," he said. "I hit it square and I wasn't braced. Now I caused a pile. But I was like roadkill. We had FieldTurf in the dome. It's comprised of ground-up rubber. I had that shit all in my face and in my mouth. My chin strap was over my nose. At first you don't know where you're at. You're trying to get up but nothing is moving. Your head is ringing. It literally sounds like a bell ringing. It's like being awake and being asleep at the same time."

Must be the way death feels. You can't move. You're trying to move but you can't. You can see the lights in the stadium. But you don't hear anything. You don't hear the crowd.

He said, "You're in this weird state until somebody comes over and taps on your helmet and they give you ammonia. I laid there two or three minutes while they gave me smelling salts. Finally I woke up and they helped me up to my feet. I started walking but I had no legs. My legs were made out of spaghetti.

"You're on the sidelines and soon your faculties come back. You start doing calisthenics. Knee bends. Stretches. Trying to make sure everything works. Then you feel it. The pain rushes through you. It comes to life. My neck started hurting. My shoulders started aching. I'm moving my head around, trying to shake out the cobwebs. I only missed about six or seven plays and I was back in. But everything ached the rest of the game."

The league saw too many of the loco players carried off the field, knocked silly, and these types, more of the unheralded, will do anything to keep their job. Players like Reese, who after that play argued so vehemently with his team's training staff to let him back in the game that they hid his helmet in a chest that held equipment pieces and uniform scraps in back of the bench.

By the end of the second quarter, Reese found his helmet. A coach asked him if he had received the blessing from the trainers to reenter the game.

"Yes," he replied, still in a fog, the kind you experience when you've been up longer than twenty-four hours.

He lied.

Then he played.

Wedge epilogue: Forever tweaking, usually with the aim of the players' best interest, the NFL Rules Committee recently attacked the wedge. So now once the ball is kicked no more than two receiving team players can be within two yards of each other on the same yard line. In other words, the shoulder-to-shoulder line of blockers, three men or more, that forms the wedge has been outlawed.

The penalty is a 15-yarder—which on the kickoff buries a team with field position—and it has effectively turned the wedge into a wafer.

Houston's Kevin Bentley—who replaced two fallen Texans, Harry Williams and Cedric Killings, as wedgebuster after both lost their football careers to frightening neck injuries—talked about the wedge wistfully. "On a kickoff return, I thought it helped immensely," he said. "You don't enjoy running into three-hundred-pound [players], but in a weird way you enjoy it."

That weird way is a grunt's way, the way of a man who judges gallantry by the sets of tire tracks on his back.

The Returner

It's every man for himself in the return game, returner Brian Mitchell preached to the young player.

"Make sure your head is like that little girl's from *The Exorcist*," he said sharply. "No joke."

Because you can't track everyone. You don't know from where the hit will come, only that it surely will. The hit is out there lurking.

Stay awake. Stay alert. Stay alive.

Yes, BMitch, as he was known, the NFL's second all-time leader in yards, on the ballot for the Hall of Fame because of his return prowess, knew all the tricks on special teams.

Ike Reese made the mistake of telling Mitchell in a game, "Dude, I've been watching you forever. I'm gonna git your ass, old man."

Said Reese, "So we're running downfield and he got me with a cheap shot in the back. Back then, the refs didn't call those types of blocks. Now the rule is both hands on the front. Before, as long as you had a hand on the side you could get away with a block in the back. So he gives me one of these cheapies and flips me over.

"Then he says to me, 'Yeah, that's right, you sorry motherfucker. Fuck you.'"

Mitchell laughed. "I said that to a lot of guys."

So did Larry Centers of the Cardinals. It's a Sunday night in Arizona, Reese's rookie year, and on the first punt return he sheds free of Centers, playing as the slot guy.

"So I'm young and stupid and I start talkin' crap," Reese said. "I say, 'Yeah old man, you ain't got nothing.'"

Centers realized that Reese was stronger than him, so the next time they matched up he hit Reese with a quick uppercut in the stomach.

"Knocked the wind out of me for a few seconds," Reese said.

Reese is still holding Centers with his right as they scuffle down the field. Centers jabs Reese two, three, four more times. Then he hits him with a quick flurry.

"Not real, real hard," Reese said. "Just hard enough for me not to retaliate with a punch. It was crazy. This cat was giving me potshots in the stomach all the way down the field."

"Yeah, I'm an old man," Centers told Reese, "but I got all the tricks."

"Yeah," Reese shot back, "you're a dirty old man."

Reese took notes from players like Centers and Mitchell. Ravens coach John Harbaugh, then special teams coach for the Eagles, offered the rest of the education: Be nasty and be aggressive. You can get away with a lot more on special teams. Push the envelope. They're standing around the pile, they get hit. Everyone is fair game.

"Sometimes you don't see that hit coming, even if it's in front of you," Mitchell said. "I can remember playing Tampa Bay when I was with Washington. Curtis Buckley was coming down and he slipped. I was thinking there was going to be a hole there. My lead blocker saw the slip, too, and figured he was out of the play and went and took on someone else. Curtis got up real quick and had a clear path to me. He got a real good lick on me. Both of us got knocked out cold because we hit each other so hard. I mean, we're out cold."

Mitchell said his teammates rushed over to his side and asked him, "BMitch, what's one plus one?"

Mitchell responded, "Damn, guys, c'mon and ask me something harder than that. I'm knocked out and I still know what one plus one is!"

Think of the mentality for special teamers. They are either fighting for a job or fighting for their career. In many cases, it's both, whether it's a veteran on the downside or some rookie free agent. They need to impress the coaches. They need to stand out.

"You don't have many opportunities to make plays and getcha shine on," Reese said. "We're gonna watch film that Monday and you want to be on that forty-five-minute session with the knockout hits on tape. Whether they're blocks or tackles, you're trying to get those. And then see who gets knocked out. Better not be you. Or you're gonna get clowned."

After the movie *Friday* came out, Ike Reese said, "Chris Tucker had all of us saying, 'You got knocked the fuck out.'"

The Uniform Police

The special teamers jog off the field toward the sidelines, where it seems like there are a million people doing a million different things. The commotion on the sidelines of an NFL game feels like the floor of the stock exchange. The flow of the throng is directionless, particularly behind the front line, because it moves in all directions simultaneously, just a mass of people moving with purpose, each with a different purpose, operating independently of one another.

Let's begin with the officials: team, league, game.

There are officials whose only responsibility is to report uniform rule-breakers, those players whose sin is vanity. Damn individualists who have this insatiable need for flare on their body, deemed insurrectionary behavior by a league that views its uniform the way Mao Zedong did the Sun Yat-sen suit in 1949 China.

Down to the socks, by the way. Players are issued a two-piece sock, one part white, the other part the team color, and if a player has only the white or the team color showing it's a violation.

And God forbid they fiddle with their jersey, like leaving it untucked or cutting it short, both finable offenses. Players want their jerseys tight but comfortable, leaving little for the opposition to grab and clutch.

In an effort to make sure their players' jerseys fit to their liking, the Philadelphia Eagles employ a tailor, a throwback tailor in his early seventies by the name of Pasquale who barely stretches past five feet

tall and speaks broken English, which perfectly accents his supreme
haberdashery skills, along with gnarled little hands and a tape measure that he wears around his neck like a rosary. It's an odd sight to
see Pasquale's shop, located on a tight, crooked city street and see the
uniforms piled on a table next to his fashionable wife, Anna, working her old-fashioned sewing machine and speaking Italian into a cell
phone, beneath racks of elegant suits and sport jackets and handmade
dress shirts. They are Eagle throwback units, in fact, that needed last-
minute alterations for a game against the Lions, and Pasquale had
visited the Eagles complex not far from his store earlier in the week to
get updated measurements from players.

But let's get back to the uniform police, the official at every single
NFL game who wields a clipboard and a checklist and a headmaster's
eye for uniform infractions, the league's ticket writer who inspects every
player up and down beginning in warm-ups and through the entire game.

For those who don't comply, the fine could be anywhere from
$5,000 to $25,000, depending on the violation, which ranges from wearing a college cap on the sideline (a $25K-er) to personalized messages
written on shoes or the tape on wrists, even if it's something as benign
as the name of a player's child. Other violations go from the obvious—
wearing any apparel other than that of Reebok, which has an exclusive
contract with the NFL—to players having one arm covered by a long
sleeve and the other bare.

Players are subject to fines as soon as they hit the field for
warm-ups.

Herein lies the case of cornerback Sheldon Brown, who was fined
$10,000 for wearing a hockey mask in the style of fictional slasher
Jason coming out of the tunnel during pregame introductions for the
2009 Philadelphia home opener.

Brown wore the mask as a symbol of his displeasure with his contract since early in the off season when team president Joe Banner
refused to talk to Brown's agent about an extension and said so publicly. A few weeks later, Banner approached Brown in a cordial manner at a team barbecue, and the player ignored him and walked away.

The hockey mask, which bears no mouth, indicated Brown wasn't
speaking to Eagles management.

When jokingly asked whether Banner would pay the fine, Brown
replied, "Who? Who? Who's that?"

Now most league officials offer a warning to offenders before reporting them, and they will circle back to check that the player made the appropriate alteration, unless they are repeat offenders or are caught on a television camera.

"They're fucking no different than meter maids," one current player said when asked of the uniform police. "But it's not their fault. The league wants us to be robots."

This all stems back to the most famous uniform rule-breaker, Jim McMahon, the brash quarterback of the Bears. During the height of the Bears' dominance and his celebrity for presiding over a team with a great defense, McMahon did for headbands gender-wise what Olivia Newton-John did for headbands, which must explain why the late 1980s brought forth headbangers.

Nonetheless, McMahon was fined $5,000 for wearing a corporate logo headband—Adidas—by then NFL commissioner Pete Rozelle. The following week he wore a headband under his helmet with ROZELLE emblazoned on it. The commissioner actually sent him a handwritten note saying the display was "funny as hell."

Then there's security. Team security and league security and stadium security and city police officers. During games that followed 9/11, some teams positioned snipers atop the stadium.

There's the game crew, the chain gang, and the ball boys, and a slew of network workers, camera crews working dollies and Steadicams, and sideline reporters and producers and assistants wandering about the sidelines, along with still photographers from media outlets and the team, and team attendants aplenty. Trainers, assistant trainers, media relations reps, equipment managers, equipment assistants, coaches' assistants and assistants' assistants, interns, and gofers, all of whom reside in constant watch mode, all the while trying to sneak-watch the game. Their jobs work within the eye of the game, down to the one responsible for making sure the communication wires that flow from the head coach remain intact and players don't trip over them. "Watch the wires," the detangler will say a thousand times during the game.

The people stretch from end zone to end zone on the sideline, though it grows markedly denser between the 40-yard-line markers, where the team resides in the middle of all this controlled chaos, engaged in its own movement and splintered into groups. Depending on which unit is on the field—offense, defense, or special teams—players usually stand or sit grouped by position on the bench tucked safely behind the thicket of bodies facing the action, with the head coach stationed at midfield, slightly in front of the pack for unimpaired sight-lines and ample pacing room.

The Edge of the Abyss

Being there inside the game, your first thought is to shrink out of the way, away from potential field traffic, which occurs nonstop between plays that sweep out of bounds and constant player substitution. They move past you from both angles, say, following a change of possession, hopped up on cleats—which adds to their height and stature, along with the helmets and protruding shoulder pads—and it's as though you're in the middle of a herd of caribou.

And when a play comes toward the sideline, you see the wave recede from danger, for standing on the sideline of an NFL game is like toeing the edge of a cliff. Usually once a game some poor unsus-pecting schlub with a field pass dangling around his neck gets trampled on the sidelines to the winces of everyone. Perhaps, too, he might have seen what was about to strike him, even processed it intellectually, only to stand there frozen by the dilemma of which way to move—the way it happens when facing a runaway railroad car.

It's that fast, you know? The game.

Rookie quarterbacks making the transition from college to pro always say it, usually referring to their reads and how time shrinks. From "one Mississippi" to "one Mi-" is how it goes, and that's for elite athletes, not schlubs. Down here, play unfolds frighteningly more fast and ferocious than your big-screen HD home masterpiece theater will have you imagine.

Even those used to the scene sometimes get caught, as was the case for Eagles security director Butch Buchanico during a game against Carolina in October 2004. Ever diligent in keeping intruders off the field, he accidentally clipped one of the officials while celebrating a long return on the game's opening kickoff. The official fell hard to the ground after colliding with the well-built Buchanico along the team's sideline and immediately flagged him for unsportsmanlike conduct, negating a 66-yard return.

I stood next to Buchanico that day like I did each time I visited the sideline while working on a magazine story. We were near the Panthers' 40-yard line following the returner—a deceptively speedy player by the name of J. R. Reed—and as he sped by us, Buchanico got tangled with the official. I looked down and he was at my feet. While on the ground, the official immediately reached for his flag and threw it to the edge of the sideline.

Coach Andy Reid shot over a menacing glare. "What the— Stay off the field!" he snapped toward us.

For a moment, I wondered if he mistakenly thought I was the culprit, and all I could do was nod dutifully.

"Sorry, Coach," said Buchanico, standing tall in his admission.

The Eagles beat the Panthers easily 30–8 that day, so the incident became something to laugh about following the game. "I was just trying to make a play," Buchanico cracked before Reid began his news conference.

"That'll be the last play you make, Butch," replied Reid.

I recall how we stayed far from the edge of the field the rest of the game. In Buchanico's defense, it's easy to become discomposed on the perfervid front lines, one of the few settings that parallels its preconception. Because the atmosphere really is that supercharged, just the way one of those marvelous NFL Films specials supposes, only in real time.

Team Violation

You can very well decipher the unwritten code of conduct on the sidelines, beginning with the damn cameras. The damn cameras recording the game scan the sidelines seeking subplots.

The damn cameras record things you don't want recorded, a coach will lecture.

So act like they're always on you, dammit!

Because they are.

So in a moment of great frustration or despair please refrain from showing up a teammate or a coach.

See, if the locker room mimics the house, then a team's sideline is the driveway. So goes the edict: Keep it inside.

Though seemingly forever the exception, the Cowboys left little to the imagination in 2009, especially during a shameful 44–6 loss in the season finale at Philadelphia with the playoffs on the line.

A game official stationed by the Cowboys bench re-created the scene of defensive tackle Tank Johnson tearing into the offense at the bench during the third quarter, especially quarterback Tony Romo.

"Y'all a bunch of pussies," Johnson screamed. "Bunch of pussy-ass motherfuckers. You suck [Romo]. Motherfuckers lost this game and y'all quit. Y'all suck!"

Johnson had to be physically nudged away from the scene by defensive teammates and assorted staff members. He fought through the circle of people and scorched the offense a second time.

"Go on, throw another fucking interception. Go on now."

Some sideline transgressions are far less conspicuous. For example, it seemed odd that DeAngelo Hall stood on the opposite side of the bench by himself away from the rest of his secondary teammates while the Falcons had the football during the second quarter against the Cleveland Browns in November 2006.

The Falcons were already down 14–0 in the game, and things were beginning to unravel on the season, with Hall already grousing. Earlier in the season, Hall had expressed displeasure during a team meeting over his assignment, crowing how he was a cover corner and would not deviate from what a cover corner does.

And so he was deep in sulk mode, off by himself, in his own place, DeAngelo's Place, lost in the music from his iPod. Upon witnessing Hall, one veteran player seethed. The veteran informed his position coach, who shrugged and did nothing. The veteran grew more angry and finally confronted then Falcons head coach, Jim Mora Jr.

Mora shook his head, looked squarely at the veteran, and chastised him for making waves.

The veteran—who had played on winning teams—could only shake his head in disgust, beaten by the system in place. At that moment, the veteran said, he knew the Falcons would implode, long before Michael Vick went to prison for charges stemming from his alleged dogfighting ring and Mora was fired and Hall was traded to the Raiders.

The difference between winning and losing can often be found by examining behavior on the sidelines.

Huddle Up

Let us help Jeff Garcia to his feet, and return with him to the huddle, the most intimate place on the field. It is here Garcia has always distinguished himself.

Leader. Fiery leader.

Diminutive, lacking the big arm of some of his brethren, Garcia enters the huddle undoubtedly in charge. He's not a joke teller and he's not pointing out celebrities in the stands. He's all energy and confidence.

"You show your nerves and anxiety and the team may see that fear in your eyes," he said. "No fear. That's how you have to be. That allows the rest of the team to be confident in you. And you need confidence in your quarterback to win."

Except that always isn't the panacea, not after an incompletion. Or when one of his wide receivers feels shunned.

"In San Francisco I had Jerry Rice on one side and Terrell Owens on the other side," Garcia said. "It's kind of hard to share the ball equally and keep them happy. You're going to hear it from the guy not getting the ball. They're always open, according to them. They're never covered and they always had a step on the defensive backs—when it just doesn't work that way. I've done my best throughout my career of reading defenses and finding the guy best to make the play. When I tried to force the issue because they're unhappy, that's when mistakes happened.

"You see the receiver moping around on the sidelines. I'd love to switch positions with him. I'd love him to have to do the things I do in the huddle. They think it's so easy. Why can't I see them? It's not as easy as they think. I can't get caught up in their feelings and emotions. When we're winning games, that's all that matters to me. Receivers, with their nature and style, would rather have a twelve-catch game and be on the losing end than catch two balls and win. I'm not feeding their ego to make them happy. It's all about team."

Meanwhile, the offensive line just blocks for him—his great protectors. They don't demean him in the media or bark in his ear.

And in the huddle, he's their best audience.

Huddle Talk

Our friend the offensive tackle who talked about how little the world knows about what transpires on a given play described happenings and conversation inside a typical huddle:

> We're usually talking about the previous play first. "Did you see me put that guy on his back? That guy was leaning on you too much. See me light him up in the ribs? I lit that guy up."
>
> That goes on early as they are running guys in and out. We're watching the replay up on the board. Figuring stuff out. Communicating football. Watching football. Having a good time. Occasionally we see a fight break out in the stands. You don't want to make it too obvious so we don't turn around. And we don't ever point. We just say, "See that up there? Look behind the left upright."
>
> People don't realize how much fun it is sometimes. It's actually entertaining out there. We'd be in the huddle cracking jokes. Passing gas, busting steam.
>
> We'd say, "Whose was that? Who shit their pants?"
>
> Then it's, "I own that one."
>
> We're keeping it light. I drop killers all the time.

Defensive Huddle Talk

Hugh Douglas remembers the conversations well inside the defensive huddle. They fancied themselves superheroes, each player with a different power. They were a tight unit, he said, brother tight.

The dialogue went like this:

Hugh Douglas: I need a sack. Ain't had one all day.

Bobby Taylor: How much time do you need, Hugh Douglas?

Hugh Douglas: Three seconds.

Bobby Taylor: I got you, Hugh Douglas.

Bobby Taylor (to Al Harris): Okay, Sheriff, it's time to put the wide receiver under lock and key.

Jeremiah Trotter: Yeah, Sheriff, arrest that man.

Al Harris: He goin' to jail.

Hugh Douglas: Superhero powers, activate.

The Line of Scrimmage

Look at them right now, down low in their stance crowding one another, separated by a man's breath over an invisible line that might as well be the Bab-e-Azadi, the border fence that separates India and Pakistan, and you are struck by their sameness. From tackle to end, and tackle to guard and center, a tight snapshot captures extra-large to mammoth men in helmets sporting similar habiliment, distinguished by only the contrast of color. There's a readiness about all of them. Soon they will collide in what feels distinctly like something out of nature.

O-linemen represent football's physicists, logical and curbed, often emotionally detached, an oddity in a game sold by many coaches—particularly the position coaches, especially the special teams coach—with bloodlust and brimstone. Offensive linemen can be described as wordless beasts, imperturbably all business as the Grenadier Guards, quite the contrast when compared to their incessantly verbal counterparts on defense.

O-linemen are also known to be detached dirty in the pile. Speaking with them, they're remorseless types too, the sociopaths of football, or as one defensive player told me, "They're sneaky fucks."

See, those who man the opposite lines in football couldn't be more opposite, Felix and Oscar opposite.

"Offensive players are more methodical," former defensive end Hugh Douglas said. "They're more thinkers. Defensive players are doers. We constantly have to change with our environment. Because defense is not an exact science. Notice how some of the guys who do their own thing they call gamers or playmakers. Because defense is more instinctive.

"Just look at the nature of offense and defense. Offense is more of a timing thing. They'll go out and sputter and sputter until they get into a rhythm. The offense has to go in at halftime and make adjustments.

A defense just adjusts on the fly. You'll see a game where a team comes out on its opening drive and the defense gets hit in the mouth, gashed for big plays. Then all of a sudden they just bow up and you can't move the ball against them. Because on defense, it's like, 'All right, let's get our shit together right now,' and we can do it."

"You have to play defense with a mean streak," linebacker Joey Porter said. "Defense is meant to be played one way: nasty and aggressive."

Yes, defensive players are hunters the way jungle cats are, tracking prey with cunning over reason, always improvising, positioning to pounce. Aggression is their fuel.

And offensive linemen act like lion tamers.

"For us, it's a mental game," Kevin Long said. "One of the biggest factors is showing the defensive linemen that you're not tired and running to the line on every play. That's something I learned from Runyan. The first play of the game, sprint to the line and show them you have the energy, even if you don't. Mess with their head. Showing them you're not tired is a big advantage. Another thing I do is grind the guy on the ground. Linebackers hate to be cut block. They hate to be on the ground. That really discourages them."

Steve Wisniewski agreed. "The first play of Junior Seau's career he lined up against me," he recalled. "I got him and drove him to the ground and sat on top of him. He got up so pissed off that he took a swing at me and was ejected from the game. It was a nice welcome-to-the-league moment.

"Later that year, we met again and I drove him into the ground twice in a row. The third time I got him again into the ground and sat on him. The coaches showed that clip all week to the team. I was just hovering over him driving him into the ground. You could see the disheartened expression on him the third time I drove him into the ground."

Now, they all imply the same thing. O-linemen versus D-linemen is intelligence versus cunning, leverage and geometry versus hostility and assailment.

"I consider the game to be mental with a slightly physical side," guard Kevin Gogan said. "It's interesting the older I got, people would hit me and then apologize to me—which was amazing to me. You shouldn't be apologizing. That is your job! I remember Simeon Rice lit me up. I never saw him coming. I literally *never* saw him. He got me in the back of the neck real good and I was down. He gets up saying, 'I'm sorry, Mr. Gogan.' Really was a good, hard hit. Best shot I ever took.

"Nice kid, good player, that Simeon Rice."

When asked of the story, Rice replied, "Don't remember apologizing to anyone. Who's Kevin Gogan?"

It's not all that surprising that Rice didn't cop to sorry-saying on the field. So much of lineplay—particularly on the defensive side—is about putting on a pose.

Meanwhile, Gogan also said, "You find a lot good people in the league. Most of those guys are the offensive linemen. Best group of guys on the team are most likely gonna be the offensive linemen. There are some good guys on the defensive line—just not as many."

Hugh Douglas tells a good war story. Like that time against the Cowboys with the game long since decided in Douglas's team's favor, when the Dallas coaches opted to plant a seed in his mind for the rematch.

Douglas had enjoyed a fine day chasing the quarterback around, and when he broke defensive huddle on this particular play—a sure running play—he noticed something different. Larry Allen, the mean and mammoth All-Pro guard, had moved outside to left tackle and lined up opposite him.

Douglas knew he was there to send a message for next time.

"Oh, okay, this how it's gonna be?" Douglas whooped. "I ain't no punk. Don't think you gonna get me. I ain't no punk."

Allen said nothing back to him. He merely smiled at Douglas through his face mask.

"Larry Allen folded me up like a cheap turban on that play," Douglas recalled.

It didn't stop Douglas from talking. He sprang to his feet because men with great pride always spring to their feet after getting mauled, and told Allen, "You got me this time, but you don't want this right here next time."

Douglas lived for trench fights. The mind games and the battle of wits and strength and courage. Like chess with blood.

That Chris Samuels of the Redskins stands out as a worthy opponent. Right from the jump, too, his rookie year in 2000. One of the league's premier pass rushers, Douglas had heard all about this big kid, selected third overall by Washington. Samuels hadn't allowed a sack through the first five weeks of that season, and Douglas was determined to get one that day, October 8, 2000.

He didn't.

Douglas: "He was writing a diary. How he was dominating everybody. One play he folded me up like a pancake and busted my chin wide open. He hit me—I don't even know how he did it, a punch, nothing. I go over to the sidelines and I thought I was just sweating. Hollis [Thomas] looked at me and said, 'You talkin' out of two mouths.' My lip was split. My chin was split. You could see inside. It was so bad they couldn't give me stitches during the game. They had to use that glue to tape my chin together. Didn't even work. Thing busted wide open later in the game.

"I didn't even know I was hurt because I was so pissed. I was like, 'Motherfucker, you ain't shit.' He just said, 'Fuck you.' And acted like nothing happened. I got crazy. We all did. That was an ugly game. Lots of "fucks" going back and forth. It's not confirmed but legend has it that even [Brian Dawkins] cussed. They beat the shit out of us. They were talking trash all week about how they were going to whup our ass and they did!"

Samuels [coolly]: "I don't remember hitting him. I just remember we won the game."

The Redskins won the game 17–14 en route to an 8–8 record, while the loss was one of only five for Philadelphia on the season.

Trench Holds

Babies, the offensive linemen call the defensive linemen. They charge that their defensive counterparts incessantly hassle the officials and forever wail one word: *"Hold!"*

"Crying game," tackle Tra Thomas called it. "I hear 'Hold!' in my sleep sometimes."

And you know what? Of course they hold. Because as one offensive tackle stated flatly, "It's only holding if you get caught."

So they develop a battery of tricks to hold without holding, and they pass them down to other offensive linemen—only to the worthy ones, mind you—as though they are company secrets.

"Sometimes you can get in their face mask," Kevin Long described, "and hold them down and catch that lower bar and hold their head down and control their movements. But you have to watch the broken fingers with that."

Benji Olson offered up his secret: Grab the opponent, pull him close really, really quick, then push him off really, really quick, bouncing him off your body.

"It usually throws them off balance just enough," Olson said.

But it's not just offensive linemen who utilize hold techniques. "When we played Baltimore, Tony Siragusa and Sam Adams would hold so bad," Long said. "They would do anything to prevent you from getting to the second level where those linebackers were. Defensive linemen hold every play of every game."

Defensive end Mike Mamula conceded that fact. "We would practice stuff—to hold doing different stunts," he said. "Our linemen would hold offensive linemen. But offensive linemen are really the ones you want to talk to. They're the dirty players."

Cheats, the defensive linemen call the offensive linemen. Maybe so.

Meanwhile, Hugh Douglas said he would work the officials to get on their good side. "I used to crowd the ball all the time," he said. "I probably lined up offside a lot. But I was pretty cool with the refs. I would always talk to the refs. See how they're doin' and shit. They liked me. I was a good player. But every now and then there was a ref who'd say, 'I don't care about that shit. You fuck up and I'm gonna get you.'"

Some players get a bad rap with the officials, Long said. "They have a history of getting in trouble with the league and the refs try to take that in their own hands. Some instances, I think the refs need to let players play. Players are bigger, faster, and stronger; they need to let them play. You can't afford to lose any players, so it wouldn't change the way we played, but it might change the way the refs call plays on certain players.

"Sometime players draw attention from the refs because of their mouth. Everyone is going to focus in on that. The O-line really doesn't want the refs watching us, because, yes, we're holding on every play."

Linemen, offensive or defensive, they all have their special ways to work the system. "In college, you do everything by the book," linebacker Ike Reese said. "You get to the pros and you learn things to help you stay in the game. Those little tricks help you stay in the game."

A Tackle's Story

One offensive tackle offered this stark view of the position under the promise of anonymity. He shook his head several times during our conversation, reiterating how little everyone knows about what goes on during play.

There's a lot of bitching to the ref that happens out on the field. Defensive guys bitch about everything. My philosophy is that there are things they will call and things they won't call. There's the vinyl belts that hold the shoulder pads. They're tight, but you can grab those. If you get your hand in there, you can control a guy no problem. He can't jump. He can't run away from you. You can do anything you want to him. There's always time when you hold. You just need to know when to let go.

You must know the threshold. What they're going to call holding and what they're not going to call holding. You have to understand angles. What the ref can see and what he can't. You have to know that the referee's angle is usually behind you and that the side judge can see certain things. You have to anticipate where the running back is and know when to let go.

The officials are usually yelling at me. "Knock that off," a ref will say.

Then I'll respond, "I'm not doing anything."

They're people too. They'll joke around with you. They're not this robot out there. They all have personalities. They're out there doing their job.

Then the defense starts again. They're always freakin' crying to the officials. "He's holding! He's holding! He's hitting me in the face mask."

You punch him in the face to slow him down. See, when you get punched in the face it stands you up. Technically it's illegal but they won't call it unless you leave your hand on them. So you do it quick. They flinch. Their eyes will blink. Their head will rattle. It gives you a second to catch up. That shit hurts, though, when it's cold outside. Know those little clamps at the top of the face mask? Catch one of those when your hand is frozen. Oh, man, that stings. Your fingertip catches the face mask and you can hear the steel of the face mask go "ting." That hurts worse than the palm of your hand.

Either way, they're going to cry. They all cry. If they're on defense, they cry.

Motivation: Fear and Paranoia

All it takes is one bad play to reverse the tide, and two bad ones for everybody to say the other guy won the battle. Especially if he's a celebrated defensive end, one of those sack guys.

According to the protectors, the biggest difference between tackle and defensive end, between offensive linemen and any defensive player, is credit. How they keep score.

They'll say it doesn't matter if you owned your man the whole game, checked him like a damn fur coat. If he finally breaks through once for the sack, God forbid twice, or even forces a throw in a hurry, you're the one, as one offensive lineman so colorfully put it, wearing the dress.

"All it takes is one slip and you're his bitch," he said.

Former guard Mark Schlereth talked of what truly motivates offensive linemen: fear and paranoia. Shame.

"It's like nothing good can happen," he said. "When you dominate a defensive player, no one notices or pays attention. I can line up in a sixty-five-play game and whup my guy's butt for sixty-four plays and that one play my guy gets the sack, he becomes the hero and I become the goat. I never met a defensive lineman that remembers getting blocked. It's always, 'Remember when I did this, remember when I got that sack.' I never met an offensive lineman who remembers blocks. Giving up sacks is what sticks with us. That fear and paranoia. If we're ever on national TV it's either for holding or for doing something bad."

To a man, it's the biggest complaint of the offensive linemen. They have to be perfect the whole game, and the defenders need only make a play or two.

"Offensive linemen are perfectionists," Wisniewski added. "I would lay awake and think a lot about the game. The bad plays or mistakes I made would run through my head all night. A defensive player can go home and think about the two or three good plays he made and be satisfied with himself. The offensive mentality is different because we think about those two or three plays we didn't make and that is what bothers us. I wouldn't have trouble sleeping from the pain but rather the plays I didn't make."

One Bad-Ass End

Michael Strahan was first-ballot great. The accomplishments, however gaudy—setting the NFL's single-season sack record with 22.5 in 2001, collecting a total of 141.5 sacks and 20 forced fumbles over a career that spanned fifteen years—only represent the by-product of his dominance.

When deconstructing a great defensive end you begin with their composition. How deep does *it* run. They all possess some degree of *it*, the way they all possess that same big-man athleticism. The body type varies, though it does seem the best boast a similar build: tall and weighty, with a wide upper body and sturdy trunk.

"You need that ass," observed Hugh Douglas, who amassed 80 sacks in 138 career games and applies as a great defensive end. "Got to have that ass. Need that foundation for the push."

Though originally somewhat undersized, the 6-foot-2 Douglas gained girth and strength as he matured, playing his best football between 260 and 280 pounds, with an ample posterior. Light and quick may get you the corner against those mammoth tackles with slow feet, but ultimately you may wear down over a long season. Jostling at the line with bigger men for all of those downs can take a toll on the body. Wear it out and sap just that whit of speed, which oftentimes marks the difference between a sack and a hurry.

For example, the lean and super-quick Jevon Kearse lived up to his University of Florida nickname and the ridiculous combine numbers he posted before the draft during his rookie year in Tennessee in 1999. Freakish how he exploded off the snap, they gushed, as he registered 14.5 sacks and earned first-team All-Pro honors. He provided instant pressure on the quarterback. Microwave pressure. He recorded 11.5 the next season and 10 more the following year, but injuries soon derailed Kearse and he hasn't seen double-digit sacks since.

The Philadelphia Eagles once let the greatest defensive end ever—Reggie White—walk over a contract dispute, all the way to Green Bay, by the way, and win a Super Bowl. It haunted the franchise through the years and ultimately through an ownership change. In 2004, the team made Kearse the highest-paid defensive end ever, signing him as a free agent as part of a huge off-season splash that also included a trade for Terrell Owens. The Eagles landed in the Super Bowl and Kearse played solid football, but he hardly proved freakish with 7.5 sacks, none coming after Thanksgiving. He produced similar results the following season, and in 2006 suffered a season-ending knee injury in week 2 against the Giants. Kearse struggled to regain his form last year and wound up with just 3.5 sacks, prompting the Eagles to release him early in the off season.

In the end, Kearse—who signed an eight-year, $65 million deal that included a $16 million signing bonus—lasted just four years in Philadelphia, producing 86 tackles and 21 sacks in 45 games. Better to save cap space than face.

Size aside, Kearse didn't exhibit a lot of *it* with the Eagles. Opposing tackles adjusted to his speed rush, forcing him farther outside, and he rarely willed a sack. Perhaps it's unfair to speculate—and perhaps totally incorrect—but you wonder if off-season life on his yacht in a Miami marina left Kearse a rather ordinary player after his first three seasons in the NFL, the good life as well as injuries sapping some of his desire.

"Jevon Kearse was terrified of me," former Ravens tackle Orlando Brown said. "That motherfucker doesn't want to get hurt. I would beat on him, and all of his buddies on my team—Ray Lewis, Deion Sanders, and these guys—are coming up telling me Jevon is afraid like a little kid to play against me."

Back to *it*, this totally subjective attribute that you can't measure with stats, something for which you can't train nor later attain. Two letters that describe a player's belly, his mettle. How unrelenting he is during a play, no matter the point in the game or the score of the game, which will ultimately prove his worth in the league.

Linebacker Jeremiah Trotter called it *that dawg*—something primal, separate from the person's comportment, something deep down that makes a ruler of the back alley or the backwoods.

Or the backfield.

There is some in every professional football player, yes, sans position or skill level. It's how they reach such a lofty level. In the great defensive end, however, *it* no longer exists like an apparition. It's for everyone to see in how he plays, a sedulous attacker. For the quarterback or the man who must block him, he's the monster of dreams come to life. Certainly it was that way with the greatest defensive end ever.

At 291 pounds, Reggie White had the body and that organic Chattanooga strength, force the push of a tractor—which doesn't necessarily go hand in hand with the body, mind you, as any bench-presser will testify. He had super quickness and dancer feet.

"That man could move like Michael Jackson," Randall Cunningham said.

What made White the best ever, however, was how he backed up his ability with play in that perdurable way, meaning you could never exhale blocking Reggie White.

Which returns us to Strahan, who attacked the quarterback with the same grimness, only wearing a gap-toothed smile while doing it. The second great defensive end of the modern era also played mind games, flopping for the ref, he too forever crying, "Hooooold!"

According to several tackles who played against him, Strahan offered a variety of techniques. He would go extra hard and suddenly let up in his version of a changeup. He would do this rope-a-dope rush thing where he had his man expend precious energy and lull him into a false sense of blocking security, then unleash something from his arsenal. Like perhaps the bull rush, where he attacks straight ahead into the protector, driving with all of his might into the man, playing the leverage game. Or maybe fake bull rush, swat away the paws that clutch him, and quickly take the outside lane to the quarterback. Or reverse, reverse psychology, which constitutes fake bull rush, fake outside move and come back for the inside route.

At 6-foot-5, around 260 pounds, and more than big-man athletic, Strahan could work every angle.

"Mike Strahan was such a great leader," said former Giants defensive coordinator Steve Spagnuolo, now the head coach of the St. Louis Rams. "I'd whisper something in his ear and he'd rally the troops. Guys listened to him."

Halftime Heroes

Down in Tennessee, where the oppressive Dixie heat lasts into early October, they call it instant air-conditioning.

Playing just one half of Sunday football in the South during Indian summer enervates the body. Down on that field for a one o'clock kick-off, the sun raging and the humidity stifling, the sideline so hot you feel it through your cleats, sixteen pounds of equipment wears the way a suit of armor does, even with short sleeves. You're literally melting, sweating away nutrients and most of the body's oomph.

It's only a matter of time before the cramps, which portend dehydration. Football players know their body the way musicians know their instrument. Most hear every bone creak and feel every muscle twitch. They can sense an impending crash. Their feet or hands may spasm and lock up for a moment. Soon it happens. Say, their hamstrings will just stop working on a given play.

It feels as though you have no power. Your muscles fall soup-noodle limp. You hit somebody and your muscle spasms and you fall to the ground. You go to fire off and your hamstrings just pop. You cramp and then you fall.

So in the locker room at halftime, the Titans would set up a M.A.S.H. unit inside the shower, with IV bags hanging off the shower heads, the stations manned by nurses. Life fills those bags, and the players wait in what resembles the line for communion at Sunday mass. One by one they extend their arms, and the nurses barely look up for a faint smile. Time is short during halftime. Twenty minutes. So the nurses perform this act mechanically. Swab the sweet spot, hit the vein, and pop a bag into a body. Disengage, and repeat on the next man.

Players will sigh with relief. The IV delivers fluids at room temperature into an overheating 102.74-degree body. Instant hydration. Instant relief. Instant air-conditioning.

"I'm from the Seattle area so I was used to the cool weather my whole life," said former Titans offensive lineman Benji Olson. "Down there, that humidity can be pretty intense. I would sweat so much, taking those IV bags became a routine before all games, and on those hot days I would go back for more at halftime."

One player put it like this: "You feel entirely normal again. You know, on those days, you lose so much fluid, you feel like you're going to die. You can't breathe. Then you start with the dry heaves. And you can't catch your breath. You get sick. It's not fun. Now you're trying to throw up and catch your breath at the same time. Now you're compounding both situations. You rip up all of the blood vessels and you start hacking up blood.

"Your body is just like that overheating engine leaking steam in that car on the side of the road, particularly for those guys who played every down or the skill players who have very little body fat. When you pop that bag, you're as good as new. You really gain a competitive advantage, and it's something that's totally legal."

The first thing you'd do at halftime is go straight to the show, jump in there and get the IV. If you're all cramped up, you get stretched, otherwise you're useless. Once you get the IV, halftime is pretty much over. Even if you're not getting an IV, you run in to use the restroom. You hear a couple of things coaches have to say. You go up to your position coach and ask, out of all that was said what pertains to me? Adjustments can be made. They're usually minor. For the player, it's just sifting through information quickly, because in a flash you're back on the field.

Extreme heat is unnatural in football. Given a choice, most players would prefer playing in extreme cold, particularly those ranch-rugged types who played in the Big 10 or deep in the prairie of, say, Nebraska, where the frigid air sweeps through the plains freely, accompanied by that whipped, biting wind.

While quarterbacks normally shrink an inch or two, diving into heavy parkas and oversized mittens on the sideline, huddled next to the heaters by the bench, linemen, particularly offensive linemen, typically embrace football cold, best described as January, Green Bay cliché cold, the way it was the night of the NFC Championship Game between the Giants and Packers at Lambeau Field in 2008.

The temperature at kickoff was one below zero with a windchill of twenty-three below and dipped further during the course of the evening. It was so cold that Eli Manning's left hand went numb during pregame warm-ups, and yet most of the linemen wore short sleeves for the game. In fact, the Packers offensive line has a rule prohibiting sleeves in any weather.

"We would fine guys if they wore sleeves," one lineman said. "Some guys just couldn't take it and paid the money. But we didn't make it that easy on them. We tortured them. Because in our eyes, O-linemen don't wear sleeves. That's a pussy thing to do. That's something guys on the defense would do."

The Fourth Time-out

So it's the fourth quarter of, say, the Super Bowl between New York and New England, and the Patriots are finally moving the football. Brady to Welker for 5. Brady to Moss for 10. Maroney up the middle for 9. Brady to Welker for 13. All on consecutive plays.

For the first time all game, the Giants defense is bending badly. The Patriots smell the momentum shift. They go no-huddle. Push the tempo. The field's starting to slant. Charge downhill.

Brady to Faulk for 4. Brady to Welker for 10. Brady to Moss for 11 more. No-huddle some more. The body language in blue reads fatigue. Guys hunched over between plays. Hands on their knees.

The desert is dry. It's been such a long, emotional evening.

No huddle.

Brady to Faulk out of the backfield again for 12. Down to the Giants 6.

And now the defense desperately needs a break, preferably without burning a precious time-out. Because if New England scores here, the offense will need the time-outs for the comeback drive.

Wait. Defensive tackle Fred Robbins remains on the ground. He lies facedown on the field wincing. The officials stop the clock.

The defense gets its rest. Now, it doesn't make a difference because the Patriots wind up scoring on the throw from Brady to Moss to take a 14–10 lead. But for this moment, the players on defense can take a breath, recoup just a little life while Robbins lies there, now with the trainer whispering something in his ear.

Suddenly Robbins springs up, the way they do it on the Sunday morning healer shows when the number to call for credit card donations flashes across the screen. He walks off the field slowly, but without any noticeable limp.

"When the defense was out there on a long drive and needed a blow," Coach Steve Spagnuolo said, "Antonio Pierce would whisper in someone's ear, 'Get hurt after this play.' Ant would then wink at me so I knew everything was okay."

Or Pierce would just wander over to the sideline and say, "Don't worry about him, Coach. He's okay. I told him to get hurt."

It's a practice that every team utilizes, so much so that the NFL has a rule in place that if a player goes down inside the two-minute warning the team is charged one time-out.

4

Slobberknockers, Misdeeds, and Regrets of Men and Monsters

M ichael Strahan yammered constantly, words flowing from him like exhaust from a sputtering car. As great as he was on the field was how good he was at talking. Before the Giants upset the Patriots, he was the toast of Super Bowl XLII, Ari Gold finger-snap-pointing his way through Media Day.

The international press and *Entertainment Tonight* and VH1 swooned as Strahan talked about pommes frites and attending the HBO party and a Suns game with Steve Nash and how the visitor's locker room inside University of Phoenix Stadium plain sucks compared to the home digs and it figures the Patriots would get that one and how that little dime-piece reporter from Mexico's TV Azteca in the stripper wedding dress who wants to marry him now that Brady and Manning are taken should know his history—then she'd leave him alone, referring to his messy divorce that played out publicly in the New York City tabloids, which went wild over that story his estranged wife told, the one about him taping her sister undress.

You can't hide following those kinds of headlines—like the one in the *Daily News* that blared his bitter defeat in divorce court, "Wife $15,000,000, Strahan 0"—and how could he? Strahan can't hide even if he could lam it into the training room every afternoon. He needs to talk. He answered all of their questions and had fun with the stupid ones, and they ate it up. You know it's bad when the media covering Media Day refer to it as the "annual circus" Media Day, as though it's a bowl game and ridiculous is the sponsor. Cheap laughs. He's good at it. He stood there looking more like Bernie Mac than a seven-time Pro Bowler.

Strahan knows how to work it. Give them a back-page headline. That's all they want. Say something about someone or some team and watch them scribble feverishly, and if another bone falls out of his closet so be it. So what if he walks around with more than a pet cemetery, if wife Jean spills more beans about more junkets with more mistresses he called "Cupcake." Hell, making the Super Bowl will cleanse state prisons, let alone athletes with a sidepiece or two or twelve, especially one as accomplished as this one, who, by the way, had to fork over more than half of his judge-decreed net worth of $22 million and still pay $311,000 in back child support—and Jean didn't account for one sack.

Keep flashing that smile and everything will be all right. Imagine that when Strahan told of his television aspirations long ago some fool in the business actually told him to fix his teeth. Stand up and whistle a few wisecracks and listen to 'em laugh, even when they're not funny.

It's a brilliant strategy by Strahan, one only a few players employ. It's best to entertain 'em instead of fight with 'em, or worse, ignore 'em, and you really don't have to be Bernie Mac to do it well. Strahan has a $2 million TV deal waiting for him when he retires, which didn't really almost happen last summer. Training Camp, Albany, is not a place to wish away the divorce blues. It could, however, happen now at any moment after the big win. Super Bowls are everlasting life, after football.

You heard the ovation when he addressed the crowd at the Giants parade. He couldn't have addressed them any better, conducting the story instead of reciting it, stretching and swallowing syllables, so that all of Gotham waited for the tagline.

"When I jump up and down, we call it. We stomp you out," he boomed. "We went on the road and we stomped out eleven straight. So just for the sake of good posture and for the fact that we are New York City and we are New Yorkers and we are very polite, we would like to extend this to every other team in the NFL, particularly for the last team we defeated. The New England Patriots. Because you know what we did to you?"

Strahan then jumped up and down in a stomping motion on the stage for effect.

"We call it. We stomp you out!"

"Strahan talks trash, but he doesn't do it directly. He does it indirectly in the press," Cowboys receiver Patrick Crayton said. "Go back and read his quotes. They're funny."

That's Strahan's charm.

There are two types of players. Those who talk on the field and those who don't.

Similarly, there are two types of talkers on the field. Those like Strahan who speak with humor, spiced by innuendo, the language of a Fox sitcom, and those who wield the wicked tongue.

The Art of Talking

Trash talkers are like graffiti artists. Some are clever and some just spray-paint the word "dick."

"People are talking shit before the game, during the play, after the play," former running back Brian Mitchell said. "I would tell them, 'Go and talk to your coach and ask him if you wanna be talking shit to me. I know how to get under your skin.'"

Mitchell was good because Mitchell was keen. While most players opt for generic insults sprinkled with profanity, Mitchell was a veritable psychologist who'd study his opponents' bios in the media guide and pick out personal information to use against them.

"There are three things that get under every man's skin," he said, "talking about his mama, his girlfriend, or his wife. Not in a degrading way, mind you. I would find out their wife's or girlfriend's name and I would say, 'How's Tammy?' They're not playing the game mentally as smart as they should be once they get that in their heads. Mind over matter. They're wondering how I know Tammy when in fact I don't know Tammy at all. I would go up to them after the game and let them know that I don't know Tammy. That I just found it in the program before the game. They cared about what I was saying. When you can affect their thoughts then you got 'em. They talked trash back to me, too. But I was always better."

Mitchell was better because Mitchell was uncurbed. Cajun spine he had, the kind born from being the youngest of seven children and fighting for seconds in a place called Fort Polk, Louisiana. Barely 5-foot-10, he jawed and jostled with everyone, and he liked engaging linemen. Sometimes his helmet wouldn't reach above their neck and he'd get in their face still, and how comical it appeared watching from above, the smaller man being evincive, decidedly more the aggressor. He had that fistfight in him. Always ready to go, no matter big or how many. His cousin was a professional boxer. And he too knew how to throw a punch, one of these guys you'd choose for your back over a thousand much bigger guys.

"Joe Gibbs used to tell me to stop talking so much trash," Mitchell said. "'Someone is going to hurt you.' I was like, 'Joe, I play to win; I don't play to be liked.'"

Foxhole guys, guys like Brian Mitchell, who squared with wide, round Warren Sapp one day, giving up somewhere near a hundred pounds. In fact, before the NFC Championship Game against Tampa in 2002, he referred to the then Buccaneer tackle as "Warren Sackless," a shot at Sapp's dramatic decline in sacks that year.

"Let his fat ass come after me," Mitchell said.

"A lot of time it's all a mental game," Jason Short said. "I look at talking trash as a veteran move, trying to get the enemy heated enough to get them do something undisciplined. Say something uncalled for."

Meanwhile, Sapp easily ranked as the biggest trash talker among players interviewed for this book.

"Warren always had plenty to talk about," Mark Schlereth said. "He was always talking. See, offensive linemen play in the concrete. Guys on the edge play in the water. Guys inside don't have a lot to say. We just go about our business because we're trying to kill each other."

"You want to be talking," Sapp once said, "because who's talking is who's winning."

And now he's retiring, after thirteen stellar seasons, including one stretch down in Tampa where he was the most dominant defensive player in the league, this incredible force of Miami mass, D-end nimble, and D-tackle fat, busting gaps and balls like no other. The announcement made on his Web site, QBKilla.com—by just the words I'M DONE! in big block letters on the home page—it does seem a fast thirteen since all of those dirty draft rumors and reports of drug use that damned him from his rightful position in the top five to the twelfth overall pick as a "gamble," like he was some Powerball ticket, and how he proved all of those draft losers wrong because he wasn't a pothead or a cokehead, or a too-slow, divisive, overeating laggard, which is not to recast him as Saint Warren Carlos from the U.

During his career, he's bumped officials and unceremoniously skipped through opponents while they stretched during pregame warm-ups and called former Packers coach Mike Sherman a "lying, shit-eating hound" and taunted and heckled and harassed and just played how a defensive tackle should—in his words, "Snot-on-snot football."

Sapp was South Florida brash and South Florida voluble. You knew how good he was because he reminded you every Sunday during the game and always thereafter. No matter what transpired against Green Bay with Chad Clifton, even if he launched himself—which he clearly did—at the prone offensive tackle during Brian Kelly's interception return and Sapp-danced while the man lay there motionless for several minutes and had the gall to gloat about his kill shot afterward, boasting, "Yeah, I was a heat-seeking missile. Boom. Boom. Boom. And I hit him."

The celebration jiggle was what prompted Sherman to chastise Sapp on the field as the game ended—and Sapp to fire back, "If I was twenty-five years old and didn't have a kid and a conscience, I would have given him an ass-kicking right there on the 30-yard line."

Upon being criticized for going over the top with Sap Yap, he replied, "I can't stop that. I'm going to do that as loud as I can for as long as I can because it just gets me going. That's the way I play the game. I can't help it."

Therein lies the motive for many who engage in talk, a way to work themselves into the right froth for the field.

"I try to get into an argument with somebody before the game," linebacker Joey Porter said. "I always pick somebody out I don't like. Then I want to go at them the whole game. I try to get 'em talking. Go ahead, talk with me. But you better back up what you're saying. That's part of the game. You better bring it.

"I got different guys on different teams. Chad Johnson always tries to make a joke out of it. Before the coin toss, he tries to act like he's gonna get into a fight. He tries to get me to go with him. Yeah,

I do that, and they kick me out. I got a lot of run-ins! That's how it's supposed to be. You're goin' into somebody's stadium, trying to take over."

Former offensive lineman Spencer Folau laughed at Porter. "He's a dumb shit," Folau said. "He was just a retard. He didn't know better. He talked when they're losing. We're kneeling the ball one time and he came over and hit LaCharles Bentley."

Bentley, Folau loved. "I remember in 2002, we played Tampa, and everyone said how good a player Warren Sapp was—his head went off the charts, and [Bentley] kicked Sapp's ass. He went right back at Sapp. He would talk so much junk. Used to help me get through the game. I laughed the whole time. He got hurt against Carolina. Somebody came in late and hit him in his ankle and as he's being carried off the field he says to [Will] Witherspoon, 'Me and you after the game in the parking lot. Me and you, dude. I'm gonna fight you.' Like it was after school at 3 p.m."

Said Hugh Douglas, "You put that helmet on, it's going to war, especially with the smaller cats. You look at those big-ass linemen and you get pissed because people told you your whole life that you're small. You don't have to be big to put your foot in somebody's ass.

"I definitely enjoyed what I did. You better enjoy it. You're throwing your body out there subjecting yourself to get fucked up.

"I'd take that anger out on the field. It's a great weapon. I got that from John Randle."

The Beast of Gevaudan

Oh, yes, John Randle.

Everybody called him Crazy John Randle, the NFL's version of the Beast of Gevaudan. By crazy, we mean football crazy, well, mostly football crazy. We remember well Crazy John Randle, who spent fourteen seasons in the NFL, eleven with the Vikings, three with the Seahawks, before retiring in 2004. Great, great player, Crazy John Randle, who recorded double-digit sacks in eight consecutive seasons during one stretch, played in 176 straight games during another, and made six Pro Bowls, even though he went undrafted and was supposedly too small at 6-foot-1, 290 pounds, to play defensive tackle.

Maybe that's why he was always a little, shall we say, off—and remains so to this day, spewing the same kind of vile things and acting again certifiable recently on a make-believe field against some backyard hack on the Spike channel game show *Pros vs. Joes*, an athletic competition of exactly what the title suggests. See, John Randle's life was never supposed to amount to much. Born in a nowhere town called Hearne, located smack-dab in the middle of the Texas Triangle, equidistant from Dallas, Houston, and San Antonio, Randle lived in a shack with his older brother, Ervin, and their single mother, Martha, who worked as a maid.

Randle worked odd jobs to help out and didn't discover football until high school, following in his older brother's path. Schooling wasn't a priority as much as survival for the Randle boys, and Jon didn't have the SAT scores to get into college. He wound up at Trinity Valley Community College for two years before transferring to Division II Texas A&M in Kingsville.

And maybe taking that difficult route to the NFL, somehow latching on with the Vikings in training camp in 1990 for just a look-see and impressing enough to be kept around like a penny stock, made him into what he was when he stayed there. Maybe it was requital for being born to Hearne, a place of four thousand folks, as painful as a hernia under Randle's circumstances, without a father and tailing his mother to her job cleaning other people's nicer homes. All that pent-up hostility worked well in the hostile environs of a football field.

Maybe that's why he wore the Halloween paint on his face that made him look terrifying. He was a warrior in life and in the game, and he wanted all of them to know it. So he lathered it on before the game and all you saw was a wicked glow from beneath his helmet.

Barry Sanders once told ESPN of Randle, "He's just flat-out crazy. He has his face painted with this warrior paint. It's not just eye black. It's actual war paint–type stuff. Like he's going into a battle. He'll get in your face and say all kinds of craziness. He's going to rip you apart, this, that, and the other."

Strahan and Sapp you sort of get, two extroverts, incessant talkers and chop-busters, heavy on the mama jokes and ugly jokes, attention hogs who viewed the field as proprietors because they were that good. Class-clown crazy.

Now, John Randle was stay-away-from crazy, the kind that borders sanity just enough to leave him be.

"I always kept my head on swivel," Kyle Turley said. "Guys were looking out for me. Guys like John Randle. He was a big talker. Great players cussing up a storm, at certain moments trying to be dirty. But it was great playing that style. You knew it was going to be fun. The competition was at its high, shit talking and all that good stuff."

Mark Schlereth said, "John Randle would talk a lot of trash, but he backed it up. He was so quick and so powerful. He was exceptionally hard to block."

Randle also used to study newspaper clippings to find dirt on his opponents. He was more like a serial stalker, however, than, say, Brian Mitchell, who was just looking for the name of a wife or a girlfriend to use as bait. Randle knew their kids' names and any past legal problems, domestic abuse issues, or DUIs. It was all fodder for Sunday.

"Nine times out of ten guys talking smack are defensive linemen," quarterback Jeff Garcia said, "and one of the biggest was John Randle. I just remember him talking smack throughout the whole game. He would tell you where you're from and who your girlfriend was. He took a lot of pride in the trash he talked."

"John Randle is the originator of violence," declared former teammate Chris Hovan, who began wearing war paint like Randle back at Boston College. "I've always given him credit. I just put my own spin on the thing."

So he's on the show *Pros vs. Joes* and he's jumping up and down and smacking himself in the head, as Average Guy is supposed to escape his clutches. It's not so much what transpires as it is what John Randle is saying and how he sounds like Zed from *Pulp Fiction*.

"Gonna put some wood on this fire. Yeah, giddy up! Giddy up! Gonna ride yo ass! Gonna ride it all night long, boy! Gonna make you one of my bitches!"

And that's exactly the sort of thing he told players in the NFL.

"He used to be on the field calling people racists," Hugh Douglas said. "Now I'm pretty sure they probably weren't racists. But he'd get himself all crazy and tell somebody, 'Motherfucker, you look like David Duke! I'm gonna get yo ass, you KKK, cross-burnin' motherfucker.' Or he'd say [to another black player], 'Ain't you that nigga coming out of my wife's car the other night?'

"Cats would look at him like, 'Dude, what's wrong with you?' And if you ever met John Randle, he's nothing like how he played. John Randle would be in a room and you wouldn't even know he was there. He was the quietest dude, the softest-spoken, coolest cat you'd ever want to know. But man, he'd put on that face paint and that helmet and he was crazy."

It's why they call it trash talking. Because sometimes it really is trash. It's vile and offensive and disgusting and sometimes racist.

"I've heard cats like Erik Williams say to Mike Mamula, 'I'm gonna kill your white cracker ass,'" Ike Reese said.

For the record, both John Randle and Erik Williams declined to be interviewed for the book. Williams had initially agreed but later expressed second thoughts, wondering aloud "whether it was such a good idea" to rehash his playing days with the Cowboys. Williams, a four-time Pro Bowler at right tackle who played the game nasty, similarly to Jon Runyan, and goes down as perhaps the only player ever to manhandle Reggie White, was involved in some of the seedy incidents that beset the Dallas dynasty team. He was extremely polite in turning down this request and said he was "in a different place now."

Several players skirted the issue of racial epithets used during the exchange of trash talking. Certainly it goes on, though now it seems to be aimed more toward white players because of the greater percentage of black players in the league.

Reese, who played his college ball at Michigan State, recalls another incident while playing LSU in a bowl game. "We're out there and their entire offensive line and the tight end—Dan LaFleur, who used to play for the Cowboys—are out there calling us porch monkeys," he said. "We went up to a couple of black players on their team, Kevin Faulk being one of them, and said, 'Your guys are out here calling us niggers. Y'all cool with that?'

"But really it hurt us. We fell for it. Stuff like that gets you out of your game. We got all kinds of personal foul penalties that day and we got beat bad."

The use of racial or homosexual slurs in taunts is not exactly shocking news. Herein lies the great paradox. The game is born unto violence, big men colliding with other big men, physically battling one another to gain their share of earth. And anger is their fuel. So how can one expect there not to be ugliness exchanged when the entire game is predicated on ugliness? Degrees of ugly are obviously varying, but anyone who has ever played sports, down to pickup basketball at the playground, knows that stuff is said between competitors that wouldn't be said during everyday life. Likewise actions on the field of play during a football game.

For a moment, forget how the NFL is marketed and imaged, and the strong moral stance taken by new commissioner Roger Goodell—which, by the way, is to be applauded—and focus on the game unplugged. All of those war analogies are apt to some degree, and when we applaud a player for knocking another's block off or simply besting him on a play, how then can we castigate him for getting caught up in the moment? The whole game resides in the moment. Short of the obvious illegal plays, the invisible line to be crossed is totally subjective, moving with motive.

Men who beat on one another are going to say vulgar things to one another. Even Eagles coach Andy Reid, a practicing Mormon who doesn't use profanity, understands that players are going to use colorful language. While he can ban booze on the charter flights to road games in the name of wholesomeness, how in the world can he ask men risking permanent limb damage, paralysis, or worse not to swear in the heat of battle? In fact, a few years back, while I was writing a magazine story, Reid granted me full access to his team with only one editorial request: Do not quote his players cursing. "You're gonna hear it," he said. "I'd rather not read it. It just doesn't look right, you know?"

And for that context, a story in a city magazine, he was probably right, though it's impossible to do so while looking through a real open window into a player's life.

"It's about getting an edge," Joey Porter said. "I say words to mess with them. Could be something on the field. Could be something off the field. Could be some nasty shit. Just to mess with their head. Freak 'em out. If he can't take talking, he better not go up against me."

Which brings us to a story of when trash talking failed to work to the talker's advantage, told by Hugh Douglas, whom Reid banned from his bus to the stadium or the team hotel on the road. He talked too much, Reid said. Douglas had to take the other bus or the buses wouldn't leave.

Douglas tells of a personal battle with Brad Hopkins of the Titans during a game in which the Eagles led with just under two minutes remaining.

"I was killing Brad all day," he said. "I had just sacked Steve McNair and I said, 'B-Hop, I own you! You scared of me!'"

Douglas then imitated Hopkins. "What? Motherfucker, what? Scared of you? Come on, motherfucker."

"He got hot," Douglas said. "I mean, he was dead before I said that. He was tired and done. I beat him like a drum all day. But he took me behind the woodshed. He whupped my ass for two minutes and we lost the game."

Meanwhile, the mistake former Seahawks tight end Jerramy Stevens made was talking before the game. The game was Super Bowl XL against the Pittsburgh Steelers and Stevens spoke about how he was going to ruin Jerome Bettis's homecoming to Detroit.

Joey Porter of the Steelers took sharp exception. "If you go down a dark alley, who do you want with you, me or Stevens?" he countered to reporters. "Don't you lie. It's going to be me, of course."

Porter's voice grows agitated even today when talking about Stevens. "He had me mad," he said. "Talking like he was a tough guy. You not tough. You know you ain't tough. You just acting. What I said was to just shut his whole program down. Prove to the world with one simple question: If you go down a dark alley, who do you want with you? Me or him? And everybody in the world knows it's me. I wanted to get him in the game, but I didn't get a shot at him. Didn't matter, though. We won and he knew the real deal."

Meanwhile, Stevens, now in San Francisco, will go down as one of the most despised players in the league. Following a game against the Raiders, in which he taunted and headbutted Oakland safety Stuart Schweigert and later got involved in a heated tussle with defensive end Tyler Brayton, prompting Brayton's ejection for kneeing Stevens in the groin, Warren Sapp said, "[Brayton] reacted like any of us would react if you were out there in a situation with this punk. This dude has been a piece of shit since he got in this league and it's never going to change about him."

The Soul Splitter

Ask a thousand players what it feels like to unleash a clean, knock-your-block-off hit and they will use the same analogy:

Like crushing a tee shot. You don't even feel it.

"When all that comes together, it's like a hot knife through butter," Mark Schlereth said. "It feels so easy and effortless, and on film it looks like you absolutely annihilated someone. All you're thinking is, 'Wow, I'd like to be able to do that again.'"

Romanowski described it as running through a cloud. So deceiving the impact. Velvety instead of vicious. Not at all like pounding the sled in practice. The victim goes down so fast, falling the way a glass does from an accidental nudge off the dinner table.

Sheldon Brown, one of the more physical corners in the league, drew national acclaim when he flattened Reggie Bush alone in the flat during a divisional playoff game between the Saints and Eagles in January 2007.

The play was designed to get Bush some space, unlocking him in the open field in a one-on-one situation. Two things went wrong: Brown read the play and Drew Brees's throw had too much air. The ball floated, leaving Bush exposed for a de-cleater. Brown exploded all shoulder and helmet into Bush's chest, sending the make-miss running back crashing to the turf.

Brown, meanwhile, continued forward with only a stumble, using the now falling Bush as balance beneath him. He compared it to running through a cardboard box. You just somehow wind up on the other side, while the box lies flat at your feet.

"I thought maybe my adrenaline was so high I couldn't feel anything," Brown said. "When I think back, I can see it but I still can't feel it."

Meanwhile, Bush sprang to his feet in valor, only to fall right back down to his knees, the wind knocked from him. His whole body echoed with a prolonged ringing, like heavy church bells at noon.

"I was dropped in coverage out there and I thought I was going to be the one who hit," said Eagles defensive end Trent Cole. "All of a sudden, I see Sheldon come right by my face and I was like, 'Oh, my God.' I've never seen anybody get hit so hard in my life. I've never seen anybody get folded up like that."

Seeing Floaties

Seeing stars is real, though seeing floaties is probably more accurate. A million specks of light buzzing around you like gnats at a country barbecue.

Spaghetti legs is real, too. Your knees wobble as you walk. Dead legs.

"As you get up," Schlereth said, "you shake out the cobwebs and you just start thinking, 'Man, that is gonna look bad on film.'"

"[I] was going downfield against the 49ers," Kyle Turley said. "There was a turnover on the play and I had the guy lined up. It was a defensive back so I knew I could get a good shot. I was hauling ass when he was right in my sights. Just as I was about to get him, I saw a shadow. Junior Bryant, a defensive end. The shadow came into the corner of my eye. I was focused on the hit I was about to give and didn't even see Bryant. My whole body did that John Elway helicopter thing and I went flying. I was really embarrassed. No one likes getting hit like that. I flopped on the ground so hard. I was so embarrassed that I shot right back up to try and make a positive out of it. I chased the guy down and got him at the 50, saving a touchdown on the play."

Some players, however, will describe a euphoric feeling that sweeps through their body following a bone-crunching collision.

"One time I was chasing a running play against the Tennessee Titans and I ran smack into Eddie George," Mike Mamula said. "At that point in the play we were both full steam ahead and we hit each other straight on. It was one of those hits where you neutralize each other's impact. It was such a rush. This really great feeling came over me. Everything went silent and it excited me. I really enjoyed it."

Let us travel inside a kill shot for a moment.

The hit occurred during a kickoff return by the Cowboys' Miles Austin during a game on December 16, 2006. You remember the date because you remember the hit, the kind of hit that happens once every game or two. See, you think you've seen a thousand of those hits but you really haven't because there aren't that many.

The hit happened in a nationally cable-televised game, which is important to the story only because of the number of text messages from around the country the Falcons' Ike Reese received following the game.

What follows is Reese's account of his flattening of poor Miles Austin that Saturday night at the Georgia Dome:

It set up so perfectly. They ran a similar return after we scored. I'm coming downfield. I figured out who's blocking me and so I'm going to set up that blocker. I'm pushing him wide to the right, acting like I'm going to stay to the right. Meanwhile, I know at the last minute I'm cutting to the left. It worked out just how I had hoped. I see the wedge coming. I could see that I'm able to slide right in behind. I'm an old man now, mind you, but I got a good jump. I'm actually out in front. I have to slow down to let the guy on my team have the wedge pick him up.

So I slow down just a little. I allow him to pass me. I cut off his back hip and slide. Then everything slows down. Totally slow-motion type of thing. All I see is his upper torso and his head and the arm carrying the ball. It's in his left hand. It's one of the rare times in my career that I see it so clearly and I'm able to form up the way they teach you and explode into the tackle. I left my feet like a rocket. I push everything into him. I caught him under his chin. I got my face mask on his shoulder blade. I extend my arms through him. I knocked him off his feet. One of those things where I can read the bottom of his shoes. I hit him so hard the arm with the ball in it stayed close to his chest, trapping it there. I didn't even feel it. I hit him flush, just like when you hit a golf ball and you don't feel like you hit it and it goes three hundred yards.

As soon as I hit him, I'm thinking the ball is out. I immediately get up and spin my head to see where the ball is. I heard the crowd say, "Oooooooh! Aaaaawww!" They saw it coming. I went into my celebration. My teammates are slapping me on the head. You could feel the electricity. It was one of those where everybody's like, "Whoooaa!"

I got my little cheer for six, seven seconds. I saw him get up, chin strap turned, helmet turned. His teammates have a hold of him, holding him up. Then I see him try to jog off and he's got that swerve-left as he heads to the sidelines.

I actually sought him out after the game. I said, "I didn't mean to have to kill you. My bad, man."

He said, "You got me!"

After the game, I went to check my phone and I had like fifteen, twenty text messages all saying they had seen the hit and I killed that guy.

After that game, Ike Reese and Miles Austin went their separate ways. Reese retired after that 2006 season, and Austin blossomed into a terrific wide receiver for the Dallas Cowboys, becoming one of Tony Romo's favorite targets. Their paths had crossed for that one brief moment.

Two passing ships.

Until a chance encounter in Las Vegas in March 2009. An oil company in Texas seeking investors sponsored a weekend junket for newly retired players and current players. So that Saturday morning following a night of revelry, Reese, Austin, and a small group of players lounged by the pool at the Bellagio.

Austin finally brought it up. "Dude, you killed me that night."

Reese just smiled. That's all he wanted.

The acknowledgment.

That's what the human part of the game is, you know? Bragging rights and one-ups, and remember this? And remember that? Because while everyone else forgets, players cling to their memories tighter than the money they made playing the game.

Diamond Girl

The real kill shot occurs on the quarterback. The poor, vulnerable quarterback left prone to a mad rusher from the blind side or under a complete jailbreak of snorting blitzers, as he tries gamely to hold on to the football long enough to deliver it at just the right time.

Ten concussions for Troy Aikman. Four liters of blood flowing into Drew Bledsoe's chest cavity. One badly mangled leg for Joe Theismann.

The Quarterback Kill Shot has left a trail of broken bodies.

For defensive players, most notably the rushing ends and blitzing linebackers, they recall each one they ever made in great detail. Somewhere in their backyard is a tree with etch marks on the trunk. Bill Romanowski turns giddy when asked about his.

Super Bowl XXXIII. His Broncos against Atlanta. The Falcons driving. Deep in Denver territory. Third down. Blitz.

The blitz was called Venus, which called for Romanowski and the cornerback to shoot after Atlanta quarterback Chris Chandler.

The Falcons' line tried to stiffen. The back staying home picked up the dashing corner. But Romanowski was disguised in the middle and he barreled through untouched on Chandler.

"And I just plastered him," he said. "To make them kick a field goal was huge for us. I nailed [Chandler] so hard that after the hit he wasn't the same. What that does to a team and momentum is huge. It really changes things."

And it feels so good. The way it did the time he fired off the outside edge on the right side on another blitz and the tackle turned to pick up someone else and set him free on another vulnerable quarterback.

Kerry Collins hurried to throw. He didn't have time to gather himself for the hit.

"I knew I was gonna nail him," Romanowski said. "I don't think you know how hard you're actually going to hit him. When he threw the ball I really nailed him. Literally his face mask was broken and his jaw was shattered and blood spilled from his mouth. I hit him so hard that everybody in that stadium heard that hit, and my teammates went nuts."

Such a play can paralyze a quarterback, particularly a young one. One devastating hit and they suddenly become St. Vitus skittish, stricken with a bad case of happy feet. Rushing their reads. Hurrying their throws.

"Quarterbacks are all scared," Hugh Douglas said. "When you do it right and hit a quarterback from the blind side—when you hit him in the small of the back and catch him just right and knock the air out of him and make him gasp—all day long he's not right. Then I'd taunt him and just say, 'Here I come. On my way to get you.'"

Then you're in his head. Messing with him.

The way Douglas did with poor Cade McNown during one game in 2000, his second and only season as the Bears' starting quarterback. The Eagles defense had battered McNown all afternoon long, working him over in an unspeakable manner. It was the kind of game all young quarterbacks must endure, lost in a wilderness tracked by wolves, praying each play call is not pass. Down in the game, blitzers loose, play moving too fast to decipher, McNown could only wish to be back in a Pac-10 place like Pullman, placid and familiar, instead of here, white-knuckle quarterbacking in the middle of jailbreak.

UCLA-quarterback smart, he understood the temporary dynamics of his situation and the need to experience firsthand this field of dread. Still, he must have thought, these growing pains leave marks.

Following yet another devastating hit that left McNown sprawled on the ground, grabbing at his helmet to make sure his head was still intact, Douglas leaned down close and told him, "You're my Diamond Girl."

"You can tell when a quarterback gets scared," Joey Porter said. "They get that look about them and they get all jittery. That's what you want them to feel—fear. You don't ever want them to get into a comfort zone. Get them jittery and they'll make simple mistakes."

It happens quite often nowadays in the age of spread the field and throw. The rules make it too attractive to chuck it fifty times a game. Three yards and a cloud of dust departed with the Mallory fedora hat. The coach now wears a hoodie.

Veteran Jeff Garcia said he purposely will put on a swagger during that nightmare scenario for every quarterback: down and desperate in the fourth quarter, the only option left to throw:

That's nut-check time. Gotta step up and be a man. If it means holding on to the ball until the last second—when you know you're going to get slammed. That's what separates the gamers and the guys that are out of the league. Guys who have been backups a long time it's because when there isn't any pressure they can look like millionaire quarterbacks. But when it comes to making plays that's when they shrivel up.

You look at the quarterbacks who always rise to the top—the Peyton Mannings and Tom Bradys—they come up big at crunch time. They have quality players around them. You can't do it alone. You have to have complete trust in your teammates. You have to know they're going to die for you. That's when those situations become fun. That every guy is going to do whatever it takes to win.

A way for a quarterback to prove his worthiness is to always stay in the game. That's what happened during a Monday Night Football game against Carolina—Garcia's first start replacing the injured Donovan McNabb in 2006—and the 350-pound Kris Jenkins picked him up and body-slammed him to the ground, flopping all of his force on the much smaller man's stomach.

"That left a lasting impression," Garcia said. "I had the wind knocked out. That struggle on the ground I remember being a tough one. And you know, you have limited time to recover. It's not easy.

You're trying to get your bearings back and recover enough to spit some words out in the huddle. Looking back on it, I needed a couple of plays to pull it together to be functional. But at the point in my season, the fans didn't know a lot about me. I felt like I needed to prove to the fans and my teammates that I wasn't going to allow them or anyone else to take me out of that game."

Crime Scene

The running back sweeps to the right, scoots through the line, and attempts to dodge the linebacker and safety who await him with arms wide open. He feels the contact first and the panic next, when he realizes he doesn't feel the ball in his arm.

It's a moment every skill player dreads.

Oh, God, no. Where is it?

Fumble.

The ball is bouncing somewhere. Somewhere unprotected. Somewhere dangerous, free for anyone on the defense to steal.

Someone jumps on it. You can't tell exactly who. Whether it's back in safe arms or the enemy's clutches. Someone else jumps in. Then another and another. Members of both teams diving into the fray. It's now a pile. A bundled mass of flesh. Arms and legs squirting out from within.

From above, it looks like a mass grave, only with desperate movement. From deep inside, it feels like a coffin. Tight and constricted and smothering. But it's worse, because things are going inside this pile. Very bad things.

"Inhumane things," Anthony Becht said. "I remember one against Atlanta. We really needed the ball and guys are grabbing all parts of the body. Doing anything to get the ball back. You could hear guys screaming. I wasn't even in the pile, but I knew by the sounds how nasty it was in there."

Added former offensive tackle Orlando Brown, "Pinching, spitting, punching, all that shit happens in there. I stay away from the pile. I've told coaches, 'I'll wreck some people, but I ain't falling on that football.' Fingers are broken all the time. I'm hitting motherfuckers. I ain't laying on the ball. I can't see who's coming to hit me, so I just clean up the pile."

Ike Reese told of a harrowing experience trying to recover a Brian Westbrook fumble during a punt return against the Patriots.

"Mike Vrabel grabbed my sac," Reese said. "We're all scrambling for the ball and Mike Vrabel had my nuts so hard I was screaming. I didn't even have the ball. He had my shit in his hands and he's squeezing. We don't wear cups. So I'm dying. Everything is fair game. The pile clears and I see him—now Mike, he's an Ohio guy, and I played against him at Ohio State when I was at Michigan State—and he's smiling and shit at me. I turned to him and said, 'You fuckin' asshole.'"

Said Simeon Rice, "I got the ball once and landed on it, and it knocked the wind out of me. I'm on the bottom and guys are grabbing groins. That shit is dumb as fuck. It's all a part of the game, I guess. The aggressive nature is a part of the game and so is getting away with it. But that's not football. That's stupidity."

"That's what happens when you have six hundred pounds all on top of you," Kevin Long said. "Ball grabbing happens all the time. You can constantly hear players bitching about their balls getting grabbed. But the worst is your hand around the pile. People step on your hands all the time with a seven-spike cleat. That's the big thing—fingers getting broken all the time in the pile."

Steve Wisniewski called the pile the most dangerous play in football. "You try and dive in those piles and everyone is trying to get at that ball and it gets real nasty in there," he said. "Every form of martial art is fair game. Pulling fingers. Poking you in the eyes. Absolutely anything necessary to get the ball. Be proactive and get the ball first was the approach I always took with the pileups."

One player said, "The worst is the pinching. You wouldn't expect it. But it really hurts. Guys are pinching guys in piles. That happens. Hurts like hell if you get the right spot. In back of the knee. Or they get the soft spot on your calf and just pinch the hell out of it. Pinching people. Fucking with people down in the bottom of the pile.

"Anything goes down there. You feel a thumb, you yank on it. Pull it and bend it back. Work the ball out. You can't grip the ball if someone is bending your thumb. Just grab something and start twisting. The officials aren't going to say anything, even if they see it. Grabbing balls is a defense mechanism. Now, spitting on people. That's very low. Spitting on someone is disrespecting someone."

"You name it," Benji Olson said with a smirk, "it's been done in the pile. I've had the ball and guys are kicking your fingers, breaking your fingers."

Added Mike Mamula, "Fumbles become survival of the fittest. Five people all trying their damnedest to rip that ball away from you. The thing I remember the most is the amount of pressure on you from every single angle. You have that attitude. You're trying to earn a living, it's a you-against-them type of mentality. Sometimes you get caught up and you try and get a job done. Bending back fingers. Twisting ankles. You don't even think about what you're doing in there. You're just trying your hardest to get the ball."

Mamula paused and warned of this next tale from the pile. "It's pretty gross," he said. "Happened [at Boston College]. There was a fumble around the goal line and my two roommates at the time ended up throwing up in each other's mouths trying to get the ball out of the pile."

Meanwhile, Chris Samuels spoke of his Alabama days. Crimson Tide against Florida at the Swamp. 'Bama trails by a touchdown early in the fourth quarter and is punting the ball back to the Gators.

Muff.

"It was a madhouse to that ball," Samuels said. "It was such a crucial point in the game and our team knew it. Our young bucks out there on special teams did great. Like three or four of them ended squeezing the punt returner's nuts until he coughed up the ball. I was so proud of the young guys out there, doing whatever it takes to win the game. That's the attitude you want all your teammates to have."

Yes, acknowledged Reese, despite playing victim to Vrabel, you must do whatever it takes. "You're scrambling for the ball and you get a returner—even if you can't get to the ball—you dive on his back," he said. "Forearm on the back of his neck. Grind him to the ground. I've poked guys in the eyes." Namely Reggie Swinton, a former return man for the Cowboys.

"We were smashing them pretty good and we kicked off and Sheldon Brown blasted him," Reese said. "Everybody's trying to cover the ball. I got Swinton. I'm on top of him. Holding him down. I'm sticking my fingers in his eyes. Pokin' 'em in and out."

"Yeah, bitch," he told Swinton, "it's gonna be like this all day with your punk ass."

"Got to do it," Reese continued. "Get him scared. If you get him scared, they're not thinking about securing the football. Get him worried about the hit as opposed to running. I did Tiki Barber like that. He fumbled four times against us. We lost 10–7 in the Meadowlands. He killed us. He rushed for, like, 200 yards.

"Anyway, he fumbled a punt return and I remember diving for the ball. He's at the bottom of the pile. So I get the heel of my hand under his face mask and I'm bending the face mask. I'm really bending his neck back—and back. Everything is fair game on the ground and scrambling. He was their starting tailback. You have a chance to hurt him—put him out of there—you do it."

Almost as disturbing is the sound that emanates from the pile. The shrieks. Bloodcurdling shrieks. The moaning. Men in pain crying out for help.

Now, it's impossible to police the pile, and you can't ask for decorum in the pile.

"If you break it down, recovering that ball could be the difference between winning and losing," Kevin Gogan said. "It could be the end of your season or your career. This is what's going on. My job is on the line. If I have to gouge or rip or pull, I'll do it. In the pile you don't even know who you're grabbing unless they wore different-colored pants. Now, if you're really into the game, sometimes it's not about getting the ball. Sometimes you have that radar of who you're going after and the pile is a great opportunity to get after them."

A player told me once that it's only dirty if you're the loser nursing swollen testicles, and then began a long diatribe about how the insatiable desire to win burns more in football than in any other game in which they keep score, because you ante up with your body. Because if you risk limb the only truly gratifying reward is victory.

"James Willis and I used to say every week, regardless of how the game is going, we're going to fight all the way to the parking lot," Douglas said. "We'll wash our ass, put our clothes on, and still fight. We were gonna whup somebody's ass. I felt like that every time I touched the field. I was mad. I wanted everybody else to be mad. You can't win on defense if you're not mad.

"We were tryin' to win. I always said it: Winner gets fucked by the prom queen. Champions fuck bad bitches."

Douglas then joked, "Hey, at the end of the day, we do what we do because we want to do the do. You can say what you want, but everybody upgraded female status playing football."

It makes a bit of sense to buy the player's argument for the idea of winning being strongest in football, especially if you factor in how unit always trumps individual and how that devalues the meaning of statistics, the great vanity plate of baseball and basketball.

Football cannot be defined by the sheer computing of passing yards and rushing yards and those YACs, despite the sweeping popularity of insidious fantasy football, something so antithetical to the game. So what if the quarterback throws for 400 junk yards, because his team fell behind by four touchdowns? And while those who travel significantly deeper than the box score may emerge wielding an acronym, however insightful, football is still not a sport ruled by a religion like sabermetrics. There are no OPBs and WHIPs, because a football player's individual success is directly linked to his teammates, which is why Tom Brady will buy his offensive line watches and steak dinners.

Meanwhile, scoring 30 a game or hitting .330 can somewhat pacify even the most ardent competitor and make them max-contract rich beyond belief—guaranteed rich, which is not the same in the NFL, even with the recent escalation of the salary cap and the up-front signing bonus. Fat designated hitters and stiff power forwards can earn up to ten times what, say, a Brian Westbrook will make, and over a much longer period of time considering the shelf life of a top-flight running back.

So peel the onion. The reckless attitude and bodily risk and trips to dark places appear in the name of winning.

"Yeah, that's how football is meant to be," Steve Wisniewski said. "It is a team game with many small battles within. I would shake anyone's hand after the game, and pray with them at midfield, but in the game everyone in a different-colored jersey is fair game. For sixty minutes, my job was to defend my quarterback and anyone else on my team against the other team."

In 1997, a *Sports Illustrated* poll of 150 NFL players named Wisniewski the dirtiest player in the league. His reputation was so bad, veteran Vikings long snapper Mike Morris told the magazine, "Wiz is a dirty bastard. He chops from behind. He'll shoot knees. I'll take sides with any old lineman, but this motherfucker had me cursing and swearing on TV. I couldn't believe the shots he took."

"I still think *Sports Illustrated* came up arbitrarily with the list," Wisniewski said. "My good friend Kevin Gogan got in the next year, and we thought it was comical. We were players that never cursed or swore, or took cheap shots. I think that a lot of the perception of offensive linemen being dirty came from the fact the linemen used to be really lazy. This was back in 1989 when these guys would take two- and three-step drops and quit on the play.

"I was lighter back then, around 282, and I would run downfield and help the running back or quarterback or receiver. I basically had a defensive mind-set. They never taught gang-blocking on offense, which is something I always believed they should. I would run downfield and take two or three players on. People would say that offensive linemen shouldn't be making plays downfield. I would say, 'Hey, man, the whistle hasn't blown. I can hit anyone until the whistle blows.' *Sports Illustrated* gave me that rep of being a dirty player because I finished plays."

Wisniewski continued, "We all expect middle linebackers to be physical. Why are offensive linemen perceived as dirty when they want to play the game like a linebacker? I wasn't dirty, but it was sure perceived as dirty. I didn't want defensive linemen to enjoy playing against me. I would cut hit him downfield until the whistle blew. Always play to the whistle. I just had the aura about me that I was going to hunt you down all over the field."

Well, defensive players definitely felt his aura, even Romanowski. "[Wisniewski's] a guy that reeled me into God," Romanowski said, "but out on the field he wanted to kill you. He and Gogan. Both of them. You couldn't stand around a pile without getting your head taken off."

Gogan—surprise—offered support for Wisniewski. "That attitude can be learned on the offensive line," he said. "You get one or two guys with that attitude and the next thing you know you have four or five guys with that same attitude. You have lazy guys in this league. When I got to the Raiders, I met Steve and Dan Turk and we were saying to each other, 'Let's go downfield and knock someone's head off.' That wasn't what the defensive backs wanted to hear and they complained to the refs and their coaches, and that was part of the reason we started getting called dirty.

"I've been to the officiating meetings and seen that side of the game. They highlighted us in film clips because they didn't like us going downfield and making that extra effort. We were doing nothing illegal. Now, we don't have high speeds and good brakes, so if we're busting our ass downfield and we're in midair and can't stop yourself, you're going to hit someone late. Steve brought incredible hustle to our teams and it was contagious. 'They' called it dirty, but we took the fines and kept hitting. Our style was not in the brochure."

Zeus: A Bad Man

One of the all-time dirty players played for only a short time, and perhaps that was best for the rest of the league.

They called him Zeus, and how fitting the nickname. You could envision him standing, striding forward, a thunderbolt leveled in his raised right hand. Mighty Zeus, ruler of the sky.

When asked about his once notorious play, Orlando Brown said exactly this:

The dirtiest thing that ever happened to me was this dude in college spit in my face. I got a cup on the sidelines and had my whole team spit in it. After the game, I walked up to that motherfucker and smacked him in the face with the cup and fucked that bitch up.

Whitney Pritchard on Jacksonville took my knees out from behind one play. It was an interception, and those are the fucking worst because the guys you've been beating on all day are looking for you on the interceptions and Pritchard went straight for my knees from behind and took them out. Man, that was a dirty fucking play.

Kevin Greene used to play a lot of psychological games. The madder they got the more they try and hurt you. They would blow me. "Oh Zeus, you're a madman. I can't get by you all day." They would suck my dick in hopes that I would stop beating on them. Kevin Greene came into my fucking locker room after a game and told me how bad I beat him down, just so that the next time we played I would take it a little easier on him. I couldn't fucking believe he came into my locker room.

That's my game, baby. Play hard, play dirty. I used to use a lot of mental stuff.

It was great for me because I can't be like that in the streets. I would go to jail if I did what I did on the field in the streets. That's why I love the game. I played the game to hurt your ass.

Coaches used to tell me, "Zeus, somebody is gonna shoot you. You're too angry. You're hurting people out there." I can fight all fucking day on the field.

On interceptions, motherfuckers would be licking their chops to get at me. Shaun King lit me up one time and all I saw was the sky. I felt like I was in the air for two minutes before I hit the ground. I said, "I'm gonna get your ass." The coaches on the sideline were all like, *"Damn!"* They never saw me get popped like that.

I hurt a lot of players. Some guy on Pittsburgh—I can't remember his name—grabbed my nuts on a run block and tried to take me down. I got him down and got on his ass. I'd never experienced some gay shit like that before. I was pissed. After the game, I went to try and find that motherfucker. Security had to pull me away from him. I wanted to kill him.

At 6-foot-7, 350 pounds, Orlando Brown was a skyscraper of a man. And he possessed a bravado that matched his size, along with the irreverence of a man-god, all of which made him the perfect offensive tackle.

"I would play with a prison attitude," says Brown. "Only the strong survive in this game."

And Zeus thrived with that mentality until that winter day in Cleveland, December 19, 1999, when he was struck in the right eye by the weighted penalty flag of an official. That was the day that everyone recalls when the subject turns to Zeus. The day official Jeff Triplette accidentally threw the flag and it flew like a homing pigeon for Brown's eye.

Brown charged Triplette.

Wounded and enraged, clawing at his eye, he staggered at the man in stripes, arms flailing. Several Browns were needed to escort Brown away from Triplette and back into the locker room for treatment.

What a frightening sight.

Peter King, the extraordinary football scribe, wrote of the incident, "And if he hadn't been stopped by teammates, Brown might have done worse [to Triplette]. I can only say that when it happened, I reacted as if I'd just seen a plane crash. This just never happens. Literally. The wind got sucked out of me, and out of most of the crowd, I assume."

Brown was suspended by then commissioner Paul Tagliabue. He had also suffered serious damage to his eye and sued the league for $200 million, settling out of court for reportedly close to $20 million.

"The infamous eye, ah, yes," Brown told me during the summer of 2008. "It took a referee to hurt me. That was the only injury that hurt me. They say my knees are like a twenty-one-year-old's. I ain't bone on bone yet. I still got lots of cartilage left in there. I wanna get back out there and play, man, but I can't because I sued the league. The Ravens want me back. Ray Lewis tells me to come back all the time, but I can't, man."

Though in fairness, four years after the incident he did return to the league. He played for the Ravens from 2003 through 2005 but wasn't the man they called Zeus.

Ray Lewis called him the ultimate gladiator. Former Rams coach Mike Martz said he couldn't think of a single football player like him.

At the height of his playing days, Brown knew how to melt men the way Mike Tyson did before Buster Douglas.

"My worst thing would be the day before games," Brown said. "I would dream about how I was going fuck the other team up. When we played Pittsburgh, I told Troy Polamalu, 'I like your hair. I'm gonna make you my bitch. I see that pretty hair sticking out your head I'm gonna rip you down. I'm gonna take that hair down and take some of that home with me.'

"I see a chain on a defensive lineman, I'm gonna get that mother-fucker. I got the chain. I would tell the line I'm gonna go get whoever's chain and I would come back to the huddle and show everyone the chain. I would tell the motherfucker whose chain it was to come and get it. I would stick the chain in my drawers and tell them to come and get it. After the games I would shake everyone's hand, but the young guys would avoid me because they thought I was crazy."

He recalled telling Dwight Freeney, the great Colts defensive end, "I'm gonna break you, bitch. I don't play football, motherfucker, I fight!"

"You make them play to you," he said. "Don't worry about his spin move. He's gonna worry about my fist in his throat. You think a fucking five-yard penalty is gonna stop me? I don't give a fuck about that penalty! I'm gonna break your nose!

"I used to hold him all day. You have to hold. I would be grabbing them by the throat, punching them in the face, throat, head, face mask. Anything to piss them off. Anytime you can get someone pissed off it takes them off their game just a little bit."

Zeus sprang on the scene in 1994 from, of all places, South Carolina State.

"Bill Belichick and Scott Paoli came to my college to work out a defensive end," he said. "I wasn't even on anyone's radar. 'You ain't a fucking pro prospect,' they told me. I worked out for them anyway, and [Belichick] wouldn't even let me change my clothes. I ended up running a 40 in my underwear. I ran something like a 5.7 in the 40.

"They said, 'You don't have shit.' They wanted me to quit. He set up a camera and I ran the camera over and told him that's what I do right there. I fucking ruined their camera. They told me, 'Ain't nobody like you, Zeus.'"

Today Orlando Brown professes his sweetness as he proudly mans the grill at the Fat Burger franchise he owns in Washington, D.C. Such a long way from the game now, Brown still looks back fondly on the days Zeus terrorized the league.

"I used to leg whup a lot and take motherfuckers down by sweeping out their legs," Brown said. "I learned how to dislocate shoulders— grab the arm in the right place and fall to the ground on my ass and rip that shoulder out.

"Belichick wouldn't let me practice with pads because I was fucking up my own teammates so bad. He developed the toughness in me. He wouldn't let me be on the practice squad because he knew I would get snatched up by another team.

"I would go against defensive end Rob Bennett in practice every day. I don't have any equipment on. I would be like, 'Coach, man, c'mon, I don't have any pads on.' I grew up next to a crack house, man. I got fucking bruises everywhere. Most of my abuse came from practice. I learned the tricks and it was payback. Bennett took off practice for the rest of the week because he was getting too beat up in practice and had to save himself for the game."

The Wrath of Mike Sellers

Dirty play resides in the eye of the accuser. Defensive linemen call offensive linemen dirty. Running backs call linebackers dirty. Receivers call safeties dirty. Cornerbacks call receivers dirty. There is also a great contradiction when it comes to what is dirty play and what isn't.

"You have to play the game mean," linebacker Joey Porter said. "Helps you stay on edge. You can never let your guard down on the football field. Cheap shots can come from anywhere, at any time. You have to be ready at all times. Stuff happens after the whistle, during the whistle. Gotta know what a guy is doing. How he's acting. If he's trying to get you to fall for something. Maybe he's smiling at you one play, trying to get you to think he's got something on you, trying to get you to fall for something. You gotta be aware.

"I have to play with a chip on my shoulder. I look for everything. When I'm alert, I'm in the game. You know what it is? There are no friends out here. Maybe after the game but not on the field. It's a contact sport. Guys do down. You get injured. One play can be your career."

Simeon Rice talks like a witness to a homicide while relaying a story involving Warren Sapp playing against the Eagles. "I've seen things," he said. "It was the Eagles. They were a nasty team and [Sapp] was getting hit late all game. I mean, he was getting kicked after plays. It was the worst I ever saw anyone get treated on a football field. Just nasty, foul play, in an overly aggressive manner. I mean, he got his eye gouged. That's not football, man. That's UFC shit. Now, he was getting it due to things he might have said.

"It is a full-contact game. It's hard to discriminate. It's so finite. It's a microscopic thing, dirty play. You can see it on the playing field. He was kicked on the ground. Just a bad display. Those players were definitely harboring some ill will towards Warren due to the things he was saying. I mean, his eye was so bad that after the game he couldn't even open it. It's a violent game but that was ridiculous."

Meanwhile, Brian Mitchell tabbed Sapp as his most infernal player. "He would be spitting and doing girlie shit like that," he said. "We were in each other's faces after a play talking shit to one another, and that motherfucker spit in my face. I said, 'Don't you worry, big man, I'm gonna get you back.'"

During the interviews, many players were asked to name the dirtiest player they ever played against.

"Rodney Harrison," Benji Olson said. "He's probably going to show up on a lot of players' lists. He's always hitting after the play. He would always be hitting guys around the pile. He caught me a couple of times after the play. Some guys play to the whistle, but Rodney was always a little more late with his contact. Funny thing is that he's always calling players dirty when in fact he is one of the dirtiest."

Mike Sellers's name came up often during the conversation. Sellers, a 6-foot-5, 260-pound fullback for the Redskins, nicknamed "the Tank," is known to stalk the field looking to maul the opponent's best special teams player.

"Mike Sellers, I can't stand that guy," Jason Short said. "He spit in my face on a special teams play. Man, I was hot. They mentioned it on TV because all they saw was me on the sidelines losing it. I spent the whole rest of the game trying to spit back in his face. He totally got me out of my game. But he had three personal fouls that game—which sure helped us win the game.

"A lot of junk goes on in the game. It was funny, the first time I had a clean shot of spitting in his face my mouth guard was in and it didn't exactly work. The second time around I made sure I took out my mouthpiece and got him back. Man, was he pissed. He got in my face and was pushing me around, and he got a personal foul for that."

Ike Reese also had several run-ins on special teams with Sellers and his partner in crime, Peppi Zellner, a 6-foot-5, 270-pound defensive end.

"These cats knew I was the best cover guy and they were after me," Reese said. "They played us twice a year so they'd pick up your tendencies. Here's this 260-pound beast running at you full speed trying to run you over. The whole time I'm thinking, 'I can't let these cats get their hands on me and get me to the ground.'"

The ground is a terrible place, one without mercy.

"Once you're on the ground," Reese said, "you get a forearm on your throat. You're pinned down and can't move. You feel like you're dying. You know they're not going to kill you. You know they're going to get up off you. They're not trying to literally kill you. But they're trying to hurt you. And you have all of this equipment on and you've been wrestling and you just ran forty yards and you're winded and you got somebody that big on top of you crushing your larynx.

"You want to do something to him for real. You're like, 'I'm gonna see your ass after the game.' I'm 6-foot-3, 230 pounds and I'm strong. I can lift weights with the best of them. Some of the cats are so big and ridiculously strong. Like He-Man [cartoon character]. And a lot of it is leverage. You're at their mercy."

Hardly a surprise, Bill Romanowski proved a popular choice among those who played against him, since he ranks as perhaps the most infamous player since the widespread state-pen pigskin that marked the 1970s era, led by the hooligan Oakland Raiders. Sick, demented, merciless Romo, they called him, while making offhanded cracks about steroids.

"Almost from the time I was a Denver Bronco on—every week, every game I was called a dirty player," Romanowski said. "I would use that to my advantage and that dark place I went to. I could reach up under the face mask and try to choke them."

He once spit in the face of 49ers receiver J. J. Stokes. "That was the only time I did that where I regretted it," Romanowski said. "He was talking shit about what a dirty player I was. What spurred that on was that I was so pissed off that he caught a ball around me and I tried to grab his nuts and break them off."

He once snapped the finger of Giants running back Dave Meggett. "I was in a pile trying to rip it off his hand, and I cracked it like a chicken bone," he said.

He threatened to maim Jonathan Avery of the Dolphins. "I hit him over the middle and then we're standing face mask to face mask," Romanowski said, "and I screamed in his face, 'I am gonna hurt you!' It was my most violent voice ever. Scariest voice I've ever heard out of myself. The darkest place I could ever go to. Anything I could do to get in someone's head I would do. It's all about winning the individual battles, which then in turn helps your team win the game. A lot of times you knew if you could get in someone's head. I heard [Avery] say later that the meanest guy he ever went against was me."

Read those words closely and you hear his pride. Affect the game. Lift your team. Whatever it takes.

Ultimately, Romanowski reached the point where Broncos coach Mike Shanahan warned him that the league would suspend him after his next "dirty play."

"Absolutely, it is a constant struggle," he said. "I was worked up about it. I was talking to my wife, Julia, and I told her I can't care about that stuff. That I can't change the way I play. That if they fine me, then so be it, they fine me."

Tight end Anthony Becht, formerly of the Jets, spoke with admiration of his physical encounters with Romanowski, singling out the year his New York team played at Denver in the AFC Championship Game.

"We played three times in eight months and Romanowski was all over me," he said. "He was hitting me from the back, stuff that had nothing to do with the play. On one crossing route completely away from the ball, he's elbowing me in the face. He would always take the extra shot trying to gain that mental edge. The next time I came back with a different style and I learned from that experience. I was a product of what he brought to the field. I couldn't wait to get back out there and give him his own medicine. Everyone wants that guy on their team."

Romanowski told his version of the encounter with Becht. "He cheap-shotted me with a push during a game," he said. "He got me. They didn't throw the ball his way and he pushed me and I went down. I got up and I told him, 'I will kill you! I will ruin your life! You will never ever touch me again like that!'

"Earlier in the season when we played the Jets, I had kicked his ass. I just nailed him so many times early in the game, he basically started going out of his way to get me. He had a holding penalty and went offsides like three times. In the playoffs I was covering him, I turned, and he nailed me to get back at me. I took him off his game and that ended up helping my team [get to the Super Bowl]."

So who was Romanowski's nominee?

"I would say Erik Williams, Cowboys," Romanowski said. "That man wanted to hurt you on every play. He was just an angry, mean son of a bitch. Whatever he could to do to hurt you he would do it. In the Pro Bowl, normally it's about taking it easy. Most guys are just trying to have fun. Well, he wanted to hurt you in the Pro Bowl."

Said Ike Reese, "We played the Cowboys on a Monday night and Erik Williams had Mamula and Jon Harris scared to go play that night. I saw Erik Williams punch Mamula in the back of the head on two consecutive plays. Right out there in the open—after the pass rush, while the play was downfield and Mamula was facing the play, and Erik banged him right in the back of the head."

Mamula didn't acknowledge any fear in playing against Williams, but he did say the Cowboys tackle easily stood out as a diabolical player during their twice-a-year meetings.

"He kept giving me extra shots after the plays and I was getting so pissed," he said. "I finally decided to take it to the ref and tell him to watch Williams because he kept getting me after the play. So now one play when I know the ref is watching I give Erik a shot in the throat right at the whistle—which the ref missed—but Erik got so pissed that he ended up taking a swing at me and sure enough the ref was watching that. He ended up getting kicked out of the game and was bitching and hollering his whole way off the field. I tried to spend as little time as possible locked up with the offensive linemen and those types of dirty players."

"I don't look at players as dirty," Simeon Rice said. "I never came across anyone that played against me dirty. They do what they need to do to get their job done. Guys always do things to try and take away speed and take away power. If guys are playing dirty, it's because they are trying to make up for a lack of skill and they're trying to level out the playing field."

Rationalization runs like a river through this subject. Anything to Win is the only commandment to memorize.

According to Kevin Gogan, no such line regarding conduct exists. "I tried to bring the fight to them, physically and mentally," he said. "So with my style of play, I never really thought of anyone as dirty. There's nothing shocking out there. It was war and a battle, and if you weren't pushing the envelope a little bit then you shouldn't be playing the game."

A Tax Write-off

The letterhead is official-looking, with the NFL logo at the top of the page and the date below the words "National Football League," and it's addressed to him in care of the Philadelphia Eagles. It begins pleasantly enough and quickly turns unnerving, just the way a Dear John letter would.

According to players, nothing stamped with the official logo could provide anything but angst, and by the way, it's written in such a stolid manner and signed with that fake "sincerely." Why not just write it in the appropriate blood and say what it is?

Just say we're taking your money.

Nowadays, the players bemoan, the league will look at the film on Monday and levy a fine, even if the infraction wasn't called a penalty on the field.

One player earned $19,000 for a divisional playoff game and was fined the exact same amount for a late hit.

Except what he earned was gross pay, and fines come off the net. The only silver lining for the players is that fine money goes to NFL charities, so they can write it off come tax time and recoup roughly 30 percent.

"I've been fined seven times in my career and it's $5,000 every time," said Jason Short, who ranked at the bottom of the NFL's pay scale. "Sometimes they say this one thing happened, something as simple as a face-mask, and you're getting fined. The refs can go back and look at tapes and pick up things that you'll get fined for. Any personal foul whatsoever and you're getting fined.

"We were involved in that pregame fight with Atlanta [to open the 2005 season], and I was fined and I wasn't even doing anything. If you're just in the fight zone, regardless of whether or not you're fighting, you're getting fined. [One of the combatants, Jeremiah] Trotter got $10,000 for that. I got $5,000."

Steve Wisniewski once racked up $65,000 worth of fines in one season. Kevin Gogan lost his Pro Bowl check for fighting and was fined a total of $20,000 in one game for various offenses, including one called "the Knife," where he and Wisniewski simulated one guy blocking a defensive lineman while the other guy cut him up and cut out his legs.

Chris Samuels said he got fined for that chop block on Chicago's Antonio Garay. "Got me for $12,500," he said. "Man, that's a lot of money for a clean play with bad results. Hopefully I can get some of that back. I am appealing that one. It's funny, our center Casey Rabach said he would actually help me pay half of the fine. When I told him how much the fine was, he kind of shied away from me."

Gogan chimed in by saying, "They should throw the dollar symbol out instead of penalty flags. There's no question that the violence sells."

Turley received a whopping $25,000 fine after a highly publicized incident in 2001 in which he attacked the Jets' Damien Robinson while attempting to aid his quarterback Aaron Brooks.

It was a wild scene that night at the Superdome. Trailing 16–9, the Saints had driven to the New York 6-yard line with inside of a minute left in the game. On second-and-3, Brooks rushed to the 5, where he was met by Robinson, who grabbed the quarterback's face mask and refused to let go.

"He was twisting Aaron Brooks's head off," Turley recalled. "The refs were blowing the whistle and he took it too far. I was standing right over top of the play. He was bending his helmet backwards. I'm screaming for him to stop it. Then Aaron let out a shriek I've never heard before on a football field."

And Turley lost it.

In a blind rage, he jumped into the mix of players and pulled Robinson off of Brooks by the face mask. He threw Robinson to the ground and kept tugging until he finally tore his helmet off and emerged with it in his hand. Blond hair flowing, his bare arms covered in tattoos, Turley looked like a Viking warrior as he held the helmet up toward the crowd like a trophy head and hurled it downfield before making an obscene gesture.

"I flipped out," he said. "I tried to choke him to death and I threw the helmet. I was taught to protect my linemen and my quarterback. I took it a little too far. But it looked like he was going to break his neck or back. He just wouldn't stop twisting his neck. Luckily Aaron didn't hurt anything too bad."

Both Turley and Robinson received offsetting personal foul penalties, but Turley drew another flag for tossing the helmet and making the obscene gesture, and was ejected from the game. The penalty pushed the Saints back to the 20-yard line and cost New Orleans a chance at winning the game.

To make matters worse, the game was being televised nationally on ESPN's *Sunday Night Football*. He became the subject of talk shows across the country as well as fodder for mainstream news programming, and was castigated publicly by his general manager, Randy Mueller.

While Turley admitted the next day that he needed to refrain from such an emotional outburst, he refused to apologize for defending his quarterback and "trying to, basically, from my point of view, save his life."

In addition to the hefty fine and the anger management classes he was forced by the club to attend, Turley now had to overcome a stigma that lasted his entire career.

"The teams I played on after that, guys thought I was an asshole before they even met me," he said. "Then you're not and they're like, 'Wow, you're a great guy.' All people saw when they saw me was me throwing the helmet.

"People don't understand how you can be one way on the field and off the field you're the complete opposite. What they see on a game day is what they perceive you as. You flip a switch when you cross that field line. You become a different person. My wife has never seen that look in my eye off the field."

Clemency Prohibited

The mind-set of the player is fascinating when it comes to determining what crosses that line into scurrilous play. For instance, attacking a player's injury is deemed a necessary evil, a by-product of winning football, and in fact it's encouraged.

"If you knew somebody was hurt, say, playing with tender ribs," Hugh Douglas said, "than you'd tenderize those ribs. Try to get him off the field. We tried to do that to Marshall Faulk once."

Gamesmanship, they argue.

While a member of the Falcons, Reese tells of purposely attacking the sore ankle of Cadillac Williams, then a rookie running back with Tampa Bay.

"I got him down by his legs on a tackle and somebody got him at the top," he said. "As I was getting up, I got up right on top of him. I stepped right on that bad ankle. We know which one hurts. We can see it all taped up."

"Ahhhh, get the fuck off my ankle," Reese recalls Williams shrieking.

"Oh, my bad, man," Reese told him.

"It's always common with the running backs, whether it's the knee or the ankle that's hurt, you go for it," he said. "You give an extra twist when you're making a shoestring tackle. You gotta go for that. That's what you want him thinking about—the injury, not securing the ball."

Reese said Emmitt Thomas, an NFL assistant coach for six different teams over the past twenty-six years, a former standout defensive back for the Chiefs, and a recent inductee into the Hall of Fame, taught his players that when quarterbacks and wide receivers ran out of bounds to dive at their knees. Don't let them get out of bounds without taking a shot. Because in the back of their mind, it will stick with them and interrupt instinctual play.

"Yeah, you have to know if your opponent has a sore knee," Wisniewski said. "Then you try to cut block him just to get him thinking about it. Not once was anyone carted off the field playing against me. Your goal was not to hurt them but rather just to get them thinking about their injury."

Wisniewski recalls playing against Bruce Smith in 1991 after the legendary defensive end was coming off major knee surgery. Wisniewski and Bruce Wilkerson drove Smith into the ground, and after the play, knowing Smith was within earshot, Wilkerson said, "Which knee is it, Steve? The right one? Oh, okay."

Wisniewski quotes Smith as saying, "Ah, man, come on. I can't believe you would go after my knee like that."

"We weren't planning on going after his knees at all," Wisniewski said, "but for the rest of the day we had one of the greatest pass rushers in history thinking about his knees.

"[This] is an extremely physical sport and any mental edge you can get is a big one. You get them thinking. You don't actually have to go after it.

"There are two types of mind-sets going against great players like that. One is that you can pat him on the ass after the play and hope that he takes it easy on you the rest of the day. Or the second one, which is the approach I usually took, is to punch him in the mouth the first play of the game and let him know you're there."

Chris Samuels is not a big trash talker, but he will tell an opponent, "You better watch your knees!"

Said Samuels, "I really don't tend to play dirty like that. If it's a knee injury I'll cut at his legs a little—but just to get him thinking about it. That will be enough to slow him down mentally. If you have him slowed down mentally, then naturally he'll slow down physically."

Benji Olson said, "If a guy's got a sore something, you tend to pick on that. More than anything I would start chirping in their ear a little bit and try and get them thinking about it. I don't try and change anything I normally do because that's when you get caught and screw up yourself. I would just ask them throughout the course of the game how their injury was feeling."

Added Rice, "That's the game of football. Exploiting your opponent's weakness. You want to take advantage of an obvious situation. If a guy has a cast on his hand you focus on that. If it's an ankle, you play with more pressure. You play with a more violent intent to get the job done—within the rules."

Orlando Brown said that if a player is banged up, "Oh yeah, you know that I'm going to work on that. Jevon Kearse's back was bothering him one time so I was trying to twist his spine up all game long. That boy hates playing hurt, and I did my homework.

"Reggie White's knee was hurting him bad once. He said, 'Ah, young buck, you coming after my knee, huh?' I said, 'No disrespect, Reg, because you the man.' But fuck that, he knew I was coming at him."

Meanwhile, Kevin Gogan used to take the opposite approach if his opponent was playing injured. Instead of attacking him, he'd lull the player into a false sense of security.

"The card I used to play in my mind was keeping this guy in the game for as long as I can," he said. "I'd even take it easy on him a little bit in the beginning of the game to make him think that he's all right, when, in fact, he's not playing at a hundred percent. I'd rather face an unhealthy starter than face some twenty-year-old kid with all the energy in the world trying to prove himself."

Field Snapshot: There May Live No Saints on Defense

The Saints were up by two touchdowns with Drew Brees and the potent offense on the field driving for more early in the fourth quarter of a week 2 game at Philadelphia when defensive coordinator Gregg Williams approached his unit, now sitting confidently on the bench.

Now, we must preface Williams's words with the backstory of the Saints defense, a definite sore spot the previous few years in New

Orleans, and Williams—known as something of a defensive guru—was brought in to fix it.

So the lesson undoubtedly centered on the mentality of playing defense. How you never let up playing defense and how you never, ever show mercy.

Williams, who coached without teeming emotion, the way it's coming out now in buckets, had noticed Philadelphia trainers across the field working on star running back Brian Westbrook.

"They're taping Westbrook's ankle over there," Williams yelled. "I want you to rip that motherfucker off! If you get a shot, hit him with your helmet. Hit that thing! Hit it! I want you to twist it! Rip the damn ankle off his leg!"

Only the Pact Can Help You Sleep

It was an accident, Chris Samuels swears. He didn't mean to put Antonio Garay's career in jeopardy.

The linebacker was supposed to hit the A gap but at the last minute veered away and Samuels's line mate, center Casey Rabach, pulled out of his assignment and rotated toward Bears defensive tackle Garay. Now they were double-teaming him because Garay was Samuels's responsibility.

Samuels performed a legal cut block, and that's when it happened, and why he will always remember the day, December 12, 2007. See, Antonio Garay's ankle got caught underneath, with both men—two very large men—draped over him, and it gave out the way a chopstick would.

Crack. The ankle snapped.

It's a hideous sound, the sound of a human bone breaking. It's something unnatural, almost evil. The shriek follows shortly thereafter, after that moment it takes for the brain to catch up to the body. Pain broadcasts the way a radio station does, on a slight delay. Then it sweeps through your entire body in a wave, an angry ocean tide, telling you something is very wrong.

Mike Mamula witnessed the Cowboys' Greg Ellis breaking his leg. "There was this loud snap," he said. "I'll never forget. I thought one of the yard markers had snapped. Mind you, this is happening fifteen yards away from me and I could hear it as clear as day."

Now, when you're the cause of that person before you moaning in agony, writhing on the field with his lower limb preternaturally crooked, guilt washes over you like pain.

When you're that close, and you can see the player's face melting from the pain and you can hear his sobs, and you know you were the cause, well, suddenly real life and compassion override the notion of football as war. Because in the end, it's not war. It's a game. And now there's a terrible casualty.

"That was something that stuck with me for a little while," Samuels said. "I felt terrible. You never like to see a player—an opposing player or not—get hurt seriously like that. And you know, he was going off on me during the course of the game, telling me I was a dirty player. The play was completely accidental and I felt pretty bad about it."

Samuels tried to call Garay and apologize thereafter. He also left a message with a Bears secretary directly following the game. "I asked her to pass along the message that I was truly sorry and it was completely accidental," Samuels said.

According to a person close to Garay, the former sixth-round pick and NFL journeyman remains extremely bitter over the incident and doesn't buy Samuels's claim that it was accidental. After the Bears waived him in March 2008, Garay finally resumed his career a season later as a bit player for the Chargers. Currently, he remains an unrestricted free agent after the Bears waived him in March.

It's a terrible feeling, guilt. Sometimes debilitating, the way it was for Ray Mancini when Duk Koo Kim died following their fight some twenty-five years ago. Mancini pummeled Kim into a coma in the fourteenth round, and five days later his mother authorized doctors to cut off his life support system. Four months later, Kim's mother was so devastated she committed suicide. The following year, the maligned referee of the fight, Richard Green, also committed suicide. Mancini was left to digest all of those tragic happenings for the rest of his life.

With the physical nature of the game, that dark possibility is very real, if not death, then paralysis or the simple fact of ending a man's career. Taking away his meal ticket.

"You can't think about that," veteran linebacker Jeremiah Trotter said. "We all know it's a possibility, a cold fact of the game. The minute you sign to play, you know there's a possibility something really bad can happen. You only pray it doesn't."

Benji Olson seriously injured a player in his second year in the league. Playoff game against Buffalo. Music City Miracle Game against Buffalo. Olson and Bruce Matthews were out to the left on a screen pass, and Olson cut blocked, a Bills player. Similar to what happened to Garay, the player's lower leg got snagged underneath Olson and snapped in half.

"It was completely accidental," Olson said. "Immediately Bruce Smith was in my face chewing me out, telling me that I ruined this guy's career and what the hell was I thinking and all of that. I was a young player and I'm telling Bruce Smith that I'm sorry and I didn't mean to hurt him. I'm all nervous about Bruce Smith. Next thing I know Bruce Matthews is in Bruce Smith's face telling him to get lost and to leave his teammate alone. I'm sitting there thinking, 'Jesus, here are these two Hall of Famers arguing about some stupid play that I caused.'"

Olson continued, "You know, I've seen some dirty plays from some of our own guys—I remember we had just thrown a 30-yard touchdown pass and one of our guys cut some guy out in the back of the legs near the end zone, clearly after the play. My jaw dropped. I'm thinking to myself, 'How could you even take a shot at somebody like that?' Individual battles get started out there and everything gets escalated. Everybody's a gladiator out there."

5

The Long Wait
for Sunday

Here at team headquarters, the week feels especially long between Sundays.

The beat of the game, the beat of a season.

The game is their reward. The rest of the week weighs on them, the way it does for everyone else who works.

Monday arrives like the day after anything momentous. You turn around and it's suddenly there, without charm, the hotel bill slipped under the door. Sunday presents a heightened emotional state, everything a blur without context, especially the end-of-game experience. The agony or exhilaration of win or lose is merely an extension of the Sunday story. Nothing crystallizes—including the Sunday pain of playing—until Monday, because Mondays are rational, analytical, and grounded.

Such a downer day, Monday, even if you win.

The Great Ache

Monday is sore day.

There is a debate under way over the Great Ache and when it arrives, the day after the game or two days after the game. It always

comes, mind you, never skipping a week. The Great Ache arrives like
an unwanted houseguest, obnoxious and pushy, with a serious attitude
of entitlement.

It drains you of will and concentration, because just as the mind
begins to focus on something it reverts back to the throbbing of something. Throbbing on top of throbbing. The Great Ache travels deep
into the body all over the body. It's all-encompassing, finding muscles
that you didn't know existed.

It's the physicality of the game, certainly, but also the various movements involved: Stop, start, make contact, backpedal, get high, get low,
make contact, sprint, cut, dive, rise, roll, make contact.

"You wake up the next day after a game and it's like you've been
in several car crashes," Ike Reese said. "You get in a car crash, even
with your seat belt on, your body is going to ache. We're going full
throttle into each other. A lot of times, body size doesn't match. More
weight, more force against you. Do that several times over three and a
half hours and the next day you can't move.

"Then you have to be in early to the complex the next morning.
You get treatment. Then cold tub. Hot tub. Ice and stim. Then you get
workout in to work out some of the soreness. Go into the training room
the day after a game and all twelve tables are filled up with guys."

"Especially after a rivalry game," added Anthony Becht. "The day
after is just brutal. You feel every block. Everything you do is magni-
fied and so you feel those games even more. By weeks 8, 9, 10, we're
not lifting as much because your body just can't take it anymore."

Kyle Turley agreed. "You would definitely feel a little more sore
than other games," he said. "Some of it also depends who you were
going up against, like for me it was Michael Strahan. I felt it after
we played the Giants. Strahan with that bull rush all day. Next day
you're hurtin'. Then there's the surface you're playing on—grass or
turf. On the old turf, your body really feels like shit on Mondays."

Mike Mamula compared the feeling of his body on Mondays to the
ground hamburger you see in the counter window of a butcher's store.
Bright red. Balled up in strands.

"Chopped meat," he said. "I remember I was living with two of
my buddies from college when I was first in the league and we would
always get take-out food on Mondays. I would struggle just to get out
to my truck to pick up the food, and by the time I would get to the

place to pick up the food I wouldn't be able to get out of the car to get the food. I would have to send my buddies in to get it.

"I tried to use the training room as little as possible, but that was almost impossible because Mondays and Tuesdays you need the help."

Good sleep is again difficult to capture Monday night. Then there are Tuesdays. It's an off day for players for a reason.

Chris Samuels said, "Going into the game you take the shots to cover the pain. The next day is really not that sore because you're still numbed up with the shots. But man, when Tuesday hits, the shots all wear off and all the soreness sets in."

Said Kevin Long, "Two days after the game was always the worst. Just like with lifting. The first day after isn't the worst. It's two days after that the injuries really start to stick out."

Said Benji Olson, "The day after you are hobbling around. But two days after is the worst. The older you get the harder it becomes. It's not very glamorous after games in the league."

Kevin Gogan reserved Mondays to get the blood flowing and wake from the undead. Feeling human, many call it, instead of a sort of bloodless mass. "Tuesday off was the best because that was the worst day for us," he said. "My first game, I'll never forget it. We were in Philly and I got the task of going against Reggie White. Waking up that Monday morning, I literally could not pick up my leg off the bed. I never felt anything like that again throughout my career. You learn quickly that it's not college anymore. For sixteen weeks you are screwed up for the rest of the year.

"You're going in [the training room] taking whatever you can take to get over the pain. There are no good days. There's no way around it. Your joints hurt. Your fat hurts."

Mark Schlereth had a similar revelation during his first game, which also took place in Philadelphia. "It was midway through the season in my rookie year and I had just been practicing all year up to that point. They had the best defense in the league. I played exceptionally well—kicked the tar out of the guy in front of me. I was so sore the next day I had a tough time doing anything. Even on Wednesday I was still sore as hell. Even Friday I was sore. I thought to myself, 'If this is how I feel after every game I'm not gonna last very long in this league.' I couldn't believe the pain."

"See," Chad Lewis explained, "Monday your body is almost in denial that you just hammered it so bad. On game day, you write checks that your body has to cash on Tuesday. You're hurting Monday and you have to run and lift. That is imperative. Keep the blood flowing and pumping. If you don't do anything until Wednesday it seems impossible to get going."

It didn't matter to Bill Romanowski whether it was Monday or Tuesday. "There were many times I couldn't get out of bed," he said. "My wife had to help me out. More than I can count. The longer I played, the worse it got. There were many times that I would acupuncture myself just so I could get out of bed. I worked with so many great therapists over the years that I learned how to do it myself."

On those Monday mornings, the training room, a football team's ER and sanctuary, is filled with battered bodies on padded tables being prodded and iced, stitched and stimmed.

Even for the others, who were lucky to escape without serious harm, the memory of the game will live for days in their bones.

"Your body is moving all day," Ike Reese said. "It's filled with adrenaline. But once the body cools and the heart rate settles that night, you can't get up off the couch. I had many nights where I slept on the couch in the basement because I was watching TV and I just couldn't make it upstairs. 'Nah, man, not tonight. Just let me lay here.'

"Some guys don't even know they're hurt until they get home. When your body cools down. That's when it begins to ache. About seven or eight o'clock that night. You feel it come on. You know it's going to be a long night. You don't want to move. You don't want to talk. You tell your wife to leave you be."

"A six-pack after the game is a great way to kill the pain," Benji Olson said.

For many, beer is the tonic.

Man rule 466: Guilt-free beer tastes better than just beer, the guilt evaporating after only a day of grinding, sweaty work—or play, mind you, since it's really only about intense exertion, and we only say work over play because the notion makes a cold one utterly deserving.

Sometimes the only way to summon sleep is to dull the soreness.

"Drinking kills that pain away," Kevin Long said.

Sleep does not come easily the night of the game. Whether it's the squealing body or racing mind that fends it away, the night of the game is just a waiting game to crash.

"Some of the worst things are body cramps that you can't expect," Long said. "Your hammy locks up on you in the middle of the night and you can't sleep. Then you can't sleep because your belly is poking out from drinking the sixteen Gatorades you needed to rehydrate yourself."

Said Olson, "I would stay up late and come down from the adrenaline of the game. It's amazing how much adrenaline your body receives in a fight for your life."

You feel like a speed freak, they will say, while the mind revs with images from the day.

"After games I wouldn't get to sleep until three or four in the morning," Chris Samuels said. "You have so much adrenaline going through your system that it's almost impossible to sleep. Plus, if there was a bad play or two that I made in the game, I would replay them over and over in my head and try and figure out what went wrong. Those plays really bother me."

Said Chad Lewis, "Even if we played in Dallas and got back to Philadelphia at midnight, I wouldn't go to bed until four a.m. My mind was flashing plays, over and over and over and over. It was a sensory overload. I would record the game and I would watch the game and process what my mind was seeing."

Obviously there are always exceptions. When told of the many players who had trouble sleeping the night of a game, Simeon Rice snapped, "Sounds like those guys need to go out and get some pussy then."

Far, Far from Sunday

The wounded from Sunday must report to the training room extra early on Monday, before 8 a.m. at most places, which means very little sleep, especially factoring in the overnight pain that depletes restfulness. Monday represents a major team day, and most of the morning and afternoon is spent in meetings and watching the film from Sunday.

The players are off on Tuesday before the longest days of the week, Wednesday and Thursday, the true work days, filled with practice, film study, treatment, and conditioning, like fulfilling their mandatory thirty-minute-apiece sessions of upper-body and lower-body workouts. Then there's the Wednesday 9 a.m. team meeting, where the head coach—who spent the previous forty-eight hours with his top coordinators formulating the game plan for Sunday—begins his main message of the week.

Following the team meeting, players splinter back into units for more meetings. Here, the game plan is reduced and translated into positional duties. The team meets back on the field at 11:15 a.m. for a walk-through practice involving the new game plan, and then breaks for a noon lunch at the cafeteria—which is a cafeteria by name only, the way it is at one of the studios in Hollywood, sort of fine dining with trays, and an especially lengthy choice of proteins.

Shortly after 1 p.m., the special teamers return to the practice field, and the second part of the day features more meetings and film study, treatment and conditioning. At any point of the day or night, especially on a Wednesday and Thursday, someone can emerge from any one of the maze of rooms inside the tastefully decorated and spectacularly immaculate two-story complex—which still smells new six years later.

The complex bustles with activity, beyond, say, football practice with football people. It feels more crowded than imagined, with attendants and assistants speed-walking with their clipboards and paperwork down wide carpeted corridors, the walls adorned with finely framed glory photos involving the team, an emphasis on the tenure of the current ownership. There is a distinct office nature here, like that of an advertising firm or any other business with a creative flare.

Thursday goes even longer than Wednesday. Thursday's practice is the most intense, because a coach likes to work the pitch of the week. From crash day on Monday down to off day on Tuesday, ramped high on Wednesday, even higher on Thursday, back down for a lighter practice and work schedule Friday, in which players usually leave the complex by 3 p.m., down further to a Saturday morning walk-through of the game plan, this block of time is what shapes a team for Sunday.

"O-linemen and D-linemen are the guys who set the tone," Turley said. "The camaraderie was great all of those years I played in New Orleans. When I was in Kansas City and our lines didn't hang out and guys didn't get along, it was a miserable experience and a miserable team to be on. The team is set by the linemen. Having fun. The battle. You have fights with the defense in practice and then you grab a beer with them afterwards, and all is forgotten. Those moments are priceless.

"I had opportunities to keep things light for the team. Outside of Sunday, it was fun. Sunday was serious. But if you got your asshole too tight, you're preparing yourself to lose. You have a fifty-fifty shot and you gotta have fun."

The Film Room Knows No Status

The lights dim in what resembles a high school classroom, the players playing students seated in their chairs with the desks attached, divided into their position groups. The position coach works the video.

Film study is now in session.

In here, the game they will see hardly resembles the one shown the day before on network television. The game is in fragments, broken down into what pertains to each position. It's raw and real, for everyone in the group to see. Mistake or magnificence.

"Better hope you played well," linebacker Jeremiah Trotter said.

Former punter Sean Landeta compared film study to "a high-level business meeting in a boardroom. There is a high level of respect during that meeting, letting the coach point out what he needs to point out. You're seeing results of so much hard work that was put in that previous week. When you win, all around life is good. When you lose, it's a very different scenario."

The film doesn't lie. Screw up Sunday and you'll hear it in here. It is Landeta's executive meeting unplugged, without the rules that govern the workplace. Motivation begins in this room, where judgment by a player's peers and their position coach is harsh and cutting. In here, unlike in the media, everyone knows the play call and knows one another's responsibility. Everyone knows whose fault it really is.

There is no hiding in the film room.

Conversely, it doesn't get any better than when you make plays and you're the king of the room and you get to wag your finger. Earning a fine living aside, the real spoils reside in here. Bragging rights.

"Obviously that one from above was embarrassing," former tackle Kyle Turley said. "You hear it all in the film room. 'You got knocked the fuck out!' I tried to make sure that never happened. But when you're on the other end of that and you get downfield and absolutely de-cleat someone, it's a beautiful thing to watch the next day."

"It's absolutely embarrassing," added former guard Mark Schlereth. "You lose sleep. You gotta watch your butt get handed to you in front of your team. Guy Diesel was this guy's nickname. Played for San Francisco. Don't even know his real name. Well, he annihilates one of our defensive backs. [Denver assistant coach, now Texans GM] Rick Smith must have rewound it twenty-five times, his only words, 'Guy Diesel is effing you up! Look at this, guys. *Guy Diesel!*'

"There's been plenty of those situations where I've been on the wrong end. The biggest thing is you feel like you let your teammates down."

Players will literally squirm in the chair, especially if they caught one or flubbed one and know that play is on the horizon.

Brace yourself. Here come the ball-breakers. They're first-class ball-breakers, city-corner ball-breakers. One-liners, foul-liners, they come in rapid fire. Feelings aren't spared. They're microwaved.

"You get burnt? You get beat real bad? That stuff doesn't go unnoticed in the film meeting," former returner and running back Brian Mitchell said. "You need tough skin to survive in a locker room and the league altogether. Nowadays the league is trying to film everything. Cameras are everywhere. In the locker room and in the huddle and in the training room. The things that are said there would be easily misconstrued in this politically correct world that we're living in now. The things would be taken entirely the wrong way.

"Language in football is different than everyday language. There is no harm meant, but you have to get your point across. We mentally try to get guys to go beyond what their body is capable of. It's like during the game— 'You're a little bitch, you're a little pussy'—you talk shit to get players off their game. It's no different with your own team in the film meeting. You say those things to make them learn not to make the same mistake."

"You know you're gonna hear it," former linebacker Ike Reese said. "And they'll look right at you. 'Damn, he's bitch-slapping you, dude. What's going on there, man?' And it doesn't stop."

And it follows you into the cafeteria and into the weight room and onto the practice field, chopping up your manhood.

Sometimes it is excessive. Sometimes it borders on torment.

And sometimes there is fallout. After all, these are men with great pride, and men with great pride you can only deride so much.

Sometimes it gets physical.

A Special Teams Meeting, Postseason 2003

The film session for Philadelphia Eagles special teamers in preparation for a divisional playoff game against the Packers began innocently enough. The film rolled forward, and rolled back to a kickoff return during the season. A group of players, led by a young defensive back named Norman LeJeune, began to chide a young wide receiver named Sean Morey on how he was blocked during the return.

"Like a little bitch," LeJeune snapped.

The barbs flew at Morey, one after another, machine-gun style, and he stewed quietly in his chair. At first he took them in stride, with a fake, defensive smile. The law of the film room says everyone has to take it because everyone is the butt of the joke sooner or later.

Now, Morey, in his first year with the Eagles, had won the special teams MVP over the regular season, while LeJeune was a rookie defensive back on the practice squad. Morey finally grew weary and snapped to LeJeune and the others, "Cut that shit out, man. No more joking."

He paused.

"No more."

But they didn't stop. All week long, they continued to mock him.

Now it was Friday morning, two days before the game. LeJeune sat behind Morey in the special teams meeting, and he started sniping at him again.

"He's whispering shit at him," said Ike Reese, the special teams captain on that team. "He's fucking with him."

Following the meeting, the players had a five-minute gap before a 9 a.m. team meeting with Coach Andy Reid, and several dawdled in the lobby of the team's practice complex. Morey circled around the group, making believe he was headed for the cafeteria, across from the large theater hall that hosted the meeting. He ducked in between a group of players, including Reese and Pro Bowl safety Brian Dawkins, and appeared in front of LeJeune.

"What was all that talking, bitch?" Morey snarled.

He then punched LeJeune square in the mouth and followed it up with a quick, savage headbutt. With LeJeune dazed and staggering, Morey unleashed a flurry of three, four more punches until Reese grabbed him from behind.

"He hit the man five, six times," Reese said. "That's how quick he hit him. Like some judo shit. Nobody knew about what had transpired between the two so everybody freaked."

"Is you fuckin' crazy?" Reese asked Morey.

Morey still seethed in Reese's arms, while LeJeune stood hunched over, his face covered in blood.

"It happened so fast Norm didn't know where he was," Reese recalled. "Sean whupped his ass so bad. To the point where Norm could've called the police and thrown his ass in jail. Norm didn't have a chance to throw a punch."

Later that day, the incident went before a players' committee meeting—a hierarchy system the head coach instituted involving leaders and key members from the offense, defense, and special teams—and a team recommendation would be made to Reid. As per the agreement, Reid would take into account his players' wishes before ultimately issuing punishment.

"Half of the cats wanted to kick Sean off the team," Reese said. "The other half were like, 'They were fuckin' with him. He got what he deserved.' Meanwhile, I told Andy, 'Coach, can't we do something else? Fine him? It's divisional round of the playoffs. I need him out there. He's our best cover guy. The guys on offense or defense don't care. He's important to us on special teams.'"

Reid wound up fining both players, Morey more than LeJeune, and let them play. Morey lost his entire game check. LeJeune considered pressing charges against Morey. The coaching staff talked him out of it, saying he didn't need to cause any more distractions.

"Norm had called his people back in Louisiana and they wanted him to press charges," Reese said. "He was lookin' sick. Both his eyes were black. His face was all swollen. He was all busted up. Looked worse than fighters I've seen. Andy made them both come out after practice to apologize to each other and to the team. Then they shook hands in front of the team."

Players Call It Instant Coma

The groundwork for a game built on so much emotion centers around tediousness of preparation.

School with hitting, one player termed it. So much class time and study time, the playbook not unlike a textbook, the film room not unlike the lecture hall. And so players begin to doze when the lights dim, especially the younger ones, just becoming acclimated to this life in the league.

Here is a snapshot of two cornerbacks drafted the same year, both out of SEC schools, sitting next to each other, already fast friends, and the one (Sheldon Brown) taken in the second round nudges the one selected in the first round (Lito Sheppard) with his elbow.

"Stay awake, man."

So it's now their second year in 2003, and the two starting cornerbacks are both hurt. Sheppard is forced to play and forced to pay attention.

"I'd see him shake his head," recalled one of the defensive coaches. "His head is going back and forth. I finally see what he's doing. He's breaking ammonia tablets and sniffing them—he's doing smelling salts to stay awake. I gave him a lot of credit."

Coffee and energy drinks only go so far. So players desperately trying to stay attentive employ either chew tobacco and spit into a cup or chew sunflower seeds and spit into a cup.

"Walk into any meeting room and you'll hear the pop of the seeds," said Coach Steve Spagnuolo. "Constant pops in the room. It's as annoying as ever."

But ever necessary, as the mind slowly wanders and drifts.

Here's one player's take on film study:

Most of the time it's just boring. So we'll get on each other. [The exchange] goes something like this: "I'm going downfield and I knocked this guy's head off, and where are you?"

The camera will move.

"Why aren't you in that frame? Why aren't you around that pile? When is the ball going to pop out? When will you save that game?"

It's not even a sprint. It's a jog. There's a defensive back who weighs 220 pounds, you have to say, "Let me put my helmet in his rib cage."

For a veteran, though, it's the shit you already know. Week in, week out, all you need to know is what is different this week.

What is your base offense? You change blocking scheme? It's just being aware. That's the hardest thing for a young guy. They don't have the base rules of the offense down. So they think it's a new offense when in reality just the details of the offense changed.

For us, when the lights come down in the room and the video pops up it's an instant coma. You're watching the same plays over and over. Now you're trying to keep yourself entertained. Sometimes you sit there and count how many times a coach runs the same play on tape. You put slash marks on a piece of paper. Just to keep yourself awake.

One play, I was in the mid-seventies. Every half second the coach pushes rewind. He's at fifty-seven. Rewind.

Fifty-eight.

Rewind.

Now the guy next to me is asking what my slash marks are.

Fifty-nine.

See, the coach is watching five guys, and he's teaching each one. Then of course some young kid has a disagreement. Now it's an argument, and I'm like, "Kid, just shut up and let him move on."

"What's wrong with your footwork? Are your hands late? Are you leaning?"

Makes for a long meeting with the lights off. If you haven't dozed off, you're not human. I wonder about the coaches. They don't get any sleep during the week. How do they stay awake? I'll drink sometimes five, six cups of coffee, and it's not for the caffeine. It's just the act of doing something. It's why a lot of guys chew. So they're doing something. You have to do something to keep awake.

In the movie of football, this scene would be sped up, the image likely a fast-moving sky from sunup to sundown, to show that a day has passed on the way to Sunday. In real life and football, the moment represents much more than merely transition. It is here that the game is won.

6

The Pain, the Price, the Glory, and the End Days

We must give you the story of pain because pain presents an embraceable job hazard, and isn't that what truly separates them from everyone else?

"I think they're wired differently," says Vikings trainer Eric Sugarman.

And now to the story, because certainly their body as their tool of trade represents an obvious notion, but the arm of a quarterback is useless if any part of the rest of him breaks. And when we talk of the skill-less positions, the hog positions, the skill of playing them rests on a man's ability to batter other men with his body, battering his own in the process.

"They have this uncanny ability to conquer the pain and actually be able to function," Sugarman said. "Man, some of the injuries I've seen guys *play* with would put a regular guy out of commission for a nine-to-five desk job for a month."

Admittedly, Sugarman is spoiled, mostly because of a man who grew up a child rodeo star, and how fitting is that? A boy who once competed in the calf roping and steer riding events at junior rodeos likely wouldn't grow to be a football player with the unflattering label of Training Table Monster.

He would be Jared Allen, a football player who suffers a grade 3 AC sprain in his shoulder, misses Wednesday and Thursday practices, works with the trainer on Friday to see if he can use his arm at all, plays on Sunday when most players wouldn't play for weeks, and records two sacks.

For the record, the AC joint is short for the acromioclavicular joint, formed by the outer end of the collarbone and a bony process that protrudes forward from the upper part of the shoulder blade. According to sportsinjuryclinic.net, a grade 1 represents a simple sprain to the AC joint; a grade 2 involves rupture of the AC ligament; and a grade 3 involves rupture of both the AC and CC ligaments, which often results in a superior displacement.

According to Sugarman, it's a most miserable injury that involves constant, throbbing pain, and signifies an automatic flat tire for a defensive end whose whole game revolves around his shoulders. It feels sort of like you have a dead wing attached to the side of your body.

"The pain is ridiculous," Sugarman says. "Then at the same time he goes through that, he gets his knee caught in the pile and sprains his MCL [medial collateral ligament]. I'm thinking, 'Yeesh, there's no way this guy answers the bell.' And of course he plays.

"He's the kind of guy who gets you in trouble with the coach. You tell him he's going to miss a couple of weeks with this deal and he plays. And the coach says to you, 'You're full of shit. You're trying to make yourself look good.'"

Really, really, he's not, Sugarman swears, and he adds that the only reason he even allowed Allen to play was that the injury couldn't get any worse, and that's sometimes the toughest part of the job. Protecting a player against himself.

For instance, Adrian Peterson, the great big running back with the breakaway speed who conjures thoughts of Eric Dickerson. After two weeks of sitting sidelined with a knee injury his rookie year, Peterson had enough and demanded to play. Sugarman semijokes that they almost got into a fistfight at the Meadowlands because Peterson wanted to play so badly.

"He was pissed," Sugarman says. "But he got over it. Contrary to public opinion, we're not going to put guys out there in harm's way."

Man Down

Around him, everyone begins to yell—his dear friends, his rivals on the team, the opposition, those he might've played against in high school, and those who have no idea of his name.

"Man down! Man down!"

He hears this and he can't stop thinking that this must be what it's like on a real battlefield where they play for keeps, where it's not just a shredded tendon or a cracked fibula. It's the closest he'll ever come to such an experience, pinned by pain to the soft ground. Everything disappears anyway during the game—the crowd, the people watching on television, the notion of ego.

Sometimes the injury is not obvious.

"What hurts?" the trainer will ask.

But the trainer is always diagnosing. He sees his guy get hit on the outside of the leg and right away he's thinking, "MCL tear?"

And most of all, the trainer must act cool. Straight cool. The way Sugarman was when Vikings cornerback Chuck Gordon dislocated his ankle, ever the gruesome injury. Gordon's ankle sprouted in different directions.

At first Sugarman thought Gordon got hit in the head, because he was lying facedown. So he grabbed his head and stabilized his neck. He could hear Gordon mumbling through excruciating pain.

Sugarman bent down closer to make out what he was saying.

"Look at my fucking ankle," Gordon rasped.

Sugarman finally saw it. Gordon's ankle traveled east-west instead of north-south.

"Those are tough ones," Sugarman says. "He's flipping out. Everyone else is flipping out. It's an emergency situation. I get a splint bag. Once I stabilize the ankle, I comfort the guy."

His tone must be soothing. "I just stabilized it," he said softly. "We're going to get you off the field and get you taken care of right away. Don't worry, I'm with you."

On those types of injuries, the trainer thinks immediately of the player's family. "What about his mom who's watching on television?" Sugarman says.

So like most trainers, in his pocket Sugarman has the emergency contact for his player—wife, mother, brother—and once he has tended to the player he'll make a phone call. When quarterback Gus Frerotte caught his hand on a helmet and pierced a vein and blood sprayed in a most frightening manner, Sugarman called his wife while he walked back to the sideline.

"Is my husband all right?" is how she answered the phone.

"He's fine," he told her. "It just looked horrible."

The Legend of Jerry O.

We pause a moment to offer a portrait of pain like no other, described by one trainer as the worst injury he has ever witnessed. By far.

They record songs about people like Jerry O., raspy American ballads that tell a tale of American perseverance in a very American town like Youngstown, hardscrabble, eat-their-Youngstown, located in northeast Ohio, equidistant from Cleveland and Pittsburgh, nestled by the river in the Mahoning Valley, where the mills once operated and produced America's steel before the great collapse that provided the subject for another raspy American ballad.

To know Jerry O. you must first know the soul of his town.

Before Springsteen sang of Youngstown's blight brought forth by lifeless mills, a steelworker and socialist named Frank Bohn in 1915 spoke of a much different Youngstown, a booming Youngstown, then a key component of thriving American Midwestern industry: "Everybody breathing dirt, eating dirt—they call it pay dirt, for Youngstown clean would be Youngstown out of work."

However bleak and life-shortening the work, Youngstown performed it with dignity, another trait of the city's dutiful and willing people, which included the many recent immigrants from Italy and Ireland who during a period of unrest in the 1920s drove the Ku Klux Klan out of town. Before the Klan finally fled the Mahoning Valley, the battle between these immigrants and the KKK became so violent and bloody that city officials declared martial law.

Throughout the years, Youngstown has radiated that sort of lawlessness, akin to the Wild West, where there were only heroes and bad guys, and women and children, and what happened in Youngstown was handled in Youngstown. Like many of the Ohio and western Pennsylvania river towns, Youngstown became a haven for organized crime during Prohibition and later an important strategic outpost because it was tucked away in the valley, set perfectly in between major mob municipalities, New York and Chicago. Mob influence in Youngstown only grew larger when the U.S. steel industry crashed in the 1970s.

Even today, the town's appellations are chilling: Crimestown, USA. Bomb City. Deathtown. In 1997, the *Wall Street Journal* called Youngstown the deadliest place in the United States.

The town has seemed forever cursed. The devil's depot.

Just like before, however, heroes remained in Youngstown, the proud workers who kept the town working and paved the way for a very recent upswing. The ones who inspired the Historical Center of Industry & Labor and the exhibit that bears the quote, "By the sweat of their brow. Forging the steel valley."

Backbone people.

Meanwhile, the Story of Jerry O. is so wholly American that it would seem prosaic if it weren't a thousand percent true. The O., by the way, stands for Olsavsky, the kind of name you would expect for the protagonist of such a story.

Jerry Olsavsky was eleven when the big steel mill closed in 1978 and Youngstown began to crumble economically. A South Sider who wanted to attend college, he was a ballplayer, though not terribly gifted athletically. He played football because football played to his attributes, which were typically Youngstown—tireless worker, overachiever, sweathog. Jerry O. became a football star at Chaney High, though he was skinny for a linebacker, with a long neck, and not very fast.

Chaney coach Ed Matey told a recruiter from the University of Pittsburgh, in town for a battle with rival Cardinal Mooney because he had an eye for a Mooney player, all about Jerry O., and Jerry O. starred in the game. Matey then sold Pitt coach Foge Fazio on him, and Jerry O. entered mighty Pitt U. as a 203-pound freshman amid hyperskepticism. In 1988, he became the first Panther in twelve years to record 100 tackles in three straight seasons.

It was the same thing all over again in the NFL after all of those tackles at Pitt. He topped out at a shade over six feet and 214 pounds as a senior, and while everyone raved about his nose for the ball and disregard for his body to make a play, the league offered players with the same instincts and fierceness, only bigger and faster.

Scouts classified him as the following: White boy. Undersized. Smart. All heart. Won't make it.

In 1989, the Pittsburgh Steelers took a shot on the local college hero in the tenth round, then a throwaway round of the NFL draft that doesn't even exist anymore (the draft ends after seven rounds now).

It didn't take long, however, for Jerry O. to draw the attention of Steelers coach Chuck Knoll. There was just something about his Youngstown ways. He was relentless in every way, in everything he did. And he was good.

So Jerry O. made the Steelers like he said he would. He played on special teams until Hardy Nickerson broke his ankle in the middle of the season. Jerry O. started in Nickerson's linebacker spot against the Chiefs and made the play of the game, stopping Christian Okoye—the hulking 260-pound running back called the Nigerian Nightmare—at the goal line to preserve a six-point victory for the Steelers. Jerry O. started the rest of the games that year and made the NFL's all-rookie team. In all, Jerry O. carved out nine years in the league on all heart.

In Youngstown and Pittsburgh and throughout mill country, they all tell a favorite Jerry O. story in the Story of Jerry O.

Like the one about the nondescript preseason game in which he was out there calling the defensive signals as the starting middle linebacker and he dislocated his little finger. He yelled to the bench to throw him some tape while he tried to pop his finger back in place. Bryan Hinkle tossed him a small roll of tape during the huddle. He broke the huddle and with the tape in his hand made the next tackle and dislocated his finger again. After the play, he taped the finger and threw the tape back to the sideline.

Or the one that illustrated his smarts that occurred in a game against Miami following a pass to tight end Troy Drayton that brought the Dolphins inside the red zone. Olsavsky and Carnell Lake had hit Drayton hard and Olsavsky's helmet popped off. The Steelers trainer at the time, Rick Burkholder, saw Olsavsky put something in his belt loop. He thought it was his mouthpiece.

On third down, Jerry O. had come off the field because it was a nickel situation—where the linebacker leaves for an extra defensive back—and Burkholder met him at the sideline.

"Give me your mouthpiece and I'll spray it down," he said.

"I don't wear a mouthpiece," Jerry O. shot back.

"What?" replied Burkholder, totally shocked. He stammered and said, "Well, what do you have in your belt loop?"

"Oh," said Jerry O., "it's Drayton's ear pad from his helmet. I was gonna throw it, but I decided to tuck it away."

Burkholder smiled.

"I look across the field and Drayton's behind their bench getting his helmet fixed," the trainer recalled. "He missed the whole series. What a brilliant guy."

Burkholder and Jerry O. became fast friends. Jerry O. was in Burkholder's wedding, and Burkholder was Jerry O.'s best man when the injury happened that Sunday in Cleveland in 1993.

Jerry O. got caught in a pile. It's every football player's great fear. Trapped in a mountain of bodies. Exposed. Helpless.

Burkholder could hear Jerry O. scream from beneath the pile.

"I rushed out to the field," Burkholder said. "Now, he's my good friend and he's laying there. His leg is mangled. One of those Theismann deals. His leg is hanging out to the side." Burkholder stood in front of Jerry O. and held a towel in front of his face so the player couldn't see his leg.

Jerry O. told his friend, "Dude, I know what it is. You don't have to shield me from it. Just do me a favor. Get me off this godforsaken field."

"He feels terrible laying on this field because it's sacred," Burkholder recalled. "It's Pittsburgh-Cleveland, the ultimate rivalry. He's dying out there and all he's worried about is getting off that field because of what it means."

Jerry O. spent three nights in a Cleveland clinic before being transported back to Three Rivers Stadium in an ambulance. His knee was a mess, dislocated entirely. He tore all three major ligaments in the knee—ACL, PCL, MCL—both sets of cartilages, and three muscles off the bone.

"Worst injury I've ever seen," Burkholder said.

A career that was never supposed to be appeared to be finished.

"Except," Burkholder said, "we're talking about Jerry O. He rehabbed his ass off. In eleven months, he was ready to play. Toughest nut I've ever been around."

"He always said, 'Listen, dude, I've got two goals. Win the Super Bowl and get in the Hall of Fame.'"

Two years later in Tempe, Arizona, during the national anthem of Super Bowl XXX between the Steelers and the Cowboys, Burkholder sought out Jerry O. on the sideline. "I had to be next to him as he was achieving one of his goals," he said.

Jerry O. played two more seasons following that Super Bowl before a hand injury forced him to retire. He's back home in Youngstown now, coaching defense at Youngstown State, still trying to be a Youngstown hero. He never made the Hall of Fame, but they all remember him. For as the railroad was built on the bodies of valiant worker men, so was the game of football on players like Jerry O.

The guy with all heart, just like his town.

We should take a moment to tell you about Jerry O.'s boy.

The Healer.

Rick Burkholder is not overly large. Under six feet, he is sturdy-trim, what you would call fit, built like someone with knowledge of the body, the nutrients and exercise that it craves to run well. However boyish-looking, with sunken eyes under a pronounced brow that forms a natural stare, he looks like a football trainer, as opposed to, say, a personal trainer, who is usually barrel-chested and overly muscled.

Healers prefer health over window dressing.

Burkholder hails from near Pittsburgh. He attended the University of Pittsburgh and his first NFL job was with the Steelers. And this is an important fact because Pittsburgh people are hardy folk. There's no pretense in Pittsburgh people, regardless of social standing, whether steeped in old mountain money or dirt from the earth's belly, those mill workers with knobby black fingers. You don't have to dote on Pittsburgh people. In fact, Pittsburgh people usually make the best doters.

Typically Pittsburgh, Rick Burkholder was born to be a football trainer, the way his father, Richard Burkholder, was. A veteran of nearly fifty years, Richard Burkholder is a member of the Athletic Trainers Hall of Fame, a forefather in the field when it was an obscure one, before the boom, before it became chic and became sports medicine.

When Rick Burkholder talked of seeking out Jerry O. on the sideline during the national anthem of Super Bowl XXX, he said that it was one of the two best moments he ever experienced in football. He added that both moments came within thirty-five seconds of each other.

For as soon as the song was over, during the rousing patriotic applause, Rick Burkholder turned toward the stands at Sun Devil

Stadium and found Richard Burkholder. And he pointed to him, the kind of gesture that pointed to deep acknowledgment. Sharing a moment from afar, without speaking or the need to speak.

"The look on his face was what you would imagine," Burkholder said. "He was a former athletic trainer. His team was the Steelers. Now he's seeing his kid work for his team at the Super Bowl."

The Man with the Lacerated Nuttocks

For a trainer, no injury is too personal. Consider what happened to Eagles tight end Chad Lewis in a game against Arizona in November 2002 after he was trapped in the bottom of the pile following an interception return by the Cardinals' Adrian Wilson.

Lewis had struggled to the sideline and stood hunched over behind the Eagles bench before wobbling to the ramp inside the tunnel that leads to the locker room, where Burkholder flagged him down. The trainer thought he had a concussion.

"Yo, C-Lew, what's up?" Burkholder asked.

Lewis responded that he got "stepped in the hole."

Burkholder figured he meant ear hole.

"Sit down over here by the fax machine and let me look at you."

"Dude, I can't sit down," Lewis said.

"What happened?"

"Somebody stepped in my a-hole," he said.

"What?"

"My butt crack."

The area was clear of people, so Burkholder told Lewis to pull down his pants.

"He's in nothing but a jock strap," Burkholder said. "The inside of his butt cheek is totally filleted open. There's a three-inch gash through to his sphincter. Split open. The bleeding is not that bad. It looks like he got hit with a fillet knife. On his right butt cheek, there are cleat marks plain as day. He had a butt-crack laceration. Somebody stepped on him with their cleat and slid down to his butthole and ripped the skin."

The team doctor came in at halftime and stitched up the wound. Lewis played the entire second half.

A week later, Burkholder received a Christmas card in the mail with cash inside. The inscription read:

> You saw something last Sunday that no athletic trainer should ever see.
>   Thanks for your help.
> C-Lew.

The Stinger

The pain is immediate, a sharp burning that flashes quickly from the neck, across the shoulder, down the arm, and into the fingers. There is accompanying numbness and tingling of the arm that can last from a moment to several minutes. The muscles in the arms and shoulders fall dead. The body suddenly feels enfeebled.

Totally disabled.

It's how you imagine getting struck by a bolt of lightning would feel. Pain on a hot griddle, instantly sapping all of your strength.

You have just suffered a stinger, one of literally hundreds of injuries a player can receive on a given Sunday.

With a stinger, the brachial plexus, a network of nerves that extends from the spinal cord across the shoulder and arms, has been stretched or compressed.

"It really lights your whole body up," Kevin Long said. "I had one in a Monday night game against Washington. I sat out the second half but I was back the next week wearing a neck brace. It's something you can play with, but it doesn't really heal properly until you fully rest it. You can hit thirty plays with no pain, then just one particular hit will catch you and light your whole body up. You can't even hold on to the football because you're so weak."

Anthony Becht once tore his plantar fascia—the thick connective tissue that supports the arch of the foot—in pregame warm-ups. He had his foot numbed and played in the game. "It felt as though I was walking around on a peg leg out there," Becht said. "Felt pretty awkward. Imagine trying to run and you can't feel your foot. Gotta do it.

Having a high pain threshold is an important part of the game. You have to be able to feel uncomfortable and play."

Mike Mamula suffered the same injury, and similarly had to get shots in his foot to finish the game. "I've had a concussion and a dislocated shoulder, but that was the most painful. It felt like my foot and the back of my foot were pulling away from each other during the course of the game."

Stemming the Violence

The back-in-the-day guys who sport their scars and crooked fingers and clicking bones like stickers of buckeye tree leaves on the Ohio State helmet would prefer to deem the current shift in the game permutation instead of, say, evolution, because of the connotation, you know?

Just think, remarks offensive lineman Jon Runyan, when he entered the league with the Houston Oilers in 1996, ashtrays dotted the inside of the Astrodome, Gatorade hadn't arrived on the sideline, and water bottles were not disposable. They were the squeeze kind that squirted, and they were passed down the bench like a grade-school flu. Beer flowed back in the locker room, and it was no big deal. It came in cans with pop tops and sat in tubs of ice, and that beer wasn't imported beer or craft beer. It was American beer brewed in the Midwest, and that's what quenched your thirst following a game.

They'd sit around the room and talk about the game and the young guys listened and were honored to retrieve the next one. And the scene told the story of the day.

Miller time.

Of course, that was before the room became the workplace and office conduct made its way down to the room. And forget the room, the whole outfit operated differently. Hell, one executive told me, when legendary coach Jimmy Johnson ran the Dolphins he had a refrigerator in his office stocked with Heinekens, and at some point, whether during those long personnel meetings or plain shootin' the shit with him, you had to have one—at least one—because Jimmy Johnson didn't trust a man who wouldn't drink a beer.

Societal shifts reach every aspect of life, including the field of play. And so it's no wonder Madden now represents an activity instead of a legendary coach and broadcaster, and the game mimics the game Madden. A second generation of football players has grown up with video games and *SportsCenter* and virtual reality, and so of course the game shifts into high energy, fast-paced pinball football. The game now seeks game moments the way movies seek movie moments—big plays, bigger hits, and oodles of points.

ADD means less D, because societal changes beget rule changes that play to a modern appetite. In a poof, the fullback goes the way of the beeper and the Wing T morphs into Five Wides and the big burly runner (John Riggins) becomes the sleek speedy back (Chris Johnson) and offense definitely usurps defense—*almost* to the point that it disproves the axiom of which always beats which.

"They want the offense to be able to score touchdowns," Bill Romanowski said. "The rules really help the offense. They want scoring and excitement and offensive plays. Touchdowns. Protect the receivers. Players are bigger, faster, and stronger and because of that the collisions are so intense they have to do everything they can to protect the offensive players or there would be more concussions, broken necks, and serious injuries.

"For me, great defensive battles are always some of the best games—where you knock the shit out of someone at the line of scrimmage. But they eliminate that from your abilities."

A once dominant defensive end, Simeon Rice stalked quarterbacks in that Chicago way. And now, he lamented, now quarterbacks too often exist in a protective shield of yellow flags and fines.

"The skirts they have put on the quarterbacks now suck," he said. "You can't even play the game the way it's supposed to be played. Cut blocks for the most part have been eliminated. They keep the quarterbacks in a cherished role. You can't even cut loose on them. Everything should be within the same framework. We're all subject to injury. If it happens, you fall victim to a blood sport."

It's true, what Rice stated, that they're all subject to injury, but all players are not viewed equally, especially with the dearth of quality quarterbacks in the league. So every once in a while you have a play like the fourth-down one a few years ago involving the Giants' Mathias Kiwanuka quitting on a sack of Tennessee's Vince Young. Wary of a penalty, Kiwanuka released Young because he thought the Titans quarterback no longer had the ball. He did and Young scampered for a big gain and a first down.

"Players become fearful of drawing that big penalty," former defensive end Mike Mamula said. "That stuff does play on guys' minds. Even when I played, William Fuller and myself hit John Elway and the corner of my shoulder pads caught John right in the head and knocked out Elway cold. We ended up winning the game, not because of it—but it sure is a lot easier to win a game when Elway is on the bench. I ended up getting fined $10,000. I was pissed and I wanted to get my money back."

Brian Mitchell said, "They're overprotecting quarterbacks. Defensive linemen and linebackers are big boys. They're running full speed at the quarterback and they have to stop themselves, even in midair some of the time. C'mon, that's ridiculous. You can't touch quarterbacks. And then there's the whole way receivers are treated nowadays. You can't touch a guy after five yards. But the receiver can get away with touching the defensive backs. Where's the logic in that?"

A quarterback, David Garrard, sounded almost sympathetic to the plight of the defender. "Basically, you're sending mixed messages," he said. "You're asking a defender not to touch the quarterback and then you expect him to hit the quarterback. You're gonna have injuries through basic play. It's something we all have to deal with. You can't take away the defender's ability to get to the quarterback."

While the league can be accused of being fine-heavy, most players understood the NFL's aim of at least trying to curb some of the unnecessary violence.

"The league has taken proactive steps to make the game less violent, which is a good thing," former offensive lineman Steve Wisniewski said. "Going after quarterbacks is controlled. Offensive linemen are much more controlled. They don't allow linemen downfield as much and you can't hit an 'unsuspecting' player."

Mark Schlereth, Wisniewski's peer from Denver, added, "Well, yeah, they're more concerned about protecting players from vicious hits. The game has become a year-round job. Guys have gotten bigger, faster, stronger. The collisions are more violent. Think about it. Shawn Merriman is an outside linebacker that weighs 270 pounds. That was a big defensive end when I started. Charles Mann was 270 and he was considered to be a big defensive end.

"The game has changed; it's amazing," he mused. "They probably have taken it away from the aggressiveness. But it also eliminates some of the dirtiness. We have a responsibility to show a game with sportsmanship to the younger generations out there. I thought it was poor judgment with Belichick walking off the Super Bowl field without shaking Tom Coughlin's hand. We don't need that poor sportsmanship."

One point of contention was the horse-collar rule adopted after Cowboys safety Roy Williams injured several players while grabbing the jersey at the neck and pulling them down to the ground.

"I think every player understands how to tackle, and how to do it properly," Anthony Becht said. "Some guys disregard that and don't care. I don't think it takes away from what we are doing. Some guys get caught up in the emotion of it and some guys just don't care. But listen, if you have to stop a touchdown and yanking his collar is the only thing that is going to work, then hey, you have to do what is best for the team and prevent that touchdown."

Countered Brian Mitchell, "The horse collar is ridiculous. You're trying to tackle someone. You're grabbing whatever you can get a hold of. Hard licks, man, is what tackling is all about. The game is violent and the league is making it softer when the guys are bigger and stronger than they've ever been."

The last decade or so will go down as one of great change in the game, beginning with the mentality of the players. Players have become less willing to risk limb—at least those who rank as upper-echelon players and wield a certain gravitas, knowing full well their job security. For example, Redskins cornerback DeAngelo Hall nursed a bum knee heading into a late November 2009 game in Philadelphia. Now, Washington's season had spiraled downward and the game essentially meant nothing. Ike Reese, a former teammate of Hall's in Atlanta, asked him during warm-ups if he was going to play. Hall, who looked rather sprightly moving about the field, shook his head and told Reese, "Nah, [the Eagles] got this [game]."

While Hall was legitimately hurt, he made it clear he wasn't going to risk his future on a game of little consequence for a team in turmoil.

Hall's mentality is more prevalent around the league. More and more players now base their decision to play or practice on their future health and earning potential.

"Why is it so hard for people to understand we play the game for money?" one current player told me. "Why is that a bad thing? Football is my job. It's not a privilege. It's not something I do for fun. It's hard work and we make good money for a short period of time. And our careers can end at any moment. The whole point of it is for us to make as much money as we can for as long as we can and not walk away a cripple. Is that wrong?"

Is it a career or a calling? Herein lies the split in the locker room. It's forever been the question. What's in a man's heart? The only difference now is that the side of career seemingly has more believers than in the past.

"Half the guys in this league just wanna make money," former tackle Orlando Brown scoffed. "They don't wanna play hurt. I went out on a mission from the start. I'd try and dislocate [a guy's] finger. I'm gonna fire something on his ass. I've made grown men cry. I had motherfuckers quit. I would dishearten players and beat them until they quit. The coaches had to come to me and tell me to relax with [teammate] Peter Boulware because I was making him want to quit. I took his confidence from him. I beat that motherfucker silly in practice.

"I was taught to play until the whistle. I ain't gonna stop until I hear the whistle. I would study my opponent. Was he soft? Does he take plays off? I wanna know his favorite move. Does he like to get hurt?"

Plenty of guys now play the game afraid, the man called Zeus added.

Seth Joyner, a linebacker for the Eagles, Cardinals, Packers, and Broncos in a career that spanned thirteen seasons, said flatly, "They don't make them as tough as we were. I played many games with injuries that would cause guys today to sit out for two, three games. There's so much money at stake in the game today. Teams are protecting guys—their investments. Guys are protecting their future.

"Back when I played, it was all about winning. You know, there's a difference between being hurt and injured. Everybody's hurt. Being injured disadvantages you to the team. They don't breed them that way. We played the game because we loved the game. We played the game for each other. If I have a knee injury, if I can limp around and play—and help the team—I will. You just don't see that anymore."

Bruising running back Eddie George retired only after the 2004 season and yet he speaks of the game today the way Art Donovan did. "Nowadays you have a 5-foot-9, 205-pound receiver sprinting down the middle of the field like a gazelle," he snapped. "Nobody's touching him. La-tee-da. Here he is . . . skipping along the sidelines. That's flag football. It's not like it used to be."

George described those wars against Pittsburgh and Baltimore, yes, the Ravens, with that nasty defense, while playing for the Tennessee franchise. "You know how there's hugging before the game between the players from both teams? We'd almost get into a fight before the game. It was war. You felt every single hit. There was bad intentions. It wasn't a catfight—wide receiver versus defensive back. It was true men. They knew we were running the football. Man-on-man is what it was, yes sir. Not like today."

While some pine over the lost days when football was football, gallant warriors wiping mud on terrible injuries to get back out there and play, the game now must answer the question: Where is the line that separates lore and liability?

And what of the coaches? They were bred in a game that still clings to the credo of team and courage. Macho code.

And oh, by the way, their job is on the line. The stakes run as high as any billion-dollar industry, from corporation down to individual.

So when is too far too far? Most coaches will answer when a player's long-term health is in jeopardy. But that's subjective.

One offensive lineman who suffered a fractured leg in 2006 said his head coach snapped at him for not playing in a game. "We're not paying you all of this money to sit out with a broken leg," the coach told him. "You're whining like a little bitch. You can't do any more damage to it. It's just pain. You can't deal with a little pain?"

The league, meanwhile, deserves credit for taking a proactive stance on concussions. Indeed, 2009 proved the year of the concussion. Zero tolerance grounded several high-profile players like Ben Roethlisberger and Brian Westbrook for a stretch of games. Players who suffer a concussion now are required to seek clearance from an independent neurologist.

Patriots linebacker Ted Johnson believes the multiple concussions he suffered while playing football have led to his severe depression and early signs of Alzheimer's disease.

Eagles safety Andre Waters, known for his devastating hits, played through a series of concussions and wound up battling depression postretirement, until he shot and killed himself at the age of forty-four in November 2006. Tests later determined that the father of three had suffered severe brain damage from playing football.

Shortly after Waters's death, Johnson's public assertions to the *New York Times*, and charges from other former players that they played through concussions, the issue of head injuries and the appropriate protection of players came to the forefront prior to last season. Last June, the league held a "concussion summit" attended by trainers and physicians from every NFL team as well as active players and medical representatives from the NFL Players Association. Commissioner Roger Goodell also invited some of the league's loudest medical critics, though Bennet Omalu was not one of them.

Omalu, a forensic pathologist from Pittsburgh, claimed the brain damage he found in four ex-players who died in recent years, including Waters, is the same condition found in punch-drunk boxers and that all of them suffered from severe depression as a result of injuries to their brain. The NFL challenged Omalu's methods and findings and commissioned its own study.

The league subsequently issued a rule before the season mandating that players undergo baseline tests of brain function as a tool in determining readiness to play following a concussion. The NFL also distributed informational pamphlets on concussions for players and their families describing symptoms to look for, set up an anonymous hotline to report information about a player forced to practice or play against medical advice, and reiterated a harder stance on player safety rules relating to the use of the helmet.

From a trainer's perspective, Burkholder has one steadfast rule in handling concussions: Hand over your helmet.

Often a player's hardiness trumps sound judgment, and he will try to hoodwink the medical staff. Such was the case with Keith Adams, a special teams kamikaze for four different teams nicknamed "Bullet" who was knocked out in the last play of a half in a game against Buffalo.

"I go out to get him and he's actually snoring," Burkholder said. "I take his mouthpiece out. He comes to. We get him up. He's totally alert. I think he's doing all right. Now, he's not allowed to play—that's always my decision after a concussion. I'm walking him down the ramp to the locker room and he seems normal. He's telling me everything that happened. Now he's trying to convince me to let him play."

"C'mon, let me go back in," Adams said.

"No."

"Aw, c'mon, Sug," he pleaded.

"Dude, you just called me Sugarman. You don't even know who you're talking to."

Adams thought Burkholder was then assistant trainer Eric Sugarman.

"It was freaky," Burkholder said. "He seemed normal, but he was really screwed up inside. That's why you can never take chances with head injuries."

"Concussions now are a big focus," said former Raider Steve Wisniewski, who played from 1989 through 2001. "In my day, it was smelling salts and shake your head and get back out there. I played through many concussions. Head-to-head contour now is great restricked."

Bill Romanowski played in 243 consecutive games, and estimated he suffered as many twenty concussions during his seventeen-year career, including one that followed a collision with Curtis Martin in which he returned to the Broncos sideline and sat on John Elway's lap. The worst came in 2003 at the end of his career against Denver while playing for the Raiders.

"I left the parking lot at the stadium and I couldn't find my home," he said. "That was how bad the concussions had gotten. They were racking up, one after another. Every time I would get a good hit on somebody I would be dazed and confused. My memory was starting to go. I couldn't remember who sang my favorite song."

Romanowski now spends his days as chairman of his Nutrition 53 supplement company and fully embraces the irony that during his NFL career he once abused steroids, spent almost $200,000 a year on supplements, doctors, and therapists, and had little knowledge of what potions he put into his body. He tried everything from acupuncture to live cell therapy in which he was injected with cells from Scottish black sheep, a practice supposed to promote healing from the physical beating he took on the field. At one point he was taking a hundred pills a day, including vitamins, herbs, enzymes, and amino acids.

"That is my passion right now," he said. "Inspired by all the concussions. After all of my concussions, basically I went around to all the specialists recommended by the NFL and they all told me, 'There's nothing you can do. Time is your friend.'

"I hired my own scientists and doctors to help turn my brain back on. That is what I have dedicated my life to now."

John Spagnola, the former Yale grad who played tight end for three teams in the league from 1979 through 1989, describes a very different approach to head injuries. "They'd wave a finger in your face to see if you're okay," he said. "They'd put three down in your face and say, 'How many?' You'd say, 'Two.'

"And they would say, 'Good. Close enough. Get back out there!'"

Bran Westbrook, who suffered two concussions in the span of three weeks, wrestled hard with the decision of when to return to game action, if at all, in 2009. Beyond medical attention, he sought the advice of several former players.

After missing five games, he eventually played on December 27 against the Broncos with the help of a specially designed helmet with extra cushioning. Leading up to the game, Westbrook admitted it weighed hard on his mind.

"I wasn't going to come back unless I was feeling comfortable," he said. "I didn't want to have a repeat situation. Of course I was very concerned. Anybody would be concerned with the long-term effects. You don't want to continue to play this game if the end result is dementia when you turn forty-five, or brain disease when you turn fifty, Alzheimer's when you turn fifty-five.

"I wanted to know why some of these players who played a long time ago have these diseases today. I wanted to know, if I play will I have these? Am I risking my future? You can never replace your brain. No matter how much money you make, you can't replace being in the right mind, having the ability to think."

Eddie George, the fellow running back, softened his stance on toughness when it came to Westbrook's dilemma. "The position is just so physically demanding," he said. "You're gonna take hits. You have to stand in there, deliver a blow and take a blow. It's always in the back of your mind. It may not come in the fifth, sixth, or seventh hit—but what about the eighth or the ninth one? You don't want to see it happen. My prayers go out to him. It's not about the money or the Super Bowl ring when your health is in question. I know plenty of broke guys with Super Bowl rings."

Suddenly everyone who ever played the game and blacked out for that nanosecond—and the list includes just about every former football player—worries in silence what the future may bring.

Would they someday wake up a vegetable? Would they get so depressed and so frightened that they would do the unthinkable, what Waters did? Put a gun to their head and fix their broken brain once and for all?

Guys like fearless Wayne Chrebet—who had to retire from the Jets because of six documented concussions and God knows how many undocumented ones—who is not out of his thirties, and every time he forgets a name or an item on the grocery list he wonders if this is it.

"I have good days and bad days," Chrebet told the *Newark Star-Ledger*. "A bad day is when you can't get out of bed and there's this dark cloud hanging over your head. A good day is anything else. But you know right away. I know as soon as I wake up what kind of day it'll be.

"Sometimes the bad days and good days go back and forth. Sometimes you get a bunch of them in a row. It's not an exact science. The bad days happen. You just try to make the best of it. But when it's bad, it's really bad. It's not the kind of thing you can talk yourself out of. If it was, I would do it."

Chrebet offers no blame and wants no pity. He told the paper, "It's my own fault. I could have gone out of bounds more. I could've ducked under tackles. They told me, Be careful. One more concussion and you're done. [But] I played the same way. Whose fault is that?"

It's the pact you make, players will say. "When you're a football player, you throw caution to the wind," Seth Joyner said. "You accept whatever comes. You just hope when the gurney comes out you can wiggle your toes. When they blow the whistle, you go and kill each other again. I'm sure I've had numerous concussions and didn't know what it was. I can remember plenty of times taking aspirin and getting back out there."

Joyner was a teammate of Waters. They were dear friends. "I remember Andre walking over center and pointing at Emmitt Smith," Joyner said. "Andre said, 'Boy, you're gonna put him on the ground twice today,' and like clockwork, he'd put it on the ground. A real football player, Andre Waters."

Joyner continued, "All that stuff, it's a part of the game. Your knee gets twisted. You just have to account with that. You play a violent game and someone's going to get hurt. The guys falling down and taking a knee in the head. Nothing you can do for that. No rule you can implement. It's the nature of the game. You know going in what it's all about. You get to do what you love for what's going to come in the future. For some guys it's much more severe than for others. That's the trade-off."

What You Remember Can Be Really Super

We move now to the New York story of a most improbable Super Bowl run, usurping the legend of Broadway Joe and the fabled underdog Jets.

Blue New York/North Jersey was quite the sizable underdog too in the biggest of games, facing the mighty unbeaten Belichicks. But what lifts the 2007 Giants to a team for the ages was the treacherous wild-card road they traveled just to reach the Super Bowl, with stops in Tampa, Dallas, and subzero Green Bay.

"You know? It actually began with the New England game that Saturday night," former Giants defensive coordinator Steve Spagnuolo said.

That Saturday night at Giants Stadium marked the final game of the regular season, and it presented a major dilemma for New York. The Giants had already clinched a playoff berth, and win or lose, they would play at Tampa the following week on Wild Weekend. Meanwhile, the Patriots were looking to trump the 1972 Dolphins by becoming the first team to go unbeaten since the schedule was expanded to sixteen games in 1978.

With nothing to play for, would the Giants just take a knee with a lineup of reserves? Or would they risk injury to key players and play the Pats straight up with history on the line?

After much deliberation, head coach Tom Coughlin walked into a team meeting that week and said, "Guys, I don't know about you, but the only way I know how to play a game is to play it to win."

That surprised many in the room, including Spagnuolo, who admitted, "I thought to myself, 'That's not how you do it. I don't care if they're 15–0. We have nothing to gain. We have nothing to play for. We need to get ready for Tampa.' I thought we'd be a tired and worn-out football team. I was petrified over it."

The Giants were just supposed to be Brady fodder that Saturday night, before a historic national television audience. The game was originally scheduled to be broadcast by the NFL Network, but with history on the line league commissioner Roger Goodell allowed CBS and NBC to televise the game as well, making it the first NFL game ever to be simulcast on more than one network.

With all of those eyes looking for Brady to set the single-season record for touchdown passes and Randy Moss the single-season record for touchdown receptions, the Giants played their hearts out. They actually led 28–16 after the third quarter, the largest deficit faced by New England the entire season, and it took a furious comeback by the Patriots to win the game 38–35.

While the Giants were lauded for their effort, Spagnuolo's fear was only heightened. Four starters were hurt in the game, including key defensive players cornerback Sam Madison and linebacker Kawika Mitchell, and center Shaun O'Hara.

Besides injury, Spagnuolo feared that his team—which relied heavily on the emotion of its attacking defense—would be flat after expending such great energy in a meaningless contest. To make matters worse, the forecast for the game in Tampa called for warm temperatures, an ominous situation for a team now conditioned to play in the winter chill.

"Nothing worse than January heat for a team in the Northeast," he said. "Your body is just not used to it."

Sure enough, the Buccaneers marched right down the field for a touchdown and the Giants managed just two yards of offense in the first quarter. But slowly New York found its legs and dominated the second quarter.

Spagnuolo's plan against Tampa centered around keeping the ever mobile Jeff Garcia from moving up in the pocket where he could buy time—and sight lines. At just over six feet, Garcia can struggle with seeing over the line, so Spagnuolo wanted to box him inside the pocket.

That would prove crucial late in the third quarter with the Giants clinging to a 17–7 lead and beginning to wilt in the unseasonable heat. The Buccaneers now driving deep into New York territory, Spagnuolo gambled with pressure from his linebackers. He called cross dog, a defense where both the strong-side linebacker and the middle line-backer blitz the quarterback.

"Gruden is a good football coach and he was ready for it," Spagnuolo said. "They picked up the blitz. But we got just enough push to bother Garcia."

The two charging backers up the middle left Garcia blindly grasping for the vulnerable spot in the Giants defense. He had to process quickly, the blitz pickup providing only an extra moment of life, and so he slung it into the end zone where there should have been opportunity.

A sliver of space closes like a door slamming shut in this league. Corey Webster, the young corner from swampy Vacherie, an unincorporated community in St. James Parish, Louisiana, filling in for the injured Sam Madison, stepped in front of the pass and corralled the game-clinching interception.

For two weeks along the Trinity River, from the Stemmons Corridor, south to the western portion of downtown and past South Dallas and Pleasant Grove, just about all the way to Houston, the palaver centered around football and threes and the rightful place of America's Team.

How the Cowboys were on the precipice of their third dynasty, from Landry and Staubach of the 1970s to Aikman and Smith of the 1990s to Romo and Owens now. How their road opened kindly with a third game against the Giants and how no way could they lose because the Cowboys had New York's number, dating back to the season opener when they put up 45 to kick off Sunday Night Football and through the rematch on a blustery late November day at Giants Stadium. That game was closer before Dallas pulled away for a 31–20 win, and afterward on the field, Tony Romo sought out Steve Spagnuolo and remarked of his defense, "It's amazing how good you guys got over the course of the season."

But this postseason was about the renaissance of the Cowboys, and no matter how much the Giants defense improved, it seemed highly unlikely, borderline impossible, that New York could keep up with the potent Dallas offense. So much so that prior to the game, Cowboys owner Jerry Jones had two tickets to the NFC Championship Game placed in each player's locker.

"I'll never forget that feeling," Spagnuolo said. "Texas Stadium. That atmosphere. The vibe. The hole in the stadium. The cheerleaders. The star in the middle of the field. Something about that roof. That place. Tom Landry. Roger Staubach. Tony Dorsett. Troy Aikman. Emmitt Smith. It transfixes you. But I remember getting there and Tom [Coughlin] told us the story of what Jerry Jones did. Our guys responded to stuff like that. Strahan. [Justin] Tuck. The offensive linemen. They didn't like it one bit."

At one point in the second quarter, however, the Cowboys held the ball for ten minutes straight and appeared poised to punch those tickets—and avoid tying an NFL record with six straight playoff losses. They drove 90 yards using a whopping twenty plays, capped by a 1-yard dive by Marion Barber in the end zone, and led 14–7.

Quicker than you can say my brother's keeper, Eli Manning brought New York right back on a boomerang possession, the Giants traveling 71 yards in just forty seconds to tie the game right before halftime.

But the Cowboys still held a dramatic advantage in time of possession and a sense of control of the game. The Giants defense couldn't get off the field.

"I told the guys at halftime that the first half was not their fault," Spagnuolo said. "I didn't call the game aggressively enough. So the guys didn't play aggressive."

In the 92nd meeting between the teams—and first in the playoffs—the Giants defense bought Spagnuolo's speech and held the Cowboys to just three points in the second half, rising up especially on the final drive of the game. With thirty-one seconds left, Dallas reached the New York 22-yard line and Spagnuolo became more aggressive with his call.

Over Spade.

It's an all-out blitz called out of the nickel or dime defense, bringing as many as eight rushers with man coverage on the outside. The middle linebacker has a read—he can either rush or drop back into coverage.

Following a false start penalty and an incompletion, Kawika Mitchell dropped back into coverage and nearly had an interception.

"I called the same all-out blitz back-to-back," Spagnuolo said. "First play almost got there. I figured, screw it, run it again."

Romo spied Terry Glenn in the end zone, but this time the rush nearly swallowed him. He threw a desperation wobbler that R. W. McQuarters, the cornerback from dusty Oklahoma nicknamed R. Dubbs, picked off to finally seal the game.

"I went back to calling the game aggressively and our players did the rest," Spagnuolo said. "Looking back on it, we got smoked defensively that first game against them—they went up and down the field on us—but we had about four or five blitzes that were right there. They were close. It was our first game and our timing wasn't there. But we laid down the seeds and it all came together in that playoff game."

Following the game, the talk centered around Romo's bye-week junket to Cabo with pop star Jessica Simpson. "You have to be careful in those bye weeks," Spagnuolo said. "Players have to have time off. They've earned it. What are you going to do? Romo in Mexico was a mistake. He probably made the wrong choice. It was good for us.

"I like Tony Romo a lot. He's legit."

Spagnuolo said following that game he texted Romo: "I think you're a helluva player."

Romo replied, "I hope you win enough games this year so you get a head coaching job and are out of the NFC East."

The Giants played interlopers again a week later in the NFC Championship Game, the next great inspirational sports movie written in reality before our eyes. The graying Packer in the winter of his career playing at home in the deep Wisconsin freeze for the right to slay the unbeaten Patriots in the Super Bowl, the perfect ending to an illustrious career for America's quarterback.

The Giants portrayed the no-name opponent in the story, nothing literary about them. The colder it dipped that Sunday leading up to kickoff, the larger Brett Favre grew, just like the week before when he and the Packers trampled the Seahawks 42–20 in a snowstorm at Lambeau Field. The pictures from that game circulated through the country all week. They were as delightful as Christmas stockings over a fireplace, the legend packing snowballs after a touchdown and throwing them playfully at his teammates.

Spagnuolo studied hard to play Scrooge.

"The biggest thing with Favre in Green Bay is to disrupt the timing of the routes of his receivers," he said. "The whole thing is timing. You have to disrupt his wide receivers. You want to pressure him but you really want his receivers off their routes. To beat him—especially there—you have to catch the ones he throws to you. At some point in the game, he's going to do it. Favre is a guy with guts. He's going to take a chance and throw you one. You just have to catch it."

The Giants caught two of them, and they caught a quarterback who looked terribly old in the cold, transforming from superhero to mortal, like anyone life-weary and weather-beaten from the northern bowl desperately seeking the calm of a lemonade on the back porch.

New York stuffed Green Bay's run game and held the Packers to just 264 total yards—90 coming on one play, a fluke touchdown catch and mostly run by Donald Driver—and stopped them on third down nine of ten times. The Giants left the game in Favre's frostbitten hands after Lawrence Tynes squandered two makable game-winning kicks, one at the end of regulation and the other early in overtime. Faure had the ball on a second-and-8 from his own 28, and Spagnuolo smelled pass and called a defense he had used for much of the day.

Fox Man.

It's a six-man pressure, born out of base defense, featuring two blitzing linebackers, with the other linebacker under and the safeties deep for help over the top. The Giants had never played that entering the game.

Favre chucked it 15 yards downfield looking for Driver, taking one of those chances Spagnuolo spoke about, and Corey Webster intercepted the pass.

The Giants, however, stalled again, and faced a fourth-and-5 from the Green Bay 29.

"Tom was on the headset talking to his guys figuring out what he was going to do when he sees the kid [Tynes] run onto the field," Spagnuolo said. "[Coughlin] thinks he must know something. That he must be confident. So he let him kick the field goal. I think if that didn't happen and it was left in the hands of Tom, he would have punted it."

Tynes's third attempt muscled through the frigid evening air—which dipped to minus-three late in the game, and minus-seventeen with the windchill—and split the uprights.

"You can't imagine how cold it was," Spagnuolo said. "I wore a stocking cap the first time ever. At the end of the game, my head was sweating so much I took it off. Within three minutes, my ears started to hurt. And then they just froze. The weather was the biggest thing. People said to me afterwards that the cameras showed that Brett was cold. You know, it's different in that kind of cold for a thirty-seven-year-old than a twenty-seven-year-old."

It was so cold that the league held the NFC Championship trophy ceremony inside the cramped visitor's locker room of mourning Lambeau.

Everyone knows well now the Miracle Drive, the coming of age of Little Brother, David Tyree's Sticky Helmet, and the 13-yard snare with thirty-five seconds left by poor imprisoned Plax to complete the most impressive slingshot victory since the relieving of Lucknow. But what still begs, even now amid the recession of the Patriot Empire, is how in the hell did the Giants hold that team to 14 points?

Two touchdowns?

By a team that scored 75 on the season? That scored at least 20 points in every single game all year long prior to the Super Bowl? That was held below 30 points only four times? That scored 56 once (Buffalo), 52 once (Washington), 49 once (Miami), 48 once (Dallas), and 38 four times (Jets, Chargers, Bills, and, uh, yes, Giants)? That produced seven AFC Players of the Week (Brady five times, Moss twice), and won the AFC Player of the Month honors for September (Brady), October (Brady), and November (Moss)? That produced five Pro Bowlers on offense (Brady, Moss, tackle Matt Light, guard Logan Mankins, and center Dan Koppen), three players on the NFL's All-Pro first team (Brady, Moss, Light), and three on the second team (Mankins, Koppen, and wide receiver Wes Welker)?

How?

The day after the NFC Championship Game, Steve Spagnuolo scribbled down on scratch paper two action items:

1. *Must* hit Brady
2. If Brady gets it off, *must* make the tackle at the catch

Meanwhile, Spagnuolo's wife, Maria, the lovely spitfire blonde, told him that day she had a good feeling about playing New England and she swore it wasn't wife's confidence.

"I was shitting myself," he said. "I thought if we held them under 30 we had a shot. Of course, I didn't know if we could hold them under 30. I thought we played well against them in game 16 and all the pressure we had in the game plan that night was not to beat the Patriots. It was to set up the Bucs—which I knew might not necessarily work against the Patriots."

Spagnuolo remembered one other thing from that regular-season finale. While he was walking off the field at the end of the game, defensive end Justin Tuck sidled up next to him and whispered, "If we play them again, just let the four of us rush."

So Spagnuolo trusted in his Blue front four, mostly consisting of rushers Strahan, Tuck, and Osi Umenyiora, and stout inside pushers Fred Robbins and Barry Cofield. He said he blitzed only about 35 percent of the time but his defense still recorded five sacks, including two by the budding young Tuck and one by Strahan. They were relentless. They bothered Brady all night, and Brady was clearly annoyed by it.

Like most great quarterbacks, Brady doesn't like to get touched, and somewhere there is a tape of Brady, miked up for the game—the aim being to record history, no doubt, supposing history—storming to the sideline more than once screaming, "What the fuck is going on? What are they doing?"

Brady began to show frustration midway through the second quarter. New England led 7–3 and took over the ball at its own 30. Conventional wisdom figured this would be the drive the Patriots would click on offense because they had clicked all year on offense and now presented the perfect opportunity, deep enough into the game to find that rhythm. But after Laurence Maroney was stuffed on first down, Spagnuolo sent his linebackers and Kawika Mitchell corralled Brady for a 7-yard loss. On third-and-long, Spagnuolo rushed four and Tuck registered the sack, minus another 7 yards.

The Patriots seemed to finally generate movement just before the half after converting a third-and-13 from their own 8-yard line. One of the rare connections between the record holders—Brady and Moss— moved the ball all the way to the New York 44. Going no-huddle and working out of the shotgun, Brady frantically tried to make a big play, but Tuck leveled him again. The ball popped free and Umenyiora fell on the fumble for the suddenly swaggering Giants.

They were excited at halftime. After all, they had just held that offense to only 7 points and 81 total yards. New England had the ball for just over ten minutes in the half—a few seconds less than the Giants' opening drive.

First of all, Steve Spagnuolo said, you really need to credit the offense. Because the Giants took the opening kickoff and held the ball for nine minutes and fifty-nine seconds, the longest drive in Super Bowl history. They only went 63 yards and didn't even score a touchdown, settling for a 32-yard field goal, but the point was to keep that offense antsy on the sideline.

"[Coughlin] figured it out," he said. "Run the ball. He's a smart football guy. He watches a lot of film. It's funny, every Friday we'd watch film together at six thirty a.m., and every other week he'd see something from an offensive point of view that would make me rethink the game plan some. Those six thirty meetings were a pain in the ass— I had a lot of stuff to do, and let's face it, you're with the boss. But I'd always go back and tell the [rest of the coaches], 'You know what? He makes a lot of sense.'"

Everything made sense during that historic run. Such a treacherous road they traveled as the wild card, through hot Tampa and chilling Dallas and chilly Green Bay, just for the right to play the Unbeatens.

"During the four-game run, we put things in game-plan-wise and it seemed like they all worked," Spagnuolo said. "It was one of those magical things. That doesn't happen all the time."

For the Love of the Game

The story of the fastest man in Florida who was always late begins with him mopping up a smelly restroom at a roadside gas station in a two-traffic-light town.

It's why he wants to write a book: *From the Toilet Bowl to the Super Bowl*.

It's his title.

It's also a story with a third act that only lasts eighteen seconds.

Because Ron Dixon overslept after the Super Bowl and missed the rest of his career. We'll talk about the Super Bowl and the seventeen seconds where America knew he was the fastest man in Florida and maybe everywhere. But what happened thereafter is what doesn't haunt him now, and perhaps that's why it ended the way it did—so prematurely—which tells you more about the game than the guy who plays through the pain to a permanent limp.

You have to love it to last in it.

Love in the sense that it defines you. Football players are football players, even if they're selling title insurance.

See, one time Ron Dixon left the alarm clock downstairs. Another time he set the little switch on the back of the clock to p.m. instead of a.m., and he missed another one of those Saturday meetings, and then it only got worse, and the coach tried harder to break him and it became this thing in the New York papers and the tabloids plastered his picture on the back page beneath the headline "Giant Pain." And he was a pain, and it's a shame because he wasn't a crook and he wasn't a creep and he wasn't a thug. He was just late or absent or absentminded, head-in-the-clouds sorts of things, maddeningly so, though. And so the coach grew more exasperated because of that speed—wasted like the Bugatti Veyron that sits in the garage because its owner can't drive—that blinding speed that makes offensive coaches like Jim Fassel drool.

Florida speed.

Synonymous with Florida players.

Players turned Gators like Reidel Anthony, Jacquez Green, Ike Hilliard—Dixon's contemporaries. He was supposed to join them at the University of Florida too. All the big schools found out about him, down there, hidden in the dead middle of the state, deep-country Florida, place called Wildwood. Located some eighty-five miles north of Tampa—and way more Mississippi—Wildwood represents the bulk of Sumter County, once tabbed Hog County because of all the wild hogs that ran free.

Dixon settled on Central Florida, a rising program at the time that produced Daunte Culpepper, but he didn't have the grades, the same way he couldn't make it to practice. See, for most of Ron Dixon's early life he intellectually understood the notion that 80 percent of life is just showing up, but he just couldn't make himself get there on time for the things in which he had little interest.

So instead of Gainesville, Dixon found himself in places like Tupelo, Mississippi, at Itawamba Community College, a rehab-for-collegiate-standing type of school that boasts Lambert Stadium, named for the late A. C. "Butch" Lambert, home of the Wolves, located about forty-five miles west of Atlanta.

He flunked out of West Georgia because he just couldn't bring himself to the classes he didn't enjoy, and the solid B's in the ones he did weren't enough to bring up his GPA, which forced him back to community college in Florida, two more, to be exact—Lake Sumter and Tallahassee.

The fastest man in Florida now cleaning toilets in that smelly restroom at the service station found his way for one year to Lambuth University, a school in West Tennessee named after a pioneer Methodist missionary bishop, Reverend Walter R. Lambuth, that proclaims "an opportunity for students to use their intelligence in the service of God and humanity."

"Hell, I knew I had to rip it to shreds," Dixon said. "I knew it was NAIA football. I knew we didn't play at nighttime. I knew we didn't have lights. I couldn't have 34 catches. I had to have astronomical numbers."

Out there by Forked Deer River, facing one last chance at salvation, he produced a season so statistically ridiculous that one NFL personnel man remarked, "I don't care if you're doing that against air, that's a lot of production."

Eighty-nine catches for 1,735 yards and 22 touchdowns—19 receiving, 2 on punt returns, 1 on a kickoff return.

Some NFL types trekked to Jackson during the season to see if some of the early numbers were the least bit real, including two scouts from the Giants. How exhilarating such a trip for a scout. The longing of the scout—any scout, for any talent—has always been to unearth that next star from some faraway land or remote outpost, though it's becoming a lost art with the world shrinking so rapidly. It used to be about discovery back in the day, say back when Jerry Rice played for Archie "Gunslinger" Cooley at Mississippi Valley State. The further back, in the days of the Colonel who discovered Elvis, the greater the challenge and the more a scout needed things like guile and underground contacts and a compulsion to know something the rest of the world didn't, schlepping to nowhere places on a whim and a whisper.

Now the trek is a click, and only the eyes get taxed—from sifting through all that video, because even the poor baseball boys of Latin America have their reels posted on YouTube. Dixon was pre–camera phone, and so it took until the end of the season before word drifted across the league.

"I had my own little combine," Dixon recalled. "First workout— fifteen teams. Second week—seventeen teams. They wanted to see whether I was legit. They didn't know if I get off the ball so they had one of the dudes line up on me—I done broke his ankles. They didn't realize what my capabilities were."

He showed everyone who was the fastest man in Florida when he replaced Laveranues Coles in the Gridiron Classic, then a highly regarded postseason all-star game. That was his coming-out party—particularly the one play where he traveled 70 yards on a 34-yard run. Everyone raved about that fast country kid. A bit of a fuckup, but boy could he run.

It was hardest on the Giants. At one point they figured they had him stashed and could wait until the seventh round to draft him. But after the private workouts and that game, his stock soared and New York selected him in the third round in the 2000 draft.

Technically, the third act of the story begins here.

His first return for a touchdown that postseason came on the open- ing kickoff of the divisional playoffs against the Eagles. The Philadelphia coverage team didn't do much wrong on the play, meaning the players mostly stayed in their lanes. They just couldn't catch Ron Dixon.

"I can still smell the grass in my face when I dove and reached for his cleat," the Eagles' Ike Reese said.

The grass was cool and a bit wet and Dixon's feet sounded like those of a racehorse, such loud steps for a slight man. Reese had the best opportunity to tackle him, and when the grass kicked up like a divot following a poor golf swing, Dixon was in the clear and effectively winning the game on the game's first play.

Super Bowl XXXV between New York and Baltimore took place in Tampa, of all places, a pleasant drive from Wildwood and Hog County. The Giants, who had crushed the Vikings 41–0 in the NFC Championship Game, couldn't do much offensively against Ray Lewis and the suffocating Baltimore defense. They trailed 17–0 after Duane Starks returned an interception 49 yards for a touchdown with 3:49 left in the third quarter.

The ensuing kickoff soared high into the sultry Florida evening. Ron Dixon looked the ball into his arms at the 3-yard line and began to move. He shot forward through the gaping hole to the left side of the wedge, slipped past a grazing hand of a tackler, cut it back to the center of the field, faking two more potential tacklers into losing their footing, and broke into the clear.

Just as he had done against the Eagles a few weeks prior to open the playoffs, he arched his back to avoid one last desperation dive at him, squared up, and raced into the end zone for a 97-yard return for a touchdown on the opening kickoff of the Giants' postseason.

Dixon had begun this incredible Giant run and now he could provide it hope during the biggest game. But when he tried to shift into that last gear—which made him such an extraordinary talent—his legs denied him. They started to pinch and suddenly feel oddly heavy.

The specter of his dream was chasing him now.

And now it's time for him to tell the rest of the story in his own words:

I wanted to show America my speed. I was on the biggest stage. Since way back in high school—when I knew I'd play in the NFL—I had this fear of getting ran down from behind because of cramps. I saw it happen to my cousin. So I was consumed by it. And as I passed the kicker and I started to feel the cramps, I started breaking down. I was like, "Oh, no, this is not happening."

I had prepared for this moment. This was my moment. I wanted to show America my speed. I closed my eyes and tried to run through it. I wasn't going to stop. I would have torn ligaments before I stopped. I get past the kicker and I see dudes running not far away beside me. I knew I was going to make it. I slow down. I score. I feel like I'm walking from the Old West or something in the end zone. Like I had on Cowboy boots.

Mike Strahan carried me off the field. I'm a Florida boy so I didn't think about it. I drank water like I was normal. I didn't think about it until afterwards that I had been in the New York snow. I got the IV right there on the sidelines. They put the needle in. I took so much liquid I peed. On the sidelines of the Super Bowl. You'd think they'd have Porta-Potties out there.

I wish we would have won the game. Since we had to lose, I'm glad I'm the only one who scored a touchdown. I know women who remember that touchdown. Women that remember that don't like football—who just go to Super Bowl parties.

What do you say to a football player who doesn't have that experience? One who plays for Cincinnati—let's be real, they're not the New York Giants. I was lucky in that respect.

Dixon's return wound up being the Giants' only points of the game. So happens, too, Jermaine Lewis for the Ravens returned the ensuing kickoff 84 yards for a touchdown in a Super Bowl back-to-back first and Baltimore won easily, 34–7.

And that was basically a wrap for Ron Dixon. He played two more tumultuous seasons for the Giants, incurring more fines for tardiness and missing rehab appointments after injuring his knee. The knee eventually derailed him. It took away that blinding speed and suddenly he wasn't worth the hassle. He never did get to show how good a receiver he could be other than a few glimpses. For his career, he averaged an impressive 19.3 yards per catch—36 receptions totaling 696 yards—and scored four touchdowns.

"What I used to hate about the whole thing is they would have plays for me," he said. "I'd tell my mom they were going to run them. They had five plays and they'd never run 'em. I'll never forget we played Chicago one game. I got a first down off a reverse on the first series. Later I come in and catch a 34-yard touchdown in the back corner of the end zone. And I didn't see the field the rest of that game.

"When the media would ask about me, Fassel would tell them, 'Oh, he doesn't know the plays.' That's the excuse they'd use. Who doesn't know how to run a go [route]? It's fucking football. And I had Kerry Collins throwing the ball all over the place. It was horrible, the not playing. I wanted to perform—and I used to give the devil in practice. I came late to practice. So what? They never seen me with pills. I never got a DUI. I just came late to practice."

Looking back, the fastest man in Florida was cursed with a gift he didn't much care for. He's an insurance salesman now, but he wants to entertain people. He says he's developing a television show—a sort of variety show—and he wants to have Jim Fassel on as a guest.

"I'm going to tell him the wrong time to make sure he's late," he said, "and then I'm going to tell him, 'I'm fining your ass!'"

Deep down, through all of the justifications and excuses, Ron Dixon knows Fassel basically did what he had to do. That the lesson of his story transcends pettiness and even his transgressions, however small and maddening, and centers on the gifts we sometimes don't choose for ourselves.

"I came from a small town," he said. "Football was all that I had. After I got there and I got to the Super Bowl, I didn't want to go to practice. I didn't mean to disrespect football. I just didn't love it the way other guys loved it. Like now—I don't want to be a coach. I don't want to be on the sidelines. I don't want to be a sports announcer.

"You can love a lot of things about football. You can love the crowds. You can love the cheers. At a certain level, you have to truly love the game."

In the Line of Duty

Let us revisit that game with another, much larger man who played offensive line for the Baltimore Ravens and walks intermittently now. He shuffles along fine until his back begins to whine—furiously so— and he hunches over until he can find a place to rest, and suddenly the black hair atop his head looks like a lie.

Spencer Sione Folau considers himself one of the lucky ones because he's close to winning his insurance claim for "line of duty" benefits and he can have that back fusion surgery and silence that bulging disc once and for all, and because he kicked his addiction to painkillers and because he's not that old teammate he saw at the championship autograph show reunion who needed to borrow cash to get home.

First, though, he wants to speak of that Super Bowl and of the entire Baltimore season, one of those once-in-a-lifetime journeys few professional athletes will ever experience.

"The Giants had no chance in that game," Folau said. "Absolutely no chance. From the beginning, we knew it."

He cited a series of early tells:

- Tiki Barber thought he had the corner on one of the first plays from scrimmage for the Giants. A patch of open green up the

sideline appeared in front of him. Folau calculated quickly—
he could go for sure for 5 yards, maybe even 10. But suddenly
Barber disappeared, sucked to the earth. Ray Lewis had tracked
him down for a 1-yard loss.

- Giants left tackle Lomas Brown couldn't block Michael McCrary,
  the Ravens' right defensive end. McCrary beat Brown three
  times in the first quarter, hounding quarterback Kerry Collins for
  a sack and two hurries.
- The entire Baltimore defense just looked too fast for the Giants,
  who managed only one first down in their first six possessions.
- Brandon Stokley caught that 34-yard touchdown from Trent Dilfer
  on a post pattern over top against Giants corner Jason Sehorn,
  who was left without safety help midway through the first quarter. Any points the dormant offense could contribute—especially
  early—only added to the fierceness of that Raven defense. Folau
  said Lewis stood up in the middle of the Saturday night team
  meeting and declared directly to the offense, "If you score 14
  points, we will win the game. That's a promise."

In a display of Super Bowl dominance that rivaled only that of the
1985 Bears, the Ravens defense battered Collins into 15 of 39 passing
for just 112 yards, picking him off four times, including one interception
returned for a touchdown.

Dilfer—the ultimate game manager, a euphemism for a quarterback
whose primary job is not to make mistakes—only completed 12 of 26
throws for 153 yards, including the toss to Stokley, and said afterward,
"I didn't throw the ball very well. But we talked about making big plays
and we made them when we needed them. We aren't pretty, like St.
Louis, but we get the job done."

To which Folau says now, "Let's be honest. We would have won if
the offense didn't set foot on the field."

When Folau thinks back to that season, he goes all the way back
to August. Former Redskins great Joe Theismann told them first during a visit to training camp. "This is a special team," he said. "I sense
it. You guys will go to the Super Bowl." Folau deemed Theismann
genuine in his belief. It was not a case of a long-ago legend in
for a chummy visit playing smoke-blower. Everyone from within felt
it, too.

Here's how Folau remembered the Ravens of 2000:

We knew the defense would be off the charts. We knew we had a good run game with Jamal Lewis and Priest Holmes. The nucleus was there. Even during the first half of the season when we were 5–4 and we barely had an offense and we didn't score a touchdown for five weeks, we knew we just needed some time for everything to come together.

There was something about that team. Felt more like a college team. Guys hung out together. It was the most team thing I ever felt playing in the league. It was fun to be in the locker room and at practice. [Tony] Siragusa was hysterical. I remember him saying to McCrary about me, "He owns you."

McCrary was a head case. He'd tape up some more and Goose would get on him again. "Spence kicked your ass yesterday."

"Quit it, Goose," I'd say. "You don't have to rile his ass up anymore."

Every Friday, we—Jonathan Ogden, Mike Flynn, and most of the offensive line—got in the cold tub. We all had to dunk our heads in at a forty-five-degree angle. When we got to Tampa for the Super Bowl, we had the other facility so there was no cold tub. So we filled garbage cans with ice and water and dunked our heads.

What an amazing ride.

Life is tenuous in the league, with teams constantly evolving, even the Super Bowl types. Players change with the frequency of the food on a supermarket shelf. And players sometimes lament the current way, despite the gift of free agency, and wonder how much fun it would have been to play back in the day—the 1970s and 1980s—when teams stayed together and you knew who occupied the locker next you from season to season and it only ended because of organic attrition.

So Spencer Folau would never come close to that experience in Baltimore—beyond the ring and the glory—for the rest of his days in the league.

He signed a one-year deal with Miami following the Super Bowl and helped the Dolphins to an 11–5 record as a starter at left tackle. Miami lost that year to his old Baltimore team in a wild-card game, but Folau proved his worth and the Saints inked him to a multiyear contract.

While the money was nice, and he had a steady job, playing in all but two games from 2002 through 2004, the seasons went by in dull color. The Saints were stuck in purgatory, finishing 9–7, 8–8, and 8–8, and New Orleans just didn't feel like Baltimore. How could it, really? Theismann called that Ravens team a special bunch, and football always feels different in Baltimore. It's bred into the landscape, the way the Phoenix Shot Tower shaped downtown. It's really Footbaltimore, you know, cemented so after World War II and certainly after the 1958 Championship Game, which inspired John Steadman to write in the *News-Post*: "You can get flowery and sentimental over the Baltimore Colts. In harsh reality, they are just a gang of professional foot-ball players representing a city known as Baltimore in a state called Maryland. But, no, the Baltimore Colts are more than that. Call them a way of life. To some of the faithful they really and truly are."

In New Orleans, still the most foreign city in America, despite the prox-imity of Bayou Ball, something wholly rooted in college, the Saints' legacy is one of beads and brown paper bags, and while bright young coach Jim Haslett always seemed on the cusp of changing that after the mess left by Mike Ditka and Ricky Williams, he could never take that final step. And think about Ditka for a moment—yes, he overpaid for Williams, but there was no reason other than a bong that Williams shouldn't have panned out as the franchise back the coach wanted to build around.

It felt that way for Folau toward the end of his time there in the late summer of 2005, the days leading up to calamity. His shoulder felt like it was hanging off its hinges. The surgery early that year hadn't really worked, and now the team pressed him to get back on the field.

Folau knew why:

They gave me four cortisone shots within a month—and you're not supposed to do that but once or twice a year in a certain area. The shots didn't help and the doctor who did my shoulder did a half-assed job. He didn't fix the whole thing. They kept pestering me to practice for one reason.

Get him on the field. Get him on film. Release him.

They can't release me if I'm injured.

The Thursday before a preseason game, Coach Haslett called me to his office. "We need you to play," he said.

"Coach, I'm not doing this. I'm not ready. You just want me to play so you can cut me."

"No, we're not. We really need to see what we got."

That preseason game on Thursday happened to be against Baltimore, and so afterward Folau took Jonathan Ogden and some of his old Raven buddies to his favorite restaurant in the French Quarter to reminisce about that night in Tampa and that magical season and all of the wonderful memories. They ate and they drank and they laughed, and they heard something about that storm the weather people had been tracking. Apparently, it had ravaged Miami and Fort Lauderdale earlier in the evening, killing four people and leaving one million without power. Apparently, it had become a Category 1 hurricane.

They were calling it Katrina.

According to the National Oceanic and Atmospheric Administration:

The projected path has the hurricane hitting the Florida panhandle. The government projection model breaks down regarding what might happen next.

Beyond three days, when Katrina is forecast to be in the eastern Gulf of Mexico, the models diverge significantly suggesting tracks which cover the coast from Mississippi eastward. The official forecast turns Katrina northward over the eastern Gulf of Mexico ahead of a strong approach trough on a track which is very close to the global model consensus. This forecast is rather difficult since one of the more reliable models—the GFS—shows that the cyclone barely touches the east coast of Florida before moving northward, while the outstanding GFDL moves Katrina south of due west across extreme South Florida and the Keys as a very intense hurricane.

On Friday, coverage of the storm dominated the newscasts, and Folau began to pay extra attention as he went about his personal life, this being an off day following the game.

By Friday evening, panic began to seep into town. Folau and his family sat transfixed watching the news that had replaced regularly scheduled programming.

Suddenly it was getting scary, and fearing a mass exodus, Folau packed the car late that night. Just in case.

Early Saturday morning, as he drove to work, Folau heard there was another slight change of the hurricane's path.

It's all everyone was talking about at Saints headquarters, and how could they not talk about it? A deadly storm loomed out there somewhere in the distance, marching toward a prone city. Weather folks said it threatened the future of New Orleans. It's unlikely they would discuss the wildcat offense or the Tampa Two at the Apocalypse.

It was a group conversation among the injured players and trainers in the training room, as Folau received treatment on his ailing shoulder.

Can you imagine living in another time? When there was no warning except the cluster of darkening clouds, the lightning off in the horizon, and the faraway crackle of thunder? When it was too late to pack up and hightail it to safer ground? What must they have done? Sat there in makeshift hovels like lambs waiting for slaughter?

About then, a member of the personnel department entered the room and approached Folau. The players eyed the trespasser spuriously.

"They need you upstairs," he said. "Coach Haslett needs to see you."

Folau knew what was going down, something other than storm contingency plans.

"Are you kidding me? What a joke!" he lashed out.

The Saints had released him.

Meanwhile, the city announced that New Orleans International Airport was now closed and offered a formal plan for evacuation on the roadways. The Louisiana State Police had activated the state contraflow plan allowing traffic to use both sides of Interstates 55, 59, and 10 to evacuate New Orleans to the north, east, and west.

Early Sunday morning, August 29, the day before the storm, the Folaus prepared to escape New Orleans. The all-news station on the radio played in the background. They slept to it and awoke to it:

Hurricane Katrina is now a potentially catastrophic Category 5 hurricane. Southeast Louisiana remains the projected landfall with 29 percent probability of the eye passing within sixty-five nautical miles of New Orleans.

The Superdome is now open as a special-needs shelter.

New Orleans mayor Ray Nagin orders a mandatory evacuation. He says, "We are facing a storm that most of us have feared. I don't want to create panic, but I do want citizens to understand that this is very serious, and it is of the highest nature."

The National Weather Service issues an urgent weather message predicting devastating damage from the hurricane. "Most of the area will be uninhabitable for weeks, perhaps longer. At least one-half of well-constructed homes will have roof and wall failure. Water shortages will make human suffering incredible by modern standards."

Like most on the choked highways that led out of New Orleans, the Folaus were headed to Houston, some 350 miles away through traffic and panic. They checked into a hotel and spent the next few days watching coverage of their city's drowning. Folau cannot forget the computer model showing an aerial map of the city color-coded with water levels. The darker the color, the deeper the water.

"They showed our neighborhood," he said. "All black with water."

A few days later, the Folaus drove back to their other family home, in Baltimore. Spencer Folau needed to devise a plan for the season. It wasn't right that the Saints had cut him.

"I needed to go to another team so they could deny me to prove the Saints did wrong," he said.

So he flew out to San Francisco for a visit with the 49ers. Following a physical, he received pretty incredulous word from the team through his agent, Tony Agnone: "Are you kidding? You have a torn labrum and a biceps problem. You can't even practice."

Usually, a player, even if he's a long shot to sign, will meet with the coaches. The process didn't even get that far. Team doctors warned San Francisco not to sign him—which only built up Folau's case against the Saints.

Folau wound up winning his grievance.

"They didn't want to pay me a salary that year so they tried to screw me over," he said. "They didn't put me on IR [injured reserve] for a couple hundred grand. I could just hear [owner Tom Benson]— 'I'm not putting him on IR. Too much money.' What a terrific guy, huh? I wound up getting 80 percent of my salary. So instead of 2005, I got paid in 2006 for that season."

Fast-forward to retirement, the big autograph extravaganza in 2008, featuring Baltimore's two favorite championship football teams—the 2000 Ravens and the 1958 Colts.

"I thought it would be awesome to see a lot of the guys again," Folau said. "But it turned out it wasn't really about the guys. Some of the guys said they came just because they needed the money."

The one guy especially, and the conversation with him—a former teammate whom Folau had genuinely looked forward to seeing that night—had been troubling.

Folau greeted him with a big smile. "Dude, what's going on?"

"Nothin' really. I just came for the check."

"It's a nice check. So—"

The man interrupted him. "Let me ask you something. You know how to get into your 401(k)?"

"Listen," Folau told him. "You don't want to do that. You'll have to pay a huge penalty. Trust me—it's a bad idea."

"Yeah, man, well, sometimes you gotta do what you gotta do."

"Dude, really, I'm sure there are ways to go."

"Spence," the man just blurted out, "I need some gas money. You got anything on you?"

Folau reached into his pocket and handed the man what he had on him. Forty or so dollars.

When Folau finished reciting the story, he paused and said, "Dude, he asked me for gas money? You believe that? I'm thinking, 'Oh, dude. Dude. Damn, dude.'

"This was in 2008. We won the Super Bowl in January 2001. That's only seven years ago. We were riding high. Now the poor guy needs a few bucks for gas? So sad to see that. Everyone thinks we make millions of dollars. They see Manning and Lewis. They see the top 10 percent. They don't talk about the other forty guys in the locker room who don't make anywhere near those guys. The money is good—but it's short-term. How long does it last? When they retire, do they have something to fall back on? Most haven't graduated. What do they put on a résumé? What do they know how to do? What's in store for them? For the rest of their lives? And that's saying they're healthy. If not, then what?"

Folau played nearly a decade in the NFL in relative obscurity, a typical lineman's life. His size gives it away that he played. That 6-foot-5, 300-something-pound frame, and the hobbled walk that came from all of the pounding and the hitting. See, the back spasms grew incrementally worse after his retirement in 2006 and made his postfootball life miserable. He couldn't work because the pain was incapacitating and he couldn't even get the benefits because the series of doctors couldn't declare him legally disabled because the MRI couldn't find anything. His other postplaying ailments that should have gone to aid his case for "line of duty" benefits—the lingering pain from two left knee surgeries, a right knee procedure to fix his MCL, and two shoulder surgeries—somehow didn't matter either.

A couple of years later, during a sitting MRI, doctors found the condition that ails him—degenerative disc disease. So he's allowed to file again, and that's a bright light in his life, along with kicking the drugs.

Folau tried every back remedy north of acupuncture and south of massage. He visited specialists and healers and witch doctors. Only the pills offered relief. He'd gulp them down every morning to get through the first part of the day. Sure, he was hooked. He knew how common the story. He knew plenty of guys who fell slave to the pain meds. But seriously, the pain, so excruciating, he just couldn't take it. He'd try to play mental games. Pretend it wasn't there. But that's the thing, the pain was always there, dominating his thoughts.

Except when he took the pills.

He didn't want to be a zombie and he didn't want his liver to quit on him at forty and he found himself taking higher and higher dosages, and so one day he decided to just make the pain part of his life. And that led to another day, and another, until he didn't take another one of those damn things.

"Been clean since January 2008," he said. "The pain still sucks. I wake up in the morning and it's brutal. Takes me a good hour or two to roll out of bed. Once I get going it's manageable—unless I'm in one place for too long, and then this sharp pain shoots down my back into my butt. My knee bothers me most of the time. My shoulder as well. But I cope with it. I'm one of the lucky ones."

The Land of Warriors

Let us travel back further with Folau—and his countrymen—to football's spectacular journey.

See, the game doesn't much import, especially compared to the other American sports. Baseball dips down into Mexico for its participants and throughout the ripe Latin basin, and now stretches to the Far East. The Japanese and the Taiwanese and the Koreans own a piece of our pastime the way China owns a piece of our debt, which is to say it's duly noted on the books.

And basketball's expansion is reminiscent of the Roman Empire in its latter days, when global domination mattered more than life inside the kingdom. Everyone plays hoops as everyone plays soccer. So the rosters of the NBA resemble a meeting of the World Trade Organization. Seventy-one different countries boast representation in the league, give or take a Gabon or Guyana.

Football buys American. Because the game is born of American fabric in wholly American pockets—the kind dubbed Main Street USA by the politicians—divided into the distinct subsets of the country, from coast to coast, spreading out to the Rust Belt and down to the Bible Belt and all of those leafy suburbs in between with high school football fields that come to life under the Friday night lights.

NFL Europe might as well have been Thanksgiving Europe. Despite filling Wembley during the annual junket back across the pond and a once aggressive approach toward global expansion, football remains a New World game played solely by New World folks, with one small exception far, far away from the house in Berea sporting the wool Browns banner in the front window.

Way, way out on the edge of the world, the game lives in a tiny cluster of islands in the South Pacific called the Friendly Islands—so named for the warm reception that Captain James Cook received upon his arrival there in 1773, though according to writer William Mariner, the local chiefs had feigned kindness to the famed British explorer and cartographer to murder him during a local festival but couldn't agree on a method. Nevertheless, the romantic notion of escaping to that exotic land that dots the ocean way, way out on the edge of the world was born, as Cook's sailing master William Bligh regrettably found out twelve years later on his excursion 86 degrees and 1,476 nautical miles north to Tahiti.

Today the islands still educe a deep curiosity. There is something about their remoteness, and the richness of the people who live so detached from the rest of the world, way, way out on the edge of the world. Nuku'alofa—the capital city of Tonga, located on the north coast of the island of Tongatapu and home to the Tonga Royal Palace—lies some 495 miles southeast of Fiji, some 1,236 miles northeast of Auckland, some 2,225 miles east of Sydney, some 3,148 miles southwest of Honolulu, some 4,758 miles south of the South Pole, and some 7,094 miles west of Green Bay, Wisconsin.

Folau hails from Nuku'alofa, a city of recent internal strife where the remnants of a bygone social structure break down into the king, nobles, and commoners—and in between, a sort of political agent for the hierarchy known as the matapule, or "talking chiefs." It's the world catching up, the evolution of life way, way out on the edge of the world.

And isn't it odd the game has now become a tradition in an isolated part of the Pacific steeped in very distinct tradition? But here in Tonga and American Samoa and Samoa, the islands of Oceania, an active earthquake zone where cyclone season runs between November and April, they produce players the way they do in western Pennsylvania and central Texas.

"You'll see all the kids wearing Polamalu jerseys right now," Folau said.

And of course, any culture that offers a Troy Polamalu would certainly embrace his game and its kids someday hoping to mimic his way— which has always been a knack for the big play, performed by a quiet man with a loud game and louder look with the long, bold folds of hair shooting out from beneath his helmet. Polamalu's greatness stems from his incredible speed and brute physicality, genetic gifts for the ultimate free safety.

Vai Sikahema, a former fearless returner, now patriarch of football's Polynesian players, believes it is his people's makeup that pushed them toward the game when American soldiers first brought it with them to the training grounds on the Solomon Islands.

"People of the islands are very physical," he said. "They're big—they eat a lot of fish and a lot of yams. And they embrace the physicality. Socially, they're very laid back, but in the field of competition they'll grab your throat. Oftentimes they don't have a lot of speed—but possess good feet. Perhaps it's from performing the native dances— which is part of family get-togethers and barbecues. It's a very rhythmic culture. So you have these huge offensive linemen who are nimble on their feet.

"Their size lends itself to football—as well as the fact that they love hand-to-hand combat. Bows and arrows weren't a part of the culture. It would be considered wimpy to shoot somebody from afar. They need to face their enemy eye to eye and defeat him with their strength, guile, quickness, and determination. They go out, swim in the ocean, and spear a shark to feed their entire village. Isn't that football?"

The culture of the political system, Sikahema surmised, adds to their natural marriage with the game.

"We're conformists in a sense," he said. "We follow orders. Because life there has a pecking order and you're expected to follow it. It starts with the elders and goes down from there."

A Man Named Tiaina

The greatest islander ever had just returned home from a little surfing at the beach in Southern California when he received the phone call from the coach he still called Coach—whose team had just gotten trounced 33–10 by the Pittsburgh Steelers and suffered another rash of injuries, this time to the defense.

"What are you doing?" Bill Belichick asked the man.

"Just got done surfing. What's up?"

"Well, we need you."

"When?"

"Now."

So Junior Seau called his kids down for a family conference, received their blessing, and landed in New England that Friday morning, the first week of December 2008. The thrill of returning to the game he so loved was enough to wipe away the fatigue of the flight, and so he arrived at Patriot headquarters, collected a playbook, and participated in a walk-through with the team. He then followed the rest of the players that afternoon back to the airport back on a flight back out west, destination Seattle this time, and played forty-one plays that Sunday.

Buoyed by Seau, the Patriots won their final four games of the season to finish at 11–5 but narrowly missed the playoffs.

Herein lies the intersection of the Polynesian culture and the game. Seau deemed it his duty to adhere to Belichick's wishes because the greatest islander ever would not rebuff such an honor.

Warrior code.

"We're fortunate to have a lot of guys that are in the league—and they respect the game," he said. "The mentality of the islands is to protect your last name. Have pride in it—not embarrassment. Whenever you have that, you have some kind of base. Things that come your way, in terms of football, in terms of any profession, in terms of life, you protect it, you embrace it, you don't take it for granted."

The Next Life Is Calling

Now, deep into the night, the mass exodus is upon us, as the flock shuffles into the clogged aisles that lead to a more clogged concourse and out to the main, even more clogged parking lots. They press the flesh as they trek, some out of celebration, others out of the sheer closeness of flesh. The bubble jackets and thick jerseys shrink space even more, as does the fact that the game was relatively close. It's a sign of competitiveness when they all stay, especially on a school night. They stay even longer when they're pleased, usually a few moments after zero just to display their satisfaction, though you needn't possess the ability to see or hear to sense the outcome of a football game.

You can tell by how the air feels, the way you can forecast a looming thunderstorm in the summer. All of that energy spilling into the air at once creates a keen vibe, particularly in an emotionally charged place like Pittsburgh or Philadelphia, Cleveland or Kansas City, plebeian towns with football souls. It matters just a little more in a Buffalo or a Baltimore, similarly, where Monday's mood will depict the football team's fortunes the previous day. It's a simple answer as to why, understandable to even the biggest get-a-lifer; it's all you have sometimes in cities without real tourism, Florida- or California-type tourism, or without super size, or even relevance or worthiness, designated nowadays by whether or not a city is listed in the world's weather report on the television inside the elevator of the ambient-crazed office building.

When it's good in these towns, the flock is festal and the adoration smothering. It's Christmas in a small town and they've gone wild with the lights again, as was the case when the Eagles acquired Terrell Owens and Jevon Kearse before the 2004 season and twenty-five thousand people trekked to watch practice at the team's training camp in a sleepy Pennsylvania town called Bethlehem, about two hours from Philadelphia.

"It's like *Field of Dreams*," Coach Andy Reid had said after almost missing practice due to fan traffic. Butch the security chief had to place a police flasher atop his SUV to navigate the snarled one-lane road that leads to the practice fields to escort Reid to the morning session on time.

Two years later, hysteria followed a wild-card victory over the Giants that capped a dramatic late-season turnaround for the Eagles after they were in jeopardy of missing the playoffs. That blustery January Tuesday, two thousand people showed up for an appearance by backup quarterback Jeff Garcia—who had endeared himself to the locals a few weeks prior with his spirited play and holiday victory over the hated Cowboys, saying afterward on national television, "Merry Christmas, Philadelphia"—at a discount clothing store in a rather remote part of town. One fan waited four and a half hours to land Garcia's autograph but left disappointed because he couldn't buy a $21.95 T-shirt bearing his likeness. All six hundred had been sold in the first hour.

Of course there is a flip side in such cities, upon disappointment, when adulation turns into ire and the flock into a mob. Before you, they grow horns and transform into gargoyles with fetid breath, like what transpired in Cleveland in a 2001 game against Jacksonville. Angered by a call on the field, fans at Cleveland Browns Stadium hurled hundreds of plastic beer and water bottles, many of them full, onto the field and at the Jaguars bench. Jimmy Smith of the Jaguars compared the incident to storming the beach in the opening scene of *Saving Private Ryan*. "We feared for our lives," he said. "It was like dodging bullets."

On this night, all is well as the Eagles beat the Giants, and Andy Reid does not endure the wrath of defeat as he would a few weeks later following a home drubbing at the hands of the Colts. The coach was rousted by fans atop the tunnel that day, one middle-aged man of ample flesh spewing, "You fat slob. You stink."

Reid refused to acknowledge the man, though a few moments later Buchanico returned and shot back, "Come back next week. We'll make you happy. And by the way, you should lose some weight yourself."

"I'm sorry," the man said.

Please allow a moment to extrapolate the story of the man who appears merely a fan lost in a make-believe land. For none of it seems real from the stands, or from the couch, which is not to speak of authenticity. The game, most certainly, is the game, with an actual winner and loser. But lost in translation, through all of the white-hot hype, the ceaseless coverage and sensory assault of the stadium show, is that those before the man are indeed men. They appear anything but mortal, most certainly. They appear in costume. They don helmets and pads and cleats and warrior paint, which makes for an elaborate getup that adds physique and ferocity to already hulking, ferocious men. The helmet is an effective disguise and makes for better anonymity in a world where numbers are really names.

And when those numbers become placeholders for more numbers, as with, say, fantasy football or a football pool, the man really struggles to see the flesh. He is desensitized at best. While he intellectually sees their humanness, he is blind to it. It's only when another man whom he recognizes because of his stark humanness—Buchanico sports a pursed-lip frown born of injustice, a cop's face—rattles him out of the Neverland of his team not winning that it dawns on him, and he apologizes.

And the man trudges away, shuffling from the aisle to the concourse to the parking lot, analyzing what happened on the field and concocting what he will tell his friends that will make for such keen insight. Sports people, those who attend it and watch it and talk about it, must always best one another for sports insight, pre or post. It's the only way sports people can compete like the sports people who provide the subject matter. It's competitive one-upping.

The man will walk by another man with grimy fingers selling soft pretzels in smudged brown bags from a shopping cart that he stole from the supermarket, now five for a dollar because it's late, and then finally reach his car in the middle of great debris because there is no bigger sty than a parking lot after a professional football game. It's irrelevant what the man drives or the zip code where he parks it, whether he's blue-collar or white-collar, because only in sport do you find the organic blurring of social barriers.

A rich man or a poor man or a smart man or a stupid man could equally become desensitized to the men to whom they had proclaimed their undying devotion in the first quarter only to curse their children to a terminal disease in the fourth. That man will muscle through stadium parking-lot traffic—which is holiday mall traffic on Tokyo traffic steroids—and drive back into his life and all of its splendor and misery. The memory of the game will soon be appropriately shelved, available only upon request.

Hours later in that parking lot, you could indeed find a few players having their own tailgate, a private postgame impromptu gathering.

It's true, you know, players in the parking lot now emptied, just a few stragglers partying in the middle of a million empties, morning leftovers from the now hungover.

The Fragile Bones

"To this day, I can't run," former All-Pro defensive end Hugh Douglas said. "I'm thirty-six and I can't run. I think you go into it knowing something might go wrong. But when you're twenty-two years old, the world is yours. You're not thinking about being thirty-six and not being able to run around with your kid. All you're thinking about is getting paid, a hot-ass sports car, and the finest bitches you could ever fuck."

Tragic stories of life after the league are plentiful and well documented. How the brutality of this game that doesn't feel like a game leaves some who play it physically wrecked. How all of those hits and collisions that are forgotten after the initial *"oooooh"* and subsequent wince and *SportsCenter* highlight leave a trail of broken bodies, knee and hip replacements, and permanent limps of men in their thirties. How those who endured the most head shots, with the worst luck, wind up in a haze, depressed, or dead. How from body to mind it all seems to expedite their lives, turning young immediately into old as quick as the NFL does their games into gold.

Collateral Damage

Kyle Turley retired at the end of the 2007 season after nine rugged years of playing offensive line in the NFL. He can't feel his right foot at this very moment because of all the sprained ankles he suffered. The fluid makes his ankle as thick as a thigh and has shut down the nerves in his foot. Tarsal tunnel syndrome.

"My foot is completely numb and I have no reflex in my right leg," Turley said. "I also have bulging discs. Herniated discs. Sciatic nerve damage. My shoulder grinds. I still need four surgeries just to clean things up a little bit in there. I also have a back surgery coming up that I'm not looking forward to."

Simeon Rice tore the labrum right from the bone. All that swimming at the line of scrimmage shredded his shoulder until the insides were like cooked chicken meat and threatened the career of the once great defensive lineman.

"Got me outta football this year and last," Rice said. "That shoulder nerve damage was the worst. I couldn't even put my hand on the ground to line up. I couldn't play at the level I wanted to play at. Your neck is out of whack. You're getting spasms. I had no strength. My arm would just collapse against any force."

Rice, who was cut by Tampa last summer, for equal parts injury and a $7.5 million salary, recorded 121 sacks in his twelve years in the league. He flirted briefly with Denver and Indianapolis but the shoulder scared teams away. He's attempting to come back this season and pitching a reality show to capture his comeback.

"Giving it a shot," he said. "Warriors go out on their sword. On their terms. You want the curtain to close when you close it. I've been a puppet master in my life for a long time."

Bill Romanowski chronicles his injuries other than concussions like achievements. He reels them off in the voice of a candidate demonstrating his worthiness:

AC separation in my shoulder against San Francisco. I had to get it shot up before every game. Six weeks straight I was getting shot up. I couldn't play in the game without it.

Eric Brown—my own teammate—nailed me in the game and gave me a hip pointer. We had Baltimore the next week. Jonathan Ogden, that bastard, would hit me so hard. It was the most excruciating pain to take him on and not be crushed by him.

I had a shoulder/neck injury against the Raiders. I almost was not able to play in the game. Coach Mike Shanahan came to me pregame and said, "I know you've never missed a game, but I don't want to put the team in jeopardy if you can't go."

I had a lower back injury in Oakland. Back and neck combo. Cortisone shots every day. I didn't think I could go. My streak was in jeopardy again. But I went back out there. It was before the first game of my final season.

Thinking back, admittedly so, it wasn't a well-thought-out plan for Kevin Long to have both shoulders repaired simultaneously. Two for one sounded best at the time, right after the Super Bowl, knowing about the recovery period and just the hassles of surgery. Who wants to endure that twice so soon apart?

The night before when they tell you not to eat anything after eight o'clock. The morning of, when you have to rise so early and your stomach is noisy and a little queasy and you haven't slept well because no matter how many times a veteran of it, the thought of surgery is unnerving. Checking into the hospital, waiting to be admitted with the other slaughtered cows in waiting, in that room with the old magazines and television turned to some morning show out of New York City where the hosts are annoyingly perky.

Don't you know I'm having surgery, people?

You're finally in the room and you're waiting some more. It's the worst kind of anticipation, as well, waiting for discomfort. Waiting to exit out of that room on a gurney, now a passenger wheeling through a color-less hallway, without any control or the ability for last-minute objections. It's like that until you drift away into unconsciousness, your last memory a cold room and stainless steel and people in masks. The last voice you hear is well meaning. It tries to soothe and it does for a moment until it turns into a growl in your dreams, where you see monsters.

Waking up is better, assuming surgical success. But you are nau-seous and terribly foggy. You've lost the ability to think, you think, at the very least concentrate on a singular thought—your girlfriend's face, your address, how many ceiling tiles are above you.

And when you're fully alert, there is the pain and the anticipation of the pain of recovery, which they refer to as a road and you a thicket of cactus.

Who wants to go through that twice?

Kevin Long felt that way until he awoke to heal and realized he lost the use of his arms for a while. "I couldn't lift them up," he said. "I couldn't do anything. You realize how helpless you are. And it was pretty embarrassing. I wasn't married at the time. I was dating my wife at the time. I couldn't ask her to help me shower or wipe my ass. I had my mom do that for me. Think about it. Your mom wiping your ass? And you're supposed to be some big professional football player. That was embarrassing. I felt pretty pathetic. I couldn't brush my teeth. I had to bend down to brush my teeth. It was pretty disgusting. Looking back on it, I should have done them one at a time so I wouldn't have lost so much daily function.

"I don't have as much functionally now, years after the surgery. I used to be able to touch my arms together behind my back. But not anymore. I've lost a lot of that. The strength never really comes back like it was before the surgery. It hurts to bench press. I use dumbbells to train because they're easier on my shoulders. People don't realize the little things you have to go through or the little things you can't do."

For Kevin Gogan, his worst experience was a broken big toe. "That was a bitch," he said. "The ball of my toe was huge—like a baseball—and you can't do anything except tough it out. I walked away from the game in relatively good shape. I was lucky I never suffered anything too substantial."

Yes, Gogan feels fortunate. He only underwent six elbow surgeries and one knee surgery during his fourteen years in the NFL.

Consider that Mark Schlereth played twelve years in the league and underwent fifteen knee surgeries. "I learned early that this game came with a price, but I never lost focus," he said. "As a society, we look at those who have succeeded and don't see all of the sacrifice. We don't see what they had to endure to get there. I never lost sight of what I wanted to be. I always played the game with one thought. Every guy I played with, I'm trying to serve. He's more important than me. I owed my teammates. I owed the organization. I always felt very passionate about that."

Said Hugh Douglas, "We were playing Chicago my last year. They were working on Soldier Field and we played in Champaign [at the University of Illinois]. I remember getting hit in the knee. It hurt so bad I had to take a time-out because I couldn't get up. I had to go out for one play, but I came right back in because I knew my team needed me. I'm like, 'I can't be hurt.' I played the whole game like there was nothing wrong. The next day I couldn't walk. There was this giant knot, like somebody put a tennis ball in the side of my left knee. My wife had to drive me to treatment. That whole season I didn't practice, but I played every game."

Jason Short is barely thirty, a part-time player in this league, and he's already suffered two broken legs—both coming against bad-luck Washington, mind you, the first a shattered fibula that ended his rookie season, the second two years later—and two fractured vertebrae, and underwent neck surgery to repair two herniated discs. He's also broken just about all of his fingers.

"I've broken just about everything," he said. "There were times I would have to take Toradol shots just to be able to get out there and run. The next day everything was aching. I'm walking around like an old man. But I didn't look as bad as Paul Grasmanis. He'd hobbled around everywhere. I don't know if one leg is shorter than the other, but that guy struggles getting around everywhere. [Then linebackers coach Steve Spagnuolo] would bust his balls in the film room, pointing out how slow he was to get to the play and how he limped around."

Grasmanis finally retired at the age of thirty-one. Injuries limited him to eight games over his final three seasons.

"I feel very free," he said at the time. "I really tried to stay positive and tell myself I could make it back. It helped being positive, but there was a line drawn where I was going home every day after rehab and I was hurting. I just decided I couldn't do this anymore."

Despite having back surgery while playing at the University of Washington that has left him with chronic pain, Benji Olson didn't miss his first game until his tenth season in the league last year. He missed three because of debilitating back spasms.

Olson once tore his groin muscle against the Packers in a Monday Night Football game and played the next six weeks on it. Against the Colts, he suffered a second-degree MCL tear in his knee after Dwight Freeney pushed quarterback Steve McNair into the back of his leg, and again he didn't miss a game.

"I just taped it up," he said. "It was a weird feeling out there playing, because you feel as though you have no stability in your leg at all. The more pain you can deal with the longer your career will be."

Olson spoke those words about three weeks before he decided to retire, during the writing of this book. He cited his back and dealing with constant pain.

Originally a fifth-round draft choice, Olson started 140 of the 152 games he played, not including nine playoff games. Only three other interior linemen—Casey Wiegmann, Alan Faneca, and Chris Gray— played more games than Olson during the span of his career from 1998 through 2007.

Former teammate Mike Munchak, now the Titans offensive line coach, thanked Olson "for playing injured the past couple years. Guys didn't realize how bad his back was the past couple years."

Brian Mitchell said that part of sustaining your career is always being on the field. "I've had four separated shoulders and played through them all," he said. "If you don't let someone else do your job then you can't lose your job. My rookie season I separated my right shoulder. Chuck Cecil hit me with his helmet right square in the shoulder and popped it out. So that's when I learned to carry the ball with my left hand.

"In Philadelphia, I busted the sac in my knee. On Wednesdays and Sundays I would have to get my knee drained. I was getting something like 80 to 100 cc's of liquid taken out of my knee. McNabb was in there one time and almost puked seeing what was taken out of my knee. He has a soft stomach."

Schlereth viewed pain as an object, no different from a lamp or, worse, a bulky couch, something to be transferred to another repository, if only for a brief period.

"For whatever reason, I could show up on crutches on Friday and play on Sunday," he said. "For whatever reason, I could block it out. I had this image. I would pray before the game. I had this imaginary jar in the top of my locker and I would ask the Lord to hold my pain in there for the course of the game. I would take it back at the end, of course."

Rice, however, believes it's all a lose-lose scenario for a player. That teams look unfavorably upon a player who won't play through "playable" pain and they don't grade a player on a curve if he plays with pain and plays poorly. Meanwhile, playing hobbled only wears the body down even more in the long run.

"It's too violent of a game to play that hurt sometimes," Rice said. "In football we have a false sense of heroism. You think you can play through everything. It's machismo. You think you're tougher than you are. You're always judged by how you play the game healthy. Even though it's not high school and college, you're giving it the ol' college try. They don't factor in your injury when evaluating how you played. Everything is compared to how you play the game when you're healthy."

Suddenly It Feels Very Cold Out Here

The great misconception is that players will contemplate retirement based on Sunday performance. It's about the appetite to do the work to get to Sunday. It's always about the appetite in professional football. In a game of grunts, it's how they get there and stay there.

It's about the resolve to wobble into work on that Monday, watch the film, study the mistakes, and replenish the body through more abuse. When want leaves a player, often a player leaves the game.

"I knew it was time to retire when I couldn't bounce back the way I used to," Steve Wisniewski said. "You used to really feel worn down Mondays and Tuesdays. In the end, it was Mondays through Saturdays."

"It's difficult the older you get," Chad Lewis added. "You heard [Brett] Favre say he was just tired during his retirement speech. It's physical and mental. It's the stress. You're tired in every way. For me, the clock in my heart clicked midnight. Teams were still giving me offers, but I told them I want to play with my kids and I don't want to be crippled the rest of my life. The reward is great but the risk/reward ratio is way out of balance. The game becomes way too violent."

A curtain will come down in every player's mind when the end is upon them. Deep inside, they just know it.

"There is a 'the end,'" Brian Mitchell said. "Playing against the Falcons, it was my last year in New York. That's when I realized it was time to hang it up. My wife was even like, 'You've never been hit that much in a game.' Usually one or maybe two guys would tackle me. I was getting gang-tackled. I could tell my instincts weren't what they used to be. That's when I said to myself this shit is real. I've always said I only worked one year that I was in the league. That year with New York. All the other years I was having fun."

One by one they fade into retirement. Just a year ago, Benji Olson called it quits. The back finally gave out.

He played for the Oilers back when they were in Houston and before the Texans suddenly appeared in a new wonder of the world, named after an energy company that connotes dependability, with its retractable roof and natural grass and New World comfort, defined by over two hundred suites, making the old Astrodome seem as dated as a running game.

"When I first came into the league I played with so many men, and you know, there's so much seniority given to guys that have been in that locker room for so many years," Junior Seau said. "Nowadays seniority is given to a player that has the biggest hit on the salary cap. That's sad— because obviously the game is being portrayed as a corporate gig."

But no matter how colossal the league grows and how many rules change and how it evolves, the essence of the game will always remain.

"This is what I tell people in the locker room," Junior Seau said. "Football is not a game that's meant for human beings to play for a number of years. So embrace it while you have it—but understand that the game of football can only be successful for you and your family if you put your mind over flesh. You have to condition your mind over your flesh because your flesh will lie to you every day. It's going to say that you're hurt. It's going to say that you're tired. It's going to say that you can't play today—you know, my hamstring hurts. Well, you have to condition your mind over your flesh. You have to condition your mind to take you through it.

"I could name so many days where the flesh is just talking to you and saying, 'I'm done.' At the same time, during the AFC Championship Game against Pittsburgh while I was with the Chargers, I had a stinger. You put a hand on a stinger and it reacts. All of a sudden I'm dead in my left arm. But I got through that, and thank God I did because that game was very crucial to us because we moved to the Super Bowl. Then of course we got beat by a better team. But there was an opportunity there, and if I hadn't kept playing we would've never known. The unknown is something that I fear every day."

On September 30, 2009, I asked Seau if he would consider playing one last season, if only to make his career one incredible round number—twenty seasons.

"Only if [Belichick] needed me for the run," he replied. "Other than that, I'm going to surf and enjoy my kids and pack a cooler and watch them. I think I'll let them entertain me instead."

Seau spoke with glee of his new reality show called *Sports Jobs*, where he performs the glamourless jobs of sport, like stadium usher and ticket taker, and he spoke again of his children. How in 2007 he asked his son whether he should return to the game and his son said, "Dad, go get it."

And how 2007 ended, so difficult to take, playing Patriot perfect for 18–0, only to lose to the Giants in the Super Bowl. And finally how at the end of the 2007 season that ended in the calendar year of 2008, his son told him, "All right, Dad, let's go home."

A veteran—any veteran—looks around the room nowadays and sees too many strangers, their faces too clean. Suddenly he notices their youth, more than his maturity, mind you. He notices the gap in their ways versus his, how entirely different their daily lives, how their commonality ends with the same jersey, and he's kind of graduated from the video games and cheap beer. And while he can still pound with the best of them, his conversation will reference fatherhood, real fatherhood over absentee fatherhood, and Disney trips and finer restaurants and capital gains tax and everything else that fills the world of a yuppie linebacker.

He's got over fifteen years on some of them, which might as well be two lifetimes in this business.

They're all signs.

But when the subject of Brett Favre arose, and the story that he told at his comeback news conference of how he sat with his daughter on the back porch discussing whether or not to play again, Seau said, "I get it. I totally get it."

Of course he did. Because two weeks later the rumors of Seau's comeback suddenly began. He tried out for the Patriots and afterward told the world, "The Pats are the team I'll answer a call for, and the only team. The reason being is the relationship between Belichick and I. Belichick, if he does call, he doesn't call anyone without having a plan, and for me, I believe in what he does. That's number one. And number two, I know the system, so if I'm ever going to stick my neck out there in the gridiron I know that I have to have a chance to succeed, not only for myself but for the team."

And of course Belichick called and coaxed Seau back for a third time.

One last pile called him.

Watch the groin.

Index